BRIDGING THE DIVIDE

BRIDGING THE DIVIDE

Working-Class Culture
in a Middle-Class Society

Jack Metzgar

ILR PRESS

AN IMPRINT OF CORNELL UNIVERSITY PRESS   ITHACA AND LONDON

First published 2021 by Cornell University Press

Printed in the United States of America

Library of Congress Cataloging-in-Publication Data

Names: Metzgar, Jack, author.
Title: Bridging the divide : working-class culture in a middle-class society / Jack Metzgar.
Description: Ithaca [New York] : Cornell University Press, 2021. | Includes bibliographical references and index.
Identifiers: LCCN 2021005647 (print) | LCCN 2021005648 (ebook) | ISBN 9781501760310 (hardcover) | ISBN 9781501760334 (pdf) | ISBN 9781501760327 (epub)
Subjects: LCSH: Working class—Social aspects—United States. | Class consciousness—United States. | Working class—United States—Social conditions. | Middle class—Social aspects—United States.
Classification: LCC HD8072.5 .M48 2021 (print) | LCC HD8072.5 (ebook) | DDC 305.5/620973—dc23
LC record available at https://lccn.loc.gov/2021005647
LC ebook record available at https://lccn.loc.gov/2021005648

"Don't Get Above Your Raising" by Lester Flatt and Earl Scruggs Copyright © 1958 by Peer International Corporation and Scruggs Music, Inc. Administered by Peermusic III, Ltd. Copyright Renewed. Used by Permission. All Rights Reserved.

An earlier version of the part 1 introduction was published as "Nostalgia for the 30-Year 'Century of the Common Man'" in *The Journal of Working-Class Studies* 1, no. 1 (December 2016): 23–27.

A portion of chapter 5, "There Is a Genuine Working-Class Culture," was published in the *Routledge International Handbook of Working-Class Studies*, edited by Michele Fazio, Christie Launius, and Tim Strangleman (Abingdon, UK: Routledge, 2020), 231–241.

For Judie Blair, as always
For Judd, Gina, Max, and Logan Metzgar, forevermore

Contents

Acknowledgments   ix

Introduction: Achieving Mediocrity   1

Part I **NOSTALGIA FOR THE THIRTY-YEAR CENTURY
        OF THE COMMON**   21

    1. What Was Glorious about the Glorious Thirty?   27

    2. The Rise of Professional Middle-Class Labor   42

    3. Working-Class Agency in Place   52

    4. "At Least We Ought to Be Able To"   66

Part II **FREE WAGE LABOR AND THE CULTURES OF CLASS**   73

    5. There Is a Genuine Working-Class Culture   77

    6. Categorical Differences in Class Cultures   100

Part III **STRATEGIES AND ASPECTS OF WORKING-CLASS
          CULTURE**   129

    7. Ceding Control to Gain Control   133

    8. Taking It and Living in the Moments   150

    9. Working-Class Realism   172

Epilogue: Two Good Class Cultures   187

Notes   193
Index   225

Acknowledgments

I have many people to thank for helping me in a variety of different ways to complete this book. But first I want to thank working-class studies and all those who have created, nurtured, and sustained it as a field of study with very few rules and many different kinds of voices—now encompassed in the Working-Class Studies Association. What they called "new working-class studies" was founded by John Russo and Sherry Lee Linkon in 1995 at Youngstown State University in Ohio and then added to institutionally by Michael Zweig at Stony Brook University in New York and Tim Strangleman at University of Kent in the United Kingdom. By collectively establishing a space where folks with extensive experience of working-class people, regardless of their own class background, could share their observations of and concerns about working-class life, working-class studies have allowed me—and so many others—to say things and think things I could not say or think anywhere else.

Personally, working-class studies gave me a fresh start in a new century with a new set of friends, many of them much younger than me, who saw things I had thought I was the only one seeing (which, if that had been the case, I would likely have been hallucinating!). The working-class studies community has enriched my life in many different ways but none more than by being among people who could sensibly correct me when I was wrong. Within this community, Russo, Linkon, and Strangleman have been with me every step of the way for this book and Russo even before that, sharing their insights, energy, and activism inside academia and out. Others who have been especially good at correcting me but who have not read the book are Sarah Attfield, Michele Fazio, David Greene, Colby King, Christie Launius, Cherie Rankin, Steve Rosswurm, and Jeff Torlina. Barbara Jensen often spiritedly corrected me as well, but mostly I value her own work, including the book she allowed me to interfere with chapter by chapter, and the couple of decades of conversations that have shaped every aspect of my interpretations; she also read the entire book at a late stage, and besides a string of helpful criticisms and suggestions, she enthusiastically gave me the approval I needed.

I have been fortunate to have people who read every word of the book in one form or another. My graduate school buddy Bill Smoot, a novelist and short story writer, wordsmithed and copyedited every chapter, sometimes more than once, immensely improving clarity and prose with the gently mocking grace only a friend of fifty years could have. Two sociologists, Betsy Leondar-Wright and Jessi Streib, read each chapter as I wrote it including a few chapters they talked me out of using, making helpful corrections, providing leads to sources, and carefully assessing each and every one of my sweeping generalizations, some of which are less sweeping now and some of which are mercifully absent here. Jefferson Cowie and Jamie Daniel also read the entire book, and even though some of my views cut against some of their grains, they both skillfully kept their criticisms (and encouragement) within a sympathetic understanding of what I was trying to do. Finally, toward the end when I thought everything was perfect, Joshua Freeman and Sherry Linkon rendered their judgments in ways that were enthusiastic but also so critically insightful that I was able to improve "the perfect"! Josh and I have been trading manuscripts for decades, and he still finds ways to sharpen my thinking, while I have been running out of criticisms to help him. Sherry Linkon deserves mention across every front. From an upper-middle-class family, Sherry has been becoming working class-ish for decades now. One of the founders of working-class studies, she has nurtured numerous voices as a skillful organizer, an even more skillful editor of the "Working-Class Perspectives" blog, and with her own writing and scholarship as well as her oral contributions to so many different conversations in the field. I was blessed to have her extensive and careful commentary on nearly every page of the book.

Those who read pieces of the book, mostly in its early stages while it was still taking shape, are Paul Barnesley, Allison Hurst, John Russo, Tim Strangleman, and Venise Wagner. They were all both critically helpful and encouraging, sometimes in that working-class not-making-a-fuss kind of way. I also appreciate the pieces my son, Judd Metzgar, read for veracity, but I benefitted even more from his wise-guy skepticism of my entire project during hours of conversation over the past several years.

I owe Fran Benson, my editor at Cornell University Press, in ways beyond the careful way she has shepherded my book through the editorial process. She has been a quiet powerhouse in working-class studies, publishing founding texts: original anthologies by Russo and Linkon and by Michael Zweig, Zweig's *Working-Class Majority*, Barbara Jensen's *Reading Classes*, Betsy Leondar-Wright's *Missing Class*, and the *Class Lives* collection as well as numerous others. These authors, all of whom are friends, are not giants—just ordinary, good people and exemplary middle-class professionals—but I stand on their shoulders nonetheless. Fran provided access to those shoulders for me and so many others.

And then there's Judie, the love of my life, who engaged in decades of dialogue with me about our class cultures, some of which she found uncomfortable and a lot of which she found tedious. She read the book in incoherent pieces, always with insight, and helped me put those pieces together. As in our life together, she seldom put her foot down in disagreement, but when she did I knew she was likely to be right. If you've ever known somebody like that, then you might have some idea what a blessing it has been to have lived more than half a century with Judie by my side.

ACHIEVING MEDIOCRITY

I knew what was about to happen as Coach Shingler reamed out one player after another as we stood in line showing our first six-week report cards. Football players could NOT be dummies, he fumed. "You might as well know that right now." And unless you could master English and math, you had "no future on this team." I dropped my notebook so I would lose my place in line, trying to work my way to the back so there would be fewer players left to witness my embarrassment. But that didn't work, as lots of guys were coming late to practice, and before I knew it I was in front of Coach, painfully raising my report card above my head so he could see. He saw.

Coach grabbed the report card with one hand and gave me a big side-hug with his other arm as he called out to half a dozen players who had just gone through the report card gauntlet but had not yet reached the locker room. Arbitrarily singling out one player, as he often did, he shouted, "Hey, Miller, you guys come back here. This may be the one time in your lives you see a report card like this," as he called everybody around to see that I had earned all A's, "even in English and math."

I liked Coach Shingler, then and ever after, because he really cared about all his guys and wanted to have a positive impact on each of our lives, even those of us who weren't such good athletes. He wasn't like a regular teacher, as he was easier for us to relate to even when he scolded us or kidded us too roughly. But I wondered even then, as a twelve-year-old, how he could do this to me. Why not just slap me on the back and say "Good job, Metzgar," as he had done with some others? Could he not know that he was branding me an outsider, not really one of the boys, as he attempted to shame others by exhibiting me, a third-string fullback with a tendency to fumble, as somebody to be emulated?

Whitey Miller, because he had been singled out, pretended to study my report card as others looked on. Fortunately he found it amusing, not humiliating, and as soon as we were in the locker room, Whitey gave me my seventh grade nickname, "AB Metzgar" (evidently he hadn't noticed that there were no B's) or "AB," which with the passage of time became "Abe," thank God, and then faded away.

In Johnstown, Pennsylvania, in 1955, seventh grade was when we all left our much smaller elementary schools and entered a mammoth building with four grades' worth of students from all over the east end of town. It was a big transition for all seventh-graders, as we all had to make a new name for ourselves and find our place in an altogether new order of things. It was worse for me, I think, because during that first six weeks my family moved from the housing project above the Moxham neighborhood, which we were *not* a part of, to a rival neighborhood across the river, which thought we were part of Moxham. Being exhibited as "a brain" got me lumped in with "teachers' pets" and "goody goodies," categories that I had learned were incompatible with being one of the boys.

Coach Shingler was not the first teacher to brand me into a group to which I no longer wanted to belong. During the first weeks of school, Miss Kreuger had passed around my math homework to show how neatly I had lined up the numbers, thereby making it less likely to make mistakes. It was not just a practical matter for Miss Kreuger, however, but a life lesson about the importance of orderliness, avoiding mistakes, and always striving to be perfect.

In my seventh grade mind these were just about the worst things that could happen to me, and I took a series of corrective actions. My next math assignment for Miss Kreuger was virtually unreadable (though all the answers were correct), and later in one of my English essays for her, I philosophized about the pain of being singled out as an example for others. She left me alone after that, and I was gradually able to go back to lining up my numbers properly (because it *does* help you avoid mistakes). The "AB Metzgar" tag was harder to shake because my father insisted I make the Honor Roll, which required all A's and B's, but because Whitey Miller had dubbed me "AB" and not "All-A," the only way to avoid that brand was to stay off the Honor Roll altogether. Fending off both my father and Whitey Miller, I worked assiduously to get one "C" in a different subject for each six-week grading period while ending the year on the cumulative Honor Roll, which only parents and teachers would ever know. I also developed a smart-ass attitude, highlighted with a "duck's ass balboa" haircut (crew cut on top and Brylcreem slicked-back hair on the sides), that fit better in my new neighborhood and earned me an appropriate degree of disdain from most teachers.

As seventh grade ended, I felt a great deal of satisfaction for my crafty accomplishment. Though I suspect I had an asterisk somewhere near my name in most of the guys' heads, I was otherwise definitely one of the boys while getting all the summertime privileges my father had promised.

Eight years later I would look back on this accomplishment as shameful evidence of what a conformist I was, of my inability to resist going along with the crowd and my fundamentally weak-charactered other-directedness. This analysis resulted in decades of trying to reverse the damage I had done to myself, struggling to achieve the potential some caring nags had warned me I was failing to live up to. But by my forties, I changed my mind again. Renewing my pride in having navigated between a seventh grade Scylla and Charybdis, I came to see it as but an early embracing of my working-class self even as I worked to earn the income and working conditions of a middle-class professional. Now I see that decision, or set of decisions, as being crucial to my achieving mediocrity.

I know that the phrase "achieving mediocrity" may seem a bit too cute, but it captures something about working-class life that is both valuable and very hard to recognize from an achievement-oriented middle-class perspective. First and most obviously, there is a kind of reverse status to being common, to not standing out, a positive value to not putting yourself above and lording it over everybody. This is actually pretty complex, because competition and showing one another up—in sports, in hunting and fishing, in fixing things, in fighting—were not only allowed but also expected. Even doing well in school, as I eventually found out, could be appreciated if you didn't buy into the teachers' program, if you didn't disdain others who were not as smart or as "well motivated" as you. The school—not everybody but rather the general ethos even in a midcentury steel town—clearly thought the good students were not just better students but also better human beings. Most teachers, themselves pretty working class by today's standards, conveyed this message in a multitude of ways, including gathering us all from time to time in "assemblies" where they would actually say something to the effect that "ending up as nothing but a mill hand" was a moral failing comparable to beating up somebody smaller than you. We knew better. It was the mill hands who were the real people, who could actually do things and knew what was what. Teachers, on the other hand, were either clueless or phonies and sometimes both.

Working-class life is antiaspirational, or at least nonaspirational or perhaps just differently aspirational, and that can be a big problem for achieving hierarchical forms of upward mobility. But there's also a strength to it—a mysterious Sancho Panza realism that mixes a vulnerable but sturdy simplicity with an easy authenticity, a freedom to be yourself, to take yourself as you are. This realism is rare (at least until old age) in a mainstream culture that provides internal and external pressures to always aspire and constantly and consistently work to achieve your potential.

And there is this paradox in American class cultures. Middle-class culture emphasizes individualism, not just rhetorically but also in hundreds of explicit and implicit ways, whereas working-class culture, as I have experienced it, emphasizes not standing out and instead finding your place in the group and being loyal to that group—solidarity in a way. The paradox is that as middle-class people, despite our radical individualism, we are all pretty similar compared to the wild diversity of characters and personalities in any sizable working-class group. The conformists turn out to be more unique and diverse than the inner-directed individualists.

Valuing Mediocrity

Let me say straightaway that an individual mediocre life like mine is not very interesting. My life in particular has lacked trauma and drama, mostly through luck but not without a little intentional design. But mediocrity in the mass is a lot more interesting than you might think—first, of course, because it is so common and second because it's not as common as it used to be either as ideal or reality. People aspire to mediocrity, and many work hard to achieve it, as I have. That sounds ridiculous only in an elite culture (which includes most of the mass media) that is constantly banging on about greatness and excellence and always looking for the extraordinary, whether a Nobel Prize winner or a mass murderer.

Among middle-class professionals, to be called mediocre or, somehow worse, "a mediocrity" is a humiliating insult, but the actual meaning of those words is not outright negative. It's the connotation that stings. Synonyms for "mediocre" include "common," "middling," "ordinary," "passable," and "adequate."[1] These are negative only if you were hoping to be outstanding or excellent. Even "second-rate" and "second-class" are not really pejorative for anyone who knows they are not as good as the best. In use, "mediocre" often simply means good, not great. In a professional setting, "good" and surely "good enough" are usually positive ways of saying "mediocre," whereas "mediocre" is a negative way of saying the same thing. Either way, you're not excellent, extraordinary, or outstanding, but you're not that bad either. In a social class whose culture is by turns anxious about and intoxicated by status, however, being a mediocrity means being "just average," which is synonymous with being a failure. In a long life of being with a variety of working-class people, on the other hand, I have never heard anyone call anyone else mediocre, partly because it is not a word in common use but mostly because their system for ranking each other is different from the middle-class professional one. "Good" is at the top of the charts in working-class culture and has moral as well as performative meanings.

What's more, mediocrity has a proud history related to modern democracy and egalitarianism. Benjamin Franklin, for example, praised revolutionary America for being "a general happy Mediocrity," a reference to what Alexis de Tocqueville would later mark as our "equality of conditions," so strikingly different from the born-and-bred class systems in Europe and the original core of what was thought to be American exceptionalism.[2] Franklin's boast and Tocqueville's observation were only about half true, of course. As Thomas Piketty points out, "the New World combined two diametrically opposed realities. In the North we find a relatively egalitarian society in which capital was indeed not worth very much, because land was so abundant that anyone could become a landowner relatively cheaply, and also because recent immigrants had not had time to accumulate much capital. In the South we find a world where inequalities of ownership took the most extreme and violent form possible, since one half of the population owned the other half."[3] Still, the rough equality of conditions in the US North inspired democratic movements everywhere beginning with the French Revolution, during which Jacobins sought "an honorable mediocrity" whereby titles would disappear and people would address one another as "citizen" rather than "monsieur" and "madame."[4] These violent eruptions at the end of the eighteenth century initiated what Raymond Williams called "the long revolution," a struggle across two centuries to assert that a society should be measured by the welfare and consent of the common, ordinary, mediocre people who constitute the vast majority.[5] From my personal perspective this long revolution culminated, without much exaggeration, in my birth.

I grew up during a thirty- or forty-year period when mediocrity was more greatly valued and also easier to achieve than at any time in human history. I was born in 1943, one of world history's bloodiest years but also in the United States a year when the Second New Deal was just starting to pay off dramatically for families like mine. My formative years were during the best three decades in human history for working classes, a golden age of collective action and shared prosperity—not only in the United States but also in Western Europe and the Soviet Union and its sphere—and an era of often tragically bloody national liberation movements that cast off imperial forms of colonialism in the decades after World War II.[6] My memory and study of this period and my bitter observation of what followed are the basis of my interpretation of the differences between working-class and professional middle-class cultures. I was born into a hard-living working-class family who, through a series of strikes against steel companies, became settled living by the time I was a teenager (something seen as affluent at the time). Then as an adult I successfully pursued middle-class professionalism, for a while with fanatical focus and dedication, but ended up just a standard-issue, mediocre professional as a night-school teacher of working adults.

It was a wonderfully open and expansive journey that few working-class sons and even fewer working-class daughters had ever been afforded before. What's as significant, however, is that as I crossed classes I experienced absolutely no survivor guilt because the working-class life I was leaving had been improving and opening up for three decades. And given how its culture and way of life were blooming, it was not so clear that becoming a middle-class professional was necessarily a net gain. I got my first full-time professional job in 1977, however, just as working-class life began to go to hell—first, dramatically with an incredibly brutal wave of plant closings and the Reagan Revolution and then slowly but surely up to the present. Like Georg Hegel's owl of Minerva or like 23.4 percent of all country and western songs, we didn't know how wonderful mediocrity was until it was gone (or, to be more accurate, severely diminished). Though I still don't experience much survivor guilt, I cannot ignore how terribly my working-class contemporaries' lives and their children's prospects have withered and are withering as my immediate family and I continue to prosper.

But achieving mediocrity is more than the absence of being excellent, extraordinary, or outstanding. It's about valuing commonness and aspiring to work hard to at least pull your own weight, do the right thing when you can, and be loyal to those with whom you belong both at home and at work. In some versions, it's also about looking out for the other guy and putting yourself in his shoes. And, above all, it's about taking satisfaction when you live up to these modest standards and about feeling a shame that is deeper than—and has nothing to do with—social status when you do not live up to them. It's also about not having the guts to stand out for fear of looking (or being) foolish in trying to be something you're not or simply from the discomfort of being noticed at all.

These are working-class values, I think, as sportswriters know when they praise offensive linemen in football and low-scoring power forwards in basketball for their "blue-collar attitudes." The opposite of stars (let alone superstars) are "role-players" and "grinders." You do your job, your part, and when you do it well nobody notices. Or, rather, there is no public notice of it, but your workmates and family sometimes acknowledge it, usually in subtle and often backhanded ways, not making too much of a fuss but in ways that encourage and nurture the value of simply doing your bit, holding up your end. These values, this way of looking at things and living a life, are not unknown among middle-class professionals, especially as we get older and figure out that we have run out of potential to achieve. But they are characteristic of working-class life and are honored and rewarded in the culture of the working class. During my formative years many newly minted middle-class professionals brought these values from their working-

class families of origin, and many of those from professional families, often re-
belling against the "bitch goddess of success," eagerly embraced some working-class
ways. For a while the working class and the standard-issue middle class, trading
back and forth, shared different versions of the "middling virtues" that were highly
valued and quite common at the time.

For twenty years or so I worked pretty hard to achieve my potential, which
I achieved a while back, and I'm done with that. I sometimes regret how much time
and effort I put into that striving, and I can still feel embarrassed and humiliated
when I remember how for a brief time I aspired to "greatness." But I was fortunate
to have a working-class culture to fall back on and so many people, especially my
wife Judie, who nurtured and enforced that culture around and within me. But I
give myself credit too for that decision I made as a seventh-grader to be "one of
the boys," a "regular guy," even though I knew I did not measure up in many respects. I was good at school, and I fit better as a teacher's pet than I ever would as
what Paul Willis called "lads," a highly masculine oppositional blue-collar culture in which working-class young men paradoxically aided (and reproduced)
their own exploitation as workers. At twelve years old I chose to be a lad, and
I became one for long enough during those formative years that, as hard as I would
eventually try, I never wholly abandoned it.

Willis's classic *Learning to Labor: How Working Class Kids Get Working Class
Jobs* is a perceptive ethnography of English working-class culture in the early
1970s, not just the culture of the school but also how its counterschool culture
was carried into blue-collar workplaces.[7] Though Willis recognized and revealed
a working-class culture that is separate and distinct from middle-class culture,
he didn't like it much. And his main purpose was to show how lads, in school and
at work, participated in their own "self-damnation"—damned to working-class
jobs that had "inferior rewards," an "undesirable social definition," and work of
"increasing intrinsic meaninglessness."[8]

I, on the other hand, liked the culture and still do. Even though I have imbibed
and embraced a lot of middle-class culture too, working-class life still seems more
real and genuine to me than the one I live. You could call it "ambivalence," but that
is no longer how I think of it. Rather, I see myself (and Judie, my wife of more than
fifty years) as having the great fortune of living our first thirty or forty years at the
juncture of a working-class culture that was working on its own terms and a professional middle-class culture that was emerging as dominant even as it challenged
and troubled itself with fundamental questions about how to live a good life. The
two cultures had a lot to offer each other in those days, and my conviction that
they still do—or could—is a great part of my motivation to write this book.

Still, the twenty-first is a very different century, and I now take Willis's con-
demnation of working-class counterschool culture very much to heart. While the

lads culture may have worked well when labor unions were strong and real wages were rising, it has always made public education difficult (for everybody) and now undermines working-class agency in making a better life and a better society. In today's circumstances I sympathize with parents and teachers as they fight the lure of the lads culture (which is present among girls as well as boys and always has been)[9], and I am grateful (usually) that my middle-class grandsons have had so little exposure to it. But it was different in my time during what the French call the Glorious Thirty (1945–1975), when working-class agency could be and was exercised in that kind of culture—a working-class culture that does indeed accept a certain kind of subordination but in a complex and crafty way that was able, for a time, to advance toward an amazing degree of freedom and dignity while maintaining the kind of taken-for-granted integrity and easy authenticity that nobody who has ever experienced it could ever want to give up.

Classes and Cultures: Concepts and Definitions

I'm trying to recognize and value a working-class culture that many people think either never existed or has now passed—or is rapidly passing—into history like dinosaurs and steel mills. I too fear that it may be passing, and it certainly is no longer as strong and vital as it has been for most of my lifetime. But I also know it has a persistence and resilience that is very easy for middle-class professionals to overlook and underestimate. And I believe that changed circumstances could bring it back, restored and renewed even better than before.

So, what do I mean by "culture," and who exactly is in the working class?

"Culture" is a slippery concept, one that cannily adjusts its meanings in different contexts and therefore is easily confused and abused. I hope to make it a bit less slippery by being very explicit about the differences in class cultures as I have experienced and observed them. I present these differences as categorical opposites mostly for purposes of conceptual clarity, not because I think they always occur in real life with such neat distinction, although in many semi-isolated precincts of American life they definitely are quite distinct. But most important concepts have multiple meanings that slip and slide as they are used by different people in different situations for different purposes. Thus, I have no hope of avoiding the slipperiness altogether, but I do hope to avoid certain slimy usages that are not uncommon in our public discourse.

When I say "culture" I am always using the term in the broad anthropological sense of "ways of life" and never to mean "artistic expression." Stories, songs, pictures, philosophies, and religions (as well as physical forms, food, and clothing) may be important expressions of a culture and may reflect, inform, reinforce, or challenge a culture as a way of life, but for me they are not culture itself. These two most common conflicting meanings of "culture" are seldom confused in context (at least not for long), but it is worthwhile noting my unslippery usage on this point.

Likewise, I do not equate "lifestyle" with culture and will never use the term. Though some lifestyles are undoubtedly more common in different classes, the term tends to focus attention on superficial matters of taste—do you prefer beer or wine, bowling or golf, NASCAR or ballet?—rather than on deeper structures that inform basic presuppositions, assumptions, thoughts, feelings, and behavior. Just because these matters of taste are superficial does not mean they are unimportant, and they are certainly part of culture as a way of life. But for good or ill, they have little or nothing to do with the class cultures I attempt to describe.

Also, I think of culture as something outside individuals that both constrains and guides individual thought and behavior. Even though we individually imbibe a culture, beginning in infancy, we do not imbibe it in exactly the same way. Neither do we always think, feel, or behave in ways prescribed by our culture—indeed, knowing what to hide and what not to say is part of how culture shapes our lives. Even when we repeatedly do, think, or feel differently from our culture, it is still "ours"; we are part of it even when we deviate from it. Furthermore, the formal oft-proclaimed belief system of a culture often does not capture and may aggressively ignore important aspects of a way of life as it is actually lived. (The authors of *Habits of the Heart*, for example, insightfully point out that middle-class American culture—which for them is all of American culture—is single-mindedly individualist even though Americans have always practiced and valued civic engagement to degrees that would seem incompatible with our individualist ideology and rhetoric.)[10] I like Alexis de Tocqueville's "habits of the heart" (though I also like to add the unalliterative "and mind" to that phrase) and Raymond Williams's "structure of feeling" because they both point to how much of culture is sensed, felt, and tacitly lived without effort while at the same time emphasizing a culture's regularity and coherence in its habitualness and structure. But "feelings" and "hearts" tend to suggest not only too much mindlessness to culture but also that culture is an individual possession that is somewhat mysteriously shared with—and transmitted to—other individuals. Thus, I believe it more accurate to think of culture as outside and beyond the individual, as a way of life is typically understood. Even though the individual carries a version of it within him/herself, a culture is wider and deeper than any individual version of it.[11]

This way of thinking about culture leaves a lot of room for individual interpretation of a somewhat ineffable collective possession, even while emphasizing how impossible it is in principle for any individual to get it right. But that is sort of the point. Cultural interpretation is itself an important part of how ways of life develop. Though people and their cultures are influenced more substantially by changes in physical, technological, economic, and institutional environments, cultural interpretation plays a role in both achieving these changes and adjusting our habits of heart and mind to them after the fact.

As for a broader class analysis, I will do some slip-sliding myself. There are too many insightful and productive ways to construe social classes in our complicated society to be stuck with just one. And besides, I am dealing with just two broad classes, not the entire class structure. Still, some basic conceptions of class and class structure have guided my thinking.

First is Karl Marx's basic conception of free wage labor versus "capital," envisioned sometimes as a class of people (capitalists or bourgeoisie), sometimes as an impersonal socioeconomic force operating independently of individual human will. As the predominant way of organizing human labor for productive activity, free wage labor is a relatively recent phenomenon of the last century or so, depending on the country. But in the United States today it is so pervasive as to be taken for granted, and because it includes almost everybody, it seems not very useful in understanding basic social differences and conflicts. Free wage labor includes everybody who works for a living as their only or principal source for sustaining themselves—all those who earn money by working under somebody else's direction. The vast majority of middle-class professionals today are free wage labor, logically part of Marx's working-class or proletariat.[12] It was Marx's understandable but great mistake that he could not envision how large, semipowerful, and well compensated this part of his "working class" would become. Not part of free wage labor are both capitalists and small business owners, including those professionals such as doctors and lawyers who independently set up shop on their own and work for themselves—thus, the traditional petty bourgeoisie. Also not included are those free wage workers such as LeBron James, Angelina Jolie, Jamie Dimon, and a million or so others who make such fabulous salaries that at some point selling their labor is no longer necessary to sustain their lives.

Within this classical context I am focused on the cultural differences between two classes, in both of which members work for somebody else because they have to. This leaves out not only capitalists and the classical middle class of small business owners but also the poor as a separate class by itself. In not seeing the poor as a separate social class but instead as part of the working class, I am following the usage of Michael Zweig's *The Working Class Majority*. For Zweig, "poverty is a condition" that "mostly happens to the working class." Because "more than half the working class experiences poverty in a ten-year period," Zweig argues that the "poor are not some persistent lump at the bottom of society; they are working people who have hit hard times."[13] Instead I use "hard living" to designate that portion of the working class who at any one time have no discretionary income and unsteady or precarious employment, including those defined in other contexts as poor, near poor, working poor, or simply struggling to get by paycheck to paycheck. Defined this broadly, the hard living are a large and growing part of the working class, probably a majority of the class at this point. But they are still part of a broad working class, and though the culture plays out differently in different economic circumstances, it is the same culture when contrasted with middle-class professionalism. Focusing on only two very broad classes within the class structure is a significant limitation, but the working class and the professional middle class as I define them include the overwhelming majority of Americans. They are also the two class cultures I have lived most of my life negotiating between.

By starting with free wage labor, I am emphasizing occupations over income, wealth, and education among the most typical ways of defining social classes, though I do not deny the importance of these other criteria, especially income. Among occupations, using the Bureau of Labor Statistics' (BLS) broadest definitions, the professional middle class is made up of some twenty-one million full-time managerial workers and some thirty million full-time professional workers who together make up more than two-fifths of the full-time US workforce. The working class is the other three-fifths, the sixty-four million workers the BLS categorizes as service; sales and office; natural resources, construction, and maintenance; production, transportation, and material-moving occupations; and the vast majority of the twenty-five million part-time workers.[14] In general, middle-class professionals have more education, more autonomy at work, and higher incomes (plus better compensation packages), and working-class occupations have less, increasingly much less.

Still, as aggregate categories do, the BLS's broad occupational designations hide a lot of important complexity—managerial workers at Red Lobster who do not make a living wage, for example, or, conversely, a union bus driver married to a union construction worker whose family income is in six digits even without overtime.[15] As I will argue, in a society dominated by free wage labor, income all by itself is a more important determinant of a person's or a family's life than power, authority, or status. Though education and (even a small amount of) inherited or accumulated wealth are also vitally important in determining one's life chances, for most people most of the time income is primary, and the primary determinant of income is occupation. In 2020, for example, the median wage for full-time, full-year managerial and professional workers was $24,000–$38,000 higher than the medians for full-time working-class occupations.[16] The proliferation of involuntary part-time work among working-class occupations makes this occupation-determines-income causality even stronger. Thus, though I frame my own definition of social class around broad occupational categories, I will from time to time slide into other markers of class such as income, wealth, and education.

I certainly wouldn't expect class cultures to line up precisely with these broad occupational categories without lots of variations and complicated exceptions. Instead, I want to add culture as an influence in determining and defining social classes—to recognize how basic ways of living a life, or trying to, should also be part of how we think about social class in twenty-first-century America.

This occupational working class is by no means exclusively blue collar or white or male and never has been. Likewise, there is a wide range of incomes and accompanying life conditions within the working class structured by race, gender, and other factors, just as there has always been. People of color are now at least 40 percent of the working class, and women are a majority.[17] Given this definition, I will have nothing to say in this book about the white working class as discussed in American electoral politics. In American politics, the multiracial working class as a whole votes about the same as the professional middle class (as defined by educational attainment), but there are huge differences in how whites and nonwhites vote in both the working and middle classes.[18] Thus, the class cultures I describe each contain a wide range of conventional political partisanship structured much more by race, ethnicity, and gender than by class.

That class—independent of race, ethnicity, and gender—is irrelevant for American electoral politics might seem to challenge the idea that there are distinct class cultures, and in some ways it does. But the class cultures as I describe and interpret them in this book are at a deeper level than electoral politics, and my argument is that these class cultures are shared across races and ethnicities. Though playing out differently and with many variations, the underlying class-cultural differences are the same regardless of race. Though empirical studies that simultaneously compare both race and class are pretty rare, those that do tend to confirm that there are distinct cultures of class that do not vary significantly by race, ethnicity, or gender.[19] So does my own observation and experience in thirty years of teaching adults of all races and a lot of different nationalities, though primarily in a white-black framework where blacks were a strong presence, often a majority. Because I draw so much on my own experience, I would be surprised if my grasp of the cultures is not inflected with whiteness, and many of my students did not hesitate to point that out. But my hope is that my interpretations will resonate broadly with all racial and ethnic groups in the United States and, if it does, that other scholars will add different inflections that advance our awareness of basic class cultures and their importance for the various ways we are and do, belong and become in the world.

Still, all these ways of defining classes are for outside interpreters like me, making arguments for how best to understand the conflicts, divisions, or simply the key breaking points in our society. If you simply ask people an open-ended question about how they would define their own social class, the vast majority will say something like "Well, I'm not rich, and I'm not poor, so I guess you'd say I'm middle class." This is the American class vernacular, the ordinary, everyday way of defining our class structure and placing ourselves within it: rich, poor, and middle class.[20] It is broadly income-based but with just a handful of "poor" people and an even smaller group of "rich" people. In answering an open-ended question, the vast majority of people see themselves and others as part of a sprawling, nearly ubiquitous "middle class" where all distinctions of income, wealth, education, status, power, and authority disappear into an amorphous but highly egalitarian notion of middleness, what Benjamin Franklin called "a general happy Mediocrity."

This is a ridiculously false notion, as it was in Franklin's time, but it makes a tacit claim for an equality of status among almost everybody, envisioning a flat, nonhierarchical class structure but with some stigma usually attached to being either "poor" or "rich." Though in other contexts it is clear that people employ various notions of class structure to fit specific situations, this vernacular sense of the United States as a middle-class society made up mostly of middle-class people is pervasive as a default conception. Within this usage, I simply want to preserve the egalitarian instinct while dividing the ubiquitous "middle class" into two parts: a working class and a professional middle class along the occupational lines explained above.

You might suspect this is just a Lefty attempt to restore "working class" as a term into a reality that most people no longer recognize, but some social scientific evidence suggests that "working class" still has an unexpectedly strong persistence in the American perception of class. One is the General Social Survey, which asks respondents to place themselves within one of four classes: upper class, middle class, working class, or lower class. Since 1972 about 90 percent of respondents have identified themselves as either "middle class" or "working class," with an equal split of about 45 percent for each of those two class categories.[21] Nearly half of our "middle class society" defines itself as working class when given that option. What's more, in a 2004 National Election Study survey, respondents were asked to rank thirty-one categories of people and institutions from least favorable to most favorable on a scale of 0 to 100. "Working-class people" were not only recognized as a class but also judged *the* most favorable of all thirty-one among choices that included women, older people, the military, middle-class people, poor people, businesspeople, rich people, labor unions, and big business (in that order).[22]

These are remarkable results in a country that for decades virtually banned the use of the term "working class" in persistently and loudly proclaiming itself a

"middle-class society." The results suggest that though unrecognized and un-
appreciated in mainstream culture, there must be another culture in our midst, a
culture that may provide an alternative to what the people who determine these
things call "the mainstream." If there is and if you believe one National Election
Study survey, that culture produces the kind of people whom Americans of all
races, genders, and stations of life view most favorably.

That's basically the argument of this book: There is a genuine working-class
culture that provides both a vital complement and an attractive alternative to professional middle-class culture, and if it's dying, it needs to be revived, rescued,
and renewed. If, on the other hand, it is persisting against all odds, as I believe,
then it needs to be recognized and appreciated within a much less imperial middle-
class culture—one capable of recognizing that we are stronger together because
we bring important differences to each other, different strengths that offset each
other's weaknesses even while providing alternative ways to live a life that's full
and meaningful.

Who Am I to Say?

Though I use a lot of economic and sociological research to support my views,
what follows is largely based on my observations and experience over more than
seven decades. I am not seeking certainty or trying to prove my views but rather
suggesting a way of understanding American society based on its primary class
cultures and the way they both clash with and complement each other. Because
I have lived my entire life in various locations of the American Rust Belt, my observations and experience may be quite limited and even useless for other regions
and generations of working-class and middle-class life. Likewise, my understanding may be more white and male than I intend. But how would I know this without putting out my interpretations for others to judge against their own
observations and experience? By relying so heavily on my own experience, I hope
to make up in intimacy of detail what I lack in breadth, but I am aware that I will
inevitably miss any possible universal mark. I hope to be interesting and insightful, even when I may be overgeneralizing or outright wrong, and I ask readers
to reflect on their own experience even as they challenge my book learning and
I challenge theirs.

My main evidentiary base is the way I have been situated in various complicated ways between and among the two class cultures across my entire life as well
as my inability and unwillingness to sustain a clear choice for one culture versus
the other. I am not somebody who grew up in the working class and then abandoned it once and for all as I became a middle-class professional, though I did

become that kind of professional and for the most part have adopted its culture, sometimes enthusiastically and sometimes with resistance. Besides growing up in a very working-class environment, two main ways that I have lived within working-class culture were as a teacher and as Judie's husband, including my adoption into her large extended and predominantly working-class family back in Johnstown. There are other less significant ways that involved where we lived and who we associated with. The friends we shared were either people from working-class backgrounds or professionals with lots of experience of working-class people, mostly as teachers or labor or community organizers. Likewise, when I was a graduate student at Northwestern University, the most thoroughly middle-class experience of my life, we lived in a working-class neighborhood on Chicago's Northwest Side, where we helped organize a neighborhood association. And when we lived in thoroughly middle-class places, including Greenwich Village in the 1960s and Oak Park since 1981, we lived in apartment buildings that included a mix of working-class and standard-issue middle-class people. Very little of this was based on self-conscious choices. More so, where we lived was based on economics and where and with whom we both felt most comfortable.

My work as a night-school teacher for thirty years, however, is my main source for a broader understanding of working-class life outside my own. If I had been taking notes, my teaching experience at Roosevelt University in Chicago would have been first-rate research based on focus group discussions. I taught general education courses—elementary and advanced writing courses as well as surveys of both the social sciences and the humanities—to adults in classes of fewer than twenty students that met twice a week for three hours each. The students in these classes ranged in age from late twenties to early sixties, and they were either in working-class occupations themselves or from working-class backgrounds in standard-issue professional or semiprofessional jobs at a time when the absence of a bachelor's degree was not nearly the obstacle to workplace upward mobility that it is today. The main campus was a building in Chicago's Loop, and the students there were an equal mix of black and white, with more Latinos and Latinas in the later years. When I started teaching in the 1970s racial issues were still raw. Chicago neighborhoods were still racially changing, and there were active struggles against racism in the police force and the building trades. Many of my students were involved in these changes and struggles on one side or the other of the racial divide, so we could not avoid discussing the issues, often in frighteningly frank terms based on their direct experiences. In the beginning the racial differences stood out, but over time I also began to notice their cultural similarities, as did many of them. My focus in this book is on those similarities by class. While I am well aware of the numerous variations within class cultures in regard to not only race and ethnicity but also gender, sexuality, region, religion, life stage, and decade, I pretty much systematically stay focused strictly on the broad class-cultural differences, not the wild variations within each class culture.

My job in all my teaching was to find demanding reading that my students would find interesting, discuss it with them as a group, and then read their papers based on whatever topics we had been discussing. Because we met twice a week for long periods in small classes and because I was reading their often innermost thoughts, I got to know most students pretty intimately. Several of the courses I taught had course-related one-on-one advising sessions built into their framework, and in addition I did a lot of academic advising, often with people I saw semester after semester. In these undergraduate classes we discussed everything from Chicago politics, neighborhood racial change, and comparative economic systems to *Oedipus the King* and *The Color Purple*. I did not get to know more than a handful of my students outside the classroom, so I had no way of verifying what they told me about themselves, their families, and their work, but they told me a lot, and when you're interested in culture, what people say is as important as observing what they do. In great measure, this book constitutes my digestion of what my students told me and each other over three decades from the 1970s into the twenty-first century.

In addition to my undergraduate general education teaching, I became involved in labor education, first in the program we had at Roosevelt and then through activism in the 1980s and 1990s around plant closings and employer demands for union contract concessions. With a group of laid-off steelworkers and academic economists I was one of the founders of the Midwest Center for Labor Research, and I was the editor of *Labor Research Review* during most of its existence.[23] This experience gave me a front-row seat to the demise of labor unions in the United States and in the way this linked up with my own and Judie's extended family, a window into the wrenching erosion of working-class conditions and prospects.

In all this teaching experience as well as my public speaking to working-class audiences, I was the middle-class professional based on my information and knowledge. In these contexts, I had both unearned formal authority and, when I was good, some earned informal authority based on what I said or how I listened and responded. In all these situations I could not succeed without recognizing the differences between my working-class audiences and myself, even as I drew both tacitly and consciously on my similarities. From my first raggedy class at Roosevelt, where I knew I belonged within the first hour, I was the spokesperson, the facilitator, the college-material socialization mechanism for a professionalism I had not realized I had so deeply imbibed. Enforcing standard English was just the most obvious and least complicated of the class functions I served.

The other primary source of this meditation on class cultures is my more than half-century marriage with Judie. The granddaughter of coal miners on both sides, Judie grew up in a large hard-living family in Johnstown in which an alcoholic father had irregular work as a mechanic, while the seven children formed intense attachments to their mother, who worked as a retail clerk at Glosser Brothers Department Store as she raised the children on her own. Judie and I were high school sweethearts and the only ones to leave town, but we were never not a vital part of that extended family as we all became adults and parents and then grand-parents together. When I say "my family" in referring to anytime after 1981, when my father died (my mother died thirteen years earlier), I am referring to the family in which I am an in-law without that making a dime's worth of difference except when the brothers and sisters reminisce about their adventures running the dense streets of the Eighth Ward as children.

After failing in my first attempt at college at Ohio University in the early 1960s, I became a serious student for the first time, becoming an obsessively self-directed learner as I worked full-time at the Johnstown newspaper and fell in love with Judie all over again. We married when I was twenty and she was nineteen. As I pursued higher and higher education, mostly as a part-time student, she worked to support my ambitions, and I fully embarked on a decades-long project of transforming myself into a writer and an intellectual, a project of becoming something I was not yet. This sense of the possibility and even necessity of becoming something different and better than what you are is at the core of middle-class professionalism and its most positive attribute by my lights. For two or three decades I bought into middle class becoming hook, line, and sinker, while Judie did not. By statistical probabilities, we should have drifted apart. There were hard times, such as when I was at Northwestern pursuing a PhD in philosophy while she had never taken a college course. She would eventually get an accounting degree as an adult in the program I taught in at Roosevelt, and though she too would eventually become a middle-class professional by occupation, earning more than I did, Judie never sought to transform herself to suit an achievement-oriented culture beyond the dress and pleasant manners of the clerical worker she was for the first decades of her adulthood. She took herself as she was, lived in the present, and, though as cute and nice as can be, didn't take shit from nobody. She frustrated me with her narrow parochialism and hesitancy to dream of a different life and a better self. I frustrated her with my head-in-the-clouds unreliability and how willing I was to test her patience discoursing on subjects she cared naught about. We both argued and fought about our experience of crossing classes, pushing and pulling each other in contrary directions, before we sorted out our differences. She began to be more tolerant and even adopt some middle-class ways, while I started, only half-consciously, to fall back to some working-class ones.

Though nobody should credit any universality to this unique occupational and marital experience, I learned a lot in the process and am hoping that what I learned may be valuable to others, especially to younger generations who are not used to thinking in these class terms. In any case, this is who I am and what I have to say.

An Argument, Not a Memoir

Though I'm going to draw a lot on my life, on my own observations and experience, this is not a memoir. Rather, it is an argument for and a defense of working-class culture as I have experienced it and an interpretation of how that culture differs from and complements the culture of the professional middle class.

As I have already indicated, my experience (and Judie's) occurred in a unique historical period with a particularly dramatic character in the ways it transformed everyday life, first for good and then for ill. The first thirty or forty years of our lives was a golden age for the American working class, including all colors and genders, followed by multiple decades of erosion and decline up to the present. One of the most dramatic ways in which this is exhibited is that during our formative years nearly everybody (90 percent) improved their incomes and life conditions compared with less than a majority today.[24] In the process the professional middle class expanded like wildfire, while at the same time working-class people, without changing their class position, bettered their lives year by year for nearly thirty years. The argument I make in part 1 is that beyond a historically unique shared economic prosperity, these three decades were also a golden age of collective action, of social movements and personal transformations, within which the two class cultures flourished. I do not want to go back to that time and place, as if that were possible, but I do want younger generations to appreciate what made it golden and see how and why we could and should extract some of that gold to move forward.

With my own life and time as context, part 2 makes the argument, against formidable opponents, that there is a genuine working-class culture that not only survived so-called affluence but also flourished in it and has retained a sturdy, if diminished, capacity to endure even as economic circumstances have deteriorated so badly. I do so by critiquing various texts that recognize the existence of an American working class (something not always noticed!) but explicitly argue that the working class has no genuine culture, being merely a receptacle, with appropriate cultural lags, of a dominant middle-class culture as it develops in a singular American mainstream. I then outline what I see as categorical differences between working-class and professional middle-class cultures. Here I draw heavily on my own observation and experience, relying primarily on a list of attributes Judie and I had worked out more than twenty years ago. But that list has since been supplemented (mostly confirmed but often productively contested) by the work of working-class studies scholars, American sociological heirs of Pierre Bourdieu, a couple of generations of labor and working-class historians, and pieces of the rich English tradition rooted in cultural studies. What emerges is but one descriptive interpretation of American working-class culture, one that may be significantly biased toward the "settled-living," "routine-seeking" parts of the working class, especially those once or now in labor unions, but also is informed by others' valuations and by different interpretations from other regions of American working-class life. My hope is that the reader will gain a larger sense of the richness and vitality of working-class life, thereby revealing what one-class interpretations of "mainstream culture" are missing when they do not see working-class habits of heart and mind as worthy and productive rivals to middle-class ones.

Part 3 attempts to deepen and broaden my analysis of certain key aspects of working-class life and culture while taking my cues from common middle-class misunderstandings, some of them self-serving and even vicious. Chapter 7, on the working-class strategy of ceding control to gain control, is probably the most original and contestable part of the book. Likewise, chapter 8, on the value of "taking it," and chapter 9, on working-class realism, treat topics rarely addressed elsewhere.

These aspects of working-class life and culture are developed against what I see as a narrowing of middle-class culture, which is more and more in a protective crouch as we simultaneously defend against our own proletarianization while watching most of our fellow citizens' work and lives become progressively harder, more constricted, degrading, and often dangerous. The economic pressures on middle-class professionals are strong to focus simply on keeping what we have and passing it on to our children with frenzied investments in their cultural capital. Not only will the math not work for many of us, but we are also losing those aspects of our culture that most gave us our claim to being a universal class, to being a justifiably dominant and mainstream culture.[25]

The epilogue suggests that middle-class aspiration, reconfigured to recover our broader vision and our own experience with collective action, can help spur a renewal of the working class's culture of belonging and broaden and build on its parochial solidarity, as has happened in the past. There is evidence from our last two decades that this *is* occurring, though without the explicit self-consciousness of class cultures that could make it stronger. Restoring the Glorious Thirty's steady expansion of *discretionary income* and *free time for what you will* is economically more feasible now than it was then. As is commonly said, we merely lack the political will to get back on the right track toward freedom and dignity for all. We lack this will, at least in part, because of our class cultural confusion. Specifically, the professional middle class mistakes its culture for the only genuine and valuable one and increasingly defines itself by its own best and brightest examples rather than by the broad extension of standard-issue middle-class mediocrity that could overlap so powerfully with an aroused working class.

Part I

NOSTALGIA FOR THE THIRTY-YEAR CENTURY OF THE COMMON

Men and women cannot be really free until they have plenty to eat, and time and ability to read and think and talk things over.

Henry Wallace, "The Century of the Common Man," May 8, 1942

In 1982 I turned thirty-nine and was making $15,000 a year, having recently given up a somewhat higher-paying administrative job to take my first full-time teaching position. My brother-in-law Albert Mikula had just been laid off as a machinist at U.S. Steel in Johnstown, where he had been making $26,000. (In today's money—2021—that would be the difference between $42,000 and $72,000.)

I remember these amounts because at a meeting of progressive academics in Chicago, I made reference to the prospects of Albert and his family if the United Steelworkers union accepted the kind of wage concessions the steel companies were asking for in the fall of 1982. I was taken aback when Joe Persky, an economist who was skeptical of our anticoncessions stance given the potential danger of mills closing, made a crack that Albert "probably makes more than you do as a professor." I responded too concretely at first, revealing Albert's wage and my salary and pointing out that Albert and Judie's sister, Peg, had six kids, while Judie and I had only one. Joe made a face that immediately alerted me to my concreteness fallacy, and I then went off in self-righteous Lefty mode about Albert's and other steelworkers' working conditions (the alternating heat and cold, the hard physical labor standing all day, the crazy swing shifts, the tight supervision) compared to my job, which hardly seemed like real work at all during the academic year and with the summers off. It was only fair that Albert should be paid more and be able to retire earlier than people like me and Joe.

Joe, as I remember, responded that fairness had nothing to do with it, arguing that steelworkers made more than we did because they were productive labor, whereas we were living off the economic surplus they produced; plus they had a union, and we didn't. Joe's point was not that we should necessarily make more than steelworkers but that the spread was large enough to allow steelworkers to take a financial haircut if it meant saving jobs and entire mills. In retrospect, Joe was probably more right than I was, but my view of fairness was popular then among our small group of academics—and was not outrageously out of whack with general professional middle-class opinion at the time. Today, of course, it would seem outrageous in middle-class settings for a factory worker to be paid more than a professor, as higher education is now a key measure of every kind of worth, including financial.

Moments such as this stick in memory for a reason. This one stuck, I think, because it occurred at a turning point in both my and Albert's lives, and part of the remembrance is about what we did not know then but do know now. I didn't know that I was at the beginning of the best decade of my life, followed by some other pretty good ones, or that Albert was at the beginning of his worst decade, followed by some more bad ones. I also didn't know the Glorious Thirty had ended seven years earlier—or indeed that it had been glorious.

My nostalgia for the Glorious Thirty and the brief glimpse of a "century of the common man" it provided is not based on how great those three decades felt at the time or even on how much was accomplished during those thirty years (which was a lot). Unlike my parents' generation, who often reminded us youngsters of how good things were in comparison to the preceding years of the Great Depression and World War II, my appreciation for 1945–1975 is founded on what has happened since: an initially dramatic but then steady erosion of working-class living standards and working conditions that by now has seeped into the standard-issue part of the professional middle class. What's more, working-class culture is not as strong and proud or as sure of itself as it once was, and middle-class culture is more crabbed and tense, more self-centered and less willing to acknowledge and explore more than its "one right way."

"Nostalgia" is a word that often has no real meaning, just a strongly negative connotation. Like "liberal," "petty bourgeois," and "mediocre," "nostalgia" simply evokes something you don't want to be and is often used to dismiss someone else's point of view without having to explain why.[1] Insofar as it has meaning, the negative aspect of nostalgia is appropriately defined as "the sentimental yearning for an irretrievable past," and this is thought to be backward-looking in a way that is unproductive for moving forward.[2] I admit to some yearning for key elements of this past, but I don't think those elements are irretrievable, and in part 1 I argue that my yearning is rational, not sentimental—or at least not only sentimental.

I have not directly experienced what Geoff Bright calls the "social haunting" of those who lost their livelihoods and have lived through the deterioration of their communities and ways of life.[3] Sometimes nostalgia is not a self-indulgent, gauzy remembrance of good old days but instead is a powerful, often overpowering, process of grieving for what has been palpably lost. I am a witness to that grieving, not a participant in it. As such, I have observed stages of grief that often end up with what I'd call a restorative nostalgia: a spontaneous sorting out of what could be and what cannot be retrieved, often expressed at the end of a reverie as "at least we ought to be able to . . ."[4]

In the first decade of the twenty-first century, when both Albert and I retired, I was making about $67,000, and he was still somewhere around $25,000—a spread in 2021 dollars between $87,000 and about $33,000 and a complete and utter reversal of where we had been in midlife.[5] Both the U.S. Steel and Bethlehem Steel mills in Johnstown were long gone, though pieces of them were still in operation by various smaller companies. Albert went back to work, after nearly three years of unemployment, at one of these pieces—back to a severely speeded-up job at a much-reduced wage and with meager benefits.[6] His younger son got work at one of the pieces that had been Bethlehem Steel's, and his older son works at a furniture store, both making less than the median wage for all full-time US workers now. Three of his four daughters have worked sporadically for Walmart, usually for much less than the median, and the other has had steady work as an administrator at a credit union with what all describe as "decent wages and benefits"—though what counts as "decent" is not what it was when she was born in the late 1960s. Albert and Peg subsist on Social Security and a collection of very small pensions, the largest one from his eighteen years at U.S. Steel before it closed, a tiny one from his twenty sporadic years at U.S. Steel's successor companies, and another bit from the National Guard for his decades as a weekend warrior operating several generations of tanks.

Albert has been through his stages of grief, and I have spent some incidental bar time with him as he expressed and recounted some of it. Shortly after he retired, he told me he was finally at peace because "there's nothing left they can take away." The "they" who had taken so much away from him was ill-defined and impersonal but clearly was not intended to include me. I had a vague but powerful sense, however, that it should.

We were once roughly equal—Albert had a higher income and a more plentiful standard of living, and I had much better working conditions and work that didn't wear me down day by day as I got older. I had greater prestige as the world goes, but in our extended working-class family he had a lot too as a decidedly better hunter of game and fixer of physical objects that had a tendency to break. Likewise, he was thought to have more common sense than me. Even though my various credentials were respected (even bragged on), my actual book learning was generally seen to be of doubtful relevance. Now I have everything—more income and more wealth as well as much better working conditions when we were working and now a more secure and fulsome retirement that includes expensive vacations (from retirement!). Even my relative prestige is enhanced, certainly as the world goes but also within their working-class culture. Four decades of deterioration in the material conditions of their lives and in the prospects for their children and grandchildren have sowed doubt about their ways of doing things and living a life.

I only occasionally feel guilty about this, and I have little inclination to give up much of what I now have. But I do have a profound sense of regret and loss and of intellectual embarrassment at not having appreciated what our society had when we had it. I really can't say it was a better world then, as a great deal was worse, much worse, especially for African Americans, women, and gays. But our trajectory, the direction we were going during those thirty years, was better, way better than the direction we are going now and have been going for the past forty years and more. It's not just the increasing standard of living and expansion of free time for what you will among the working classes that I'm nostalgic for but also the way shared prosperity from the bottom up tends to enhance both aspiration and generosity across the board.[7]

I have my own class interests to protect, and a good part of what I'm nostalgic for is a time when middle-class professionalism had not only its characteristic status-anxiety and competitive success ethic but also a countervailing willingness and drive to conscientiously explore what a good life might be in the absence of scarcity. Today there's little time for that, as nearly all our conscientiousness is forced into mobilizing our social and cultural capital so we can maintain our position and pass on our class advantage to our children and, in my case, grandchildren for fear they might fall into that swirling downward economic spiral that is working-class life today. But with middle-class professionalism's increasing isolation from and active avoidance of working-class life and culture, it's harder and harder for middle-class generations to see the attractions and value of working-class ways, let alone learn from and borrow some of those ways. This was not always so, and that too is a reason to be nostalgic for thirty years that were not so bad in themselves and actually pretty glorious compared to the directions we're heading now.

This is the nostalgia I feel, and my argument is that you should feel it too—or at least acknowledge it as a legitimate spur for the kind of golden age thinking that has long been productive in informing the present and charting a future. Since at least the Renaissance in Europe, golden age thinking has been used to criticize present situations, find past examples of better ways of doing things, and urge the work of recovery, restoration, and renewal.[8] Seldom has it been a simple pining for a past that is experienced as irretrievable. More often, golden age thinking has spurred serious intellectual and practical endeavors to imitate some admired quality or aspect of the past, whether an ineffable spirit or a gritty capacity for working with stone.

Golden age thinking is rife today and very much focused on various parts of the Glorious Thirty. Conservatives wish to recover the "family values" and religiosity of the 1950s along with its rigid gender and sexual "normalcy." Liberals point to the widespread benefits of labor unions and an active government in bettering people's lives especially in the 1960s, with many grieving for the passing of a "social democratic moment" that extends back to the 1930s. Much of the reaction against nostalgia—the counsel to forget the past, get over it, and forge ahead—is based on the supposed exhaustion of this debate. But on the progressive side of this nostalgia, my side, a formidable literature has developed that picks through the specific policies of those times and calls for their restoration as part of a renewed commitment to shared prosperity. Much of it is golden age thinking at its best, and I hope to build on it in what follows.

The exhibits here are too numerous to mention, but Jacob Hacker and Paul Pierson's *American Amnesia: How the War on Government Led Us to Forget What Made America Prosper* is a recent progressive compendium of golden age thinking across a wide front. Hacker's earlier *The Great Risk Shift* and, with Pierson, *Winner-Take-All Politics* use the history of postwar prosperity as a kind of touchstone for compelling critiques of what is often called "neoliberalism," whereas *American Amnesia* is a thorough reconstruction by nonhistorians of the policy history from the Progressive Era (1896–1916) through the Glorious Thirty.[9] For Hacker and Pierson "the goose that laid the golden age" is a "mixed economy," which is very like what Tony Judt in *Ill Fares the Land* defines as "social democracy," an "acceptance of capitalism—and parliamentary democracy—as the framework within which the hitherto neglected interests of large sections of the population would now be addressed."[10] A somewhat more politically ambitious history by a nonhistorian, Sam Pizzigati's *The Rich Don't Always Win: The Forgotten Triumph over Plutocracy That Created the American Middle Class, 1900–1970*, focuses on popular movements that won explicit policies to redistribute income, wealth, and opportunity especially through progressive taxation.[11] Other nonhistorians nostalgically reference a golden age of shared prosperity, not to yearn for an irretrievable past but instead to advocate for practical political economic programs of restoration and renewal, adjusted for current circumstances. Thomas Piketty's *Capital in the Twenty-First Century*, for example, is positively wistful, like Pizzagati, for the steeply progressive and "confiscatory" income tax rates in the United States under President Dwight D. Eisenhower. Bob Kuttner, Robert Reich, and Paul Krugman all advocate massive stimulative investment in public works (now called "infrastructure"), harkening back to Eisenhower's long-term investment in the interstate highway system and President John F. Kennedy's space program. The living wage movement is nostalgic for steady increases in the federal minimum wage like we had until 1968. David Weil's *The Fissured Workplace: Why Work Became So Bad for So Many and What Can Be Done to Improve It* harkens back to a time before workplaces were cracked apart with part-time, contingent, temporary workers and "independent contractors," a time when high turnover and quit rates were not goals for low-wage employers but rather symptoms of problems that needed to be addressed.[12] Even financial writers such as Steven Pearlstein fondly remember the good old days of "managerial capitalism" versus today's narrow-minded, mean-spirited "shareholder capitalism."[13] Kuttner's *Can Democracy Survive Global Capitalism?* is especially compelling in showing how what he calls the "vulnerable miracle" of the Glorious Thirty was based on "suppressing speculative finance" at both national and international levels.[14]

These authors and many others are insistent, often passionately so, on remembering this historical period not to pine or yearn for it—and not, like many progressive historians, to uncover opportunities lost and construct narratives of what went wrong—but instead to use this past to expand the range of the possible in our current circumstance and make arguments for practical proposals for future action based on past successes. Some or all of them may be wrong, but they cannot be simply dismissed as nostalgic and therefore irrelevant. Their nostalgia is justified, even necessary. Without it, the future is narrower and meaner in prospect.

My goal in part 1 is to add to this literature by showing how working- and middle-class cultures developed during this period in a kind of dialectical opposition and unity that was both cause and consequence of some of the glories of the Glorious Thirty.

WHAT WAS GLORIOUS ABOUT THE GLORIOUS THIRTY?

The lost U.S. paradise is associated with the country's beginnings: there is nostalgia for the era of the Boston Tea Party, not for Trente Glorieuses and a heyday of state intervention to curb the excesses of capitalism.

Thomas Piketty, *Capital in the Twenty-First Century*

Les Trentes Glorieuses. I had been talking and teaching about "postwar prosperity" and "the postwar boom" for decades before I came across this French usage that derives from a 1979 book that in English would be titled *The Glorious Thirty, or the Invisible Revolution from 1946 to 1975.*[1] I immediately adopted the usage for two reasons. One is the precise dating for the meaning of "postwar." The other is the "Glorious" tag, which strikes English-speaking ears as hyperbolic and for that reason establishes a much higher bar for evidentiary support than the weak and exclusively economic terms "prosperity" and "boom."

I've been riding this hobby horse for a while in teaching and in public speeches, and it is amazing how even with use of the "Glorious Thirty" people think I'm talking only about the 1950s, which is seen as an especially repressive time for both blacks and women, not to mention gays, Latinx Americans, disabled people, and even Catholics, Jews, and non-WASP ethnic groups. When I had previously used "postwar" I recognized the ambiguous timeframe—sometimes meaning just the most formative years of the late 1940s and more often just the fifteen years from 1945 to 1960 that evokes "the '50s"—so I had been scrupulous in defining "postwar prosperity" as lasting from 1947 to 1973, as tracked by the rise and fall of real weekly wages for production and nonsupervisory workers. Even so, people had difficulty detaching my "prosperous twenty-six" from "the '50s."

Maybe that is at least in part because I am a straight white guy, and that naturally engenders a suspicion that what I'm nostalgic for is the good old 1950s when straight white guys were uncontested kings, even among the poor and working class. Who knows what's going on in my unconscious, but I am the kind of male who benefited from women's liberation, both financially and culturally, in not having to be a sole breadwinner and not having to live up to a narrower view of masculinity than I was suited for. And in a variety of ways, both in youth and as an adult, I was profoundly influenced and positively affected by the civil rights movement, which added so much to and took nothing away from me. What's more, us straight white guys still have a lot of our kingly advantages, even when we don't explicitly claim them. No, I am nostalgic not for a better country, a better world, than we have now but instead for one going in a better direction—one that is more inclusive than in the past but one that would have a robust respect for the common and a constantly confirming sense that things could and should get progressively better for mediocrities, who constitute the vast majority of humanity.

Likewise, I am nostalgic not for a mere decade but instead for the entire expanse of the three decades from 1945 to 1975 that included *both* the 1950s and the 1960s, particularly for how those decades were linked not just as opposites but also in a unity of material prosperity and a transformation of moral and spiritual values, a unity of impersonal economic forces and highly personal social movements. As I see it, the unprecedented improvements in material conditions unleashed a flood of grand expectations, to use James Patterson's telling title for his history of the period, and made these years not only a golden age of shared prosperity but, as both cause and consequence, a golden age of collective action as well.[2] Like a flood, our grand expectations eventually overwhelmed us for a time, but we are still living in the enriched soil that those expectations left behind.

So, what was so glorious about those times—glorious not compared to some ideal world we can envision but rather compared to what preceded it (going back as far as you can go) and to what has followed and is following it? To what extent was it a thirty-year "century" of the common?

Though my primary interest is in what was happening back then to the two wings of free wage labor—the one I grew up in and the one I've spent the bulk of my life in since—I'll start with the macroeconomic base.

These were years of superior economic growth, during which the GDP averaged better than 4 percent a year, while unemployment averaged under 5 percent and inflation around 2 percent until the oil shock of 1973–1974. Those are not perfect or even ideal numbers, but they are much better than anything before or since. During the nineteenth-century industrial revolutions in the United States, for example, economic growth averaged only 1.6 percent a year from 1839 into the twentieth century and then hovered around 3 percent for the first half of the twentieth century.[3] Likewise, we have not seen anything like Glorious Thirty numbers since the early 1970s, averaging about 3.1 percent GDP growth in the last thirty years of the twentieth century and a little less than 2 percent in the first eighteen years of the twenty-first century.[4] There have been important periods when *either* unemployment or inflation did as well or better but *never both for such a sustained period* as during the Glorious Thirty.[5]

Sustained low levels of unemployment and inflation during a strong period of economic growth is really, really good, but it would stretch even the French language to call it "glorious." Though improvements in the general standard of living are likely during such a period, they are not inevitable, as we know from more recent if much shorter growth periods. Rising general standards of living (and working) during the Glorious Thirty are the core glories that led to other glories. The gold of this golden age came in two primary forms, money and time, namely the steady increases in real incomes, including the emergence and spread of discretionary income, and the overall increase in free time for what you will, including the emergence of what for most people was a whole new stage of life: retirement. Thus, it was not just prosperity itself that was glorious but also the way that prosperity was shared.

Real wages for all employees began their sustained rise in 1940 with the onset of World War II in Europe. Wages at that time were only slightly better than they had been in 1929, as the Great Depression had halted a substantial increase in real wages since the beginning of the century. In 1940 the average wage in 2020 dollars was about $24,000, but by 1970 it had climbed 110 percent to nearly $51,000—about $1,000 more than it is today (2020).[6] These are "real" wages and incomes, meaning they are adjusted to take account of the corrosive effects of inflation on spending power; thus, they record a more than doubling of the general standard of living, a doubling of the amount of money people had to cover the costs of living their lives. Managerial and professional workers did somewhat better than the average during those thirty years, manufacturing workers about average; and domestic workers, farmworkers, retail sales, clerical workers, and others somewhat worse, but all advanced, and almost everybody advanced substantially.[7]

Though poverty (as we have measured it since the 1960s) was undoubtedly reduced during the full-employment years of World War II in the United States, we don't have numbers that go back that far. The official series begins with 1959, but Frank Levy has calculated that the US poverty rate in 1949 was 32 percent and would have been higher than that in the preceding decades.[8] By 1971 it had steadily declined to about 11 percent before it stopped declining and started creeping back up.[9] That's a 65 percent decrease in poverty in twenty-two years, from one of every three men, women, and children being poor to one of every ten. If that rate of decrease had continued, poverty would have been eliminated well before the dawn of the twenty-first century.[10] The most recent poverty rate as I write is about 12 percent (during the COVID-19 recession), so on this score I might like to go back to 1971 when it was a point lower, but much more important

TABLE 1.1 Average annual real family income growth by income group, 1947–2013

PERIOD	BOTTOM FIFTH	2ND FIFTH	MIDDLE FIFTH	4TH FIFTH	TOP FIFTH	TOP 5%
1945–1979	2.6%	2.3%	2.5%	2.5%	2.3%	2.0%
1979–2007	0.0%	0.4%	0.6%	0.9%	1.5%	2.0%
2007–2013	[−1.9%]	[−1.4%]	[−1.3%]	[−1.0%]	[−0.2%]	0.1%

Source: Adapted from Economic Policy Institute, "Average Real Family Income Growth, by Income Group, 1947–2013," *The State of Working America*, September 25, 2014, http://www.stateofworkingamerica.org /charts/real-annual-family-income-growth-by-quintile-1947-79-and-1979-2010/.

than any particular state that was achieved by the end of the Glorious Thirty is that trajectory: the steady rise of wages and incomes and the steady reduction in poverty. The direction and its steadiness are what we should be nostalgic for.

The Economic Policy Institute's series *The State of Working America* has for years been gathering data that compare US family incomes by quintiles across various time periods, always with the purpose of contrasting the tremendous growth of family incomes from the 1940s through the 1970s with what has happened since. The most recent version gives average annual growth rates by quintile, as shown in table 1.1.

Table 1.1 shows a thirty-two-year period, 1947 to 1979, when real family incomes at every level increased by more than 2 percent a year, followed by a twenty-eight-year period (1979–2007) during which incomes increased much more slowly, especially for the bottom 80 percent. This stagnation was followed by a much briefer period from the onset of the Great Recession in 2007–2009, when incomes for everybody except the top 5 percent actually declined. It also shows a dramatic reversal in the distribution of income growth, from the bottom fifth of families having the greatest gain during the glorious period to their losing income faster than any other group in the most recent period. That last row of table 1.1 shows a clear hierarchy of loss nowadays—the less you have, the more you lose.

Because these are small numbers, it is easy to look past them and see just the reversal of trend. But try to imagine how different living a life is when your real income goes up 2 percent a year versus one where it goes down 1 percent or so every year. In the former, life gets a little bit easier to live each year; in the latter, it gets a little bit harder. The annual change is fairly small—instead of having $100 you have either $102 or $99—so it is easy not to notice the change. But living in the first situation can make you feel like a genius and in the second like a failure. This is why Jean Fourastie called the Glorious Thirty an "invisible revolution." These small annual changes accumulated into a series of transformations in everyday life, a revolution that because it was both slow and steady lacked drama and thus had limited visibility. What's more, even though life was improving steadily, relentlessly, so too were expectations. An earlier version of *The State of Working America* showed that from 1947 to 1973 those small annual increases had more than doubled the family incomes of the bottom two and the middle quintiles, while the second and top quintiles increased by 97.5 percent and 88 percent, respectively. That's right. For those twenty-six years the poor got richer faster than the rich, and so did the middle. Though founded on a longer revolution beginning nearly a century before, these years are when, in the words of Jacob Hacker and Paul Pierson, "We broke from the entirety of prior human existence, in which life was nasty, brutish, and short for almost everyone."[11] How could that not be glorious? And how could it be irrational and unrealistic to be nostalgic for that trajectory and its steadiness?

That steadiness had a certain weight of its own, independent of specific magnitudes of increase. Steady jobs with steadily increasing incomes came to be taken for granted not long after World War II, opening up the floodgates of consumer debt—from installment buying of cars and appliances to the emergence of the credit card including for people with blue collars, people who had not previously been deemed credit-worthy mostly because they had not previously been credit-worthy. Historian Louis Hyman calls the 1950s Charga-Plate "a new kind of social democracy at the checkout counter."[12] As Hyman shows, postwar consumer debt was a virtuous circle as long as real wages were rising, and it took a while for that debt to turn vicious after wages and incomes began to stagnate and then decline.[13] Part of debt's virtue during the Glorious Thirty was its macroeconomic effects in further fueling economic growth, but I'm not as nostalgic for that as I am for the way it piled on to an already expanding discretionary income.

Disposable income is simply your income after taxes are taken out—it may be a little or it may be a lot, but everybody has some of it. *Discretionary income* is different—it's what's left over after *all* your regular expenses have been paid (not just your taxes but also your rent or mortgage, food, clothing, etc.). Though I could not find a clear history of discretionary income, it's safe to say that most people didn't have any until somewhere in the middle of the twentieth century. Discretionary income is the money you have available to spend however you want. In a money economy based on free wage labor and a cash nexus, the expansion of discretionary income (both in individuals' lives and in the proportion of people who have some of it) is a great leap forward for human freedom. And the widespread availability of credit added to that freedom. You could waste your money at the race track, or you could put it in your church's donation plate; you could buy baubles and beads on impulse, or you could invest in cars and refrigerators, TVs, and automatic washers and dryers, things that would transform your daily activities and life; you could drink your discretionary income at the local bar, or you could save it for your children's education. Discretionary income is that part of your wages that is "for what you will." Its expansion during the Glorious Thirty was an enormous increase in freedom and one of the most glorious of the glories that have been and still are being eroded.

If discretionary is the better part of income, then it surely is also the better part of time. Most of the effort, the movement politics and government policies, that achieved the forty-hour workweek occurred before the Glorious Thirty, but it was not until the fall of 1945 that the five-day week and two-day weekend finally emerged as "a fixture of American life" and then remained so for three or four decades.[14] The manufacturing workweek had declined from nearly seventy hours to about sixty during the nineteenth century, and the forty-eight-hour, six-day workweek had been achieved in great measure by the 1920s. The Great Depression posed the opposite problem—not enough and sporadic work, when many workers were basically day laborers who might work Monday through Wednesday one week, Thursday and Friday the next, and not at all the week after that. When the Fair Labor Standards Act established the forty-hour standard in 1938, the average workweek in manufacturing was actually only about thirty-five hours. Then during the full-employment economy of World War II there was so much overtime that the forty-eight-hour workweek of the 1920s was restored (though with the crucial difference that workers were paid 50 percent more for those "extra" eight hours, as required by the Fair Labor Standards Act).[15] Though in a steel town with its rotating swing shifts there was no uniform Saturday and Sunday weekend, I grew up taking for granted and not appreciating that extra day off— that is, until as a professional worker I lost my weekends as my work steadily bled into them and until I watched as working-class jobs experienced increasing wage theft with overtime hours not being paid, while others had insufficient hours with irregular, contingent employment. Today we increasingly have the worst of both the Great Depression and World War II economies—not enough paid work for some and too much paid (and unpaid) work for others. It's not yet worse than back in the day, but it's heading that way. What was glorious about the weekend back then was not just the increase in leisure time it afforded (which many social scientists worried at the time might be misused and abused!) but rather the relative steadiness and reliability of that swath of time for what you will.

The official standard workweek for nonsalaried workers is still forty hours today, so there was no progress during the Glorious Thirty on this score, just the enjoyment of that extra day off. The American labor movement has often been criticized for failing to focus on reducing it further, but unions worked steadily during this period to reduce the work year by increasing days of paid vacation and holidays, much of which spilled over to nonunion workers. This was nothing to brag about compared to what unions would achieve in European countries, but it did have the effect of gradually expanding free time for what you will over a worker's lifetime. Much more significant, however, was the emergence of retirement as a new stage of life after you were done with work—something very few workers had ever experienced or anticipated before 1950 or 1960.

The increasingly widespread availability of retirement during the Glorious Thirty had its foundations in earlier times in the increasing lifespans made possible by advances in sanitation and public health, the continuing miracles of modern medicine, and the creation of Social Security in 1935 as a foundation for private pensions. As Robert Gordon explains, "In earlier eras, workers often died before the age of retirement or had no financial resources enabling them to enjoy retirement, leaving them confined as dependents in the dwellings of their children."[16] In 1940 barely over half of men and about 60 percent of women survived from age twenty-one to age sixty-five, and at sixty-five their life expectancies were seventy-seven and eighty; by 1980 more than two-thirds of men and 81 percent of women survived those years, and their life expectancies at age sixty-five had increased an additional two and four years, respectively.[17]

But retirement could not have become a universal expectation and widespread reality without the spread of private pensions and health insurance during the postwar era—again largely as the result of the efforts of union workers, which came to benefit most other workers (but by no means all). In 1940, for example, only 7 percent of the labor force had private pensions, but by 1970, 45 percent did; this later declined to 35 percent by the early 1990s and then to 18 percent by the second decade of the twenty-first century.[18] Likewise, we now have unarguably the least effective and most expensive health care system among advanced capitalist countries, but going into World War II most people did not have health care of any sort because they could not afford it. Fewer than 10 percent of private-sector workers were covered by health insurance in 1940, but by 1973, 87 percent were covered for hospital and 81 percent for surgical expenses. Private insurance coverage has been declining ever since, though Medicare and Medicaid (both passed during the Glorious Thirty) and the Affordable Care Act of 2010 have significantly filled some gaps.[19] Medicare and the continuing advances in medical treatments get the bulk of the credit for life expectancy at age sixty increasing "more rapidly after 1940 than before," but regardless of who or what gets the credit, adding a brand-new stage to life, whether complete with fancy vacations or just getting by, is a glorious increase in free time for what you will.[20]

This is what I'm nostalgic for—the enormous increase in net freedom for almost everybody based on the steady increase in both wages and "the time and ability to read and think and talk things over"—or to go fishing in the afternoon and write poetry in the evening, or to just simply hang out with your friends in a bar or at a prayer meeting, all the while cultivating your backyard garden or the window flower box in your apartment. You can criticize people for their consumerism, their rediscovery of fundamentalist religion, or their eventual evolution into couch potatoes—which many scholars, especially on the Left, have done to an exaggerated degree—but that newfound freedom of time and money was there and was gradually expanding for people to use, misuse, or both. That's what I'm nostalgic for.

The Gold in Social Movements

Presenting these facts and figures in class and in public settings, at this point I often get complaints that all this might be true for whites or even just white men but that the Glorious Thirty was not such a golden age for black people, women, and gays.[21] There is, of course, truth to this, as racial and gender inequalities of every sort, especially of the ideological or cultural sorts, were much worse for the entirety of this period than they are now. But such complaints also seem strange to me, since every January we celebrate the heyday of the civil rights movement from 1955 through 1968, which coincides with the public life and movement activism of Martin Luther King Jr., right at the heart of the Glorious Thirty. Likewise, gay pride parades in every major city each year are held in June because the Stonewall Riots during that month in 1969 are seen as the activist kickoff for gay liberation. And most histories of second-wave feminism (known as women's liberation back then) locate the roots of the movement in the 1960s.[22] Golden ages are times when important things turn and start moving in new and better directions (the original meaning of "revolution"), and if you're looking for three decades when the arc of history got bent toward justice, you're not going to do better than the Glorious Thirty.

Economics is part of it, the foundational part of it as I see it, but the upsurge of liberatory social movements during the Glorious Thirty is very much part of what makes those decades so glorious in retrospect. It may not have felt so great at the time, though there were moments of exhilaration and joy alongside those of frustration, confusion, and grief and a fair amount of fear and trembling. Those racial, gender, and sexual revolutions continue today, some such as LGBTQ rights still vigorously, but others are stalled or at best grinding out day-to-day progress against the grain of relentless economic deterioration for all but the top 20 or 10 or 5 percent. It wasn't that way back in the day. The steady and over time enormous increases in money and time did not lead to complacency and mindless consumerism, as was feared at the time and still often claimed today, but instead to a golden age of organized collective action. And this is one of the most urgent lessons to be learned from harking back to the Glorious Thirty: shared prosperity didn't co-opt common people with roast beef and apple pie; rather, it expanded their sense of the possible and their willingness to fight for it. Not everybody, of course, maybe not even a majority if you're counting and definitely not all at the same time, but looking back over this thirty-year period the mainline of causation involves working-class agency creating shared prosperity, which on a sustained basis did exactly what Alexis de Tocqueville saw as the foundation of the French Revolution:

> As the prosperity of France developed . . . , men's minds appeared meanwhile more anxious and more unsettled. Public disquiet sharpened; the loathing of all ancient institutions was on the increase. . . . [T]he French found their situation all the more intolerable the better it became. . . . [E]xperience teaches us that the most hazardous moment for a bad government is normally when it is beginning to reform[,] . . . setting out to relieve [its] subjects' suffering after a long period of oppression. The evils, patiently endured as inevitable, seem unbearable as soon as the idea of escaping them is conceived. Then the removal of an abuse seems to cast a sharper light on those still left and makes people more painfully aware of them; the burden has become lighter, it is true, but the sensitivity more acute."[23]

By the 1950s the American labor movement had lost whatever revolutionary edge it might once have had, but it was not afraid to strike to make sure that whatever prosperity there might be would be shared with its members and the working class more broadly. No decade in American history saw more strikes than the supposedly placid 1950s, and the Glorious Thirty in fact opened and closed with two of the greatest strike waves in our history, 1945–1946 and 1967–1971.[24] I have argued elsewhere that this enforced sharing of economic growth actually contributed to that growth, and without it there might not have been much "postwar prosperity" at all.[25] That view is not even in the parking lot of the ballpark of mainstream economics today, but there is no doubt that union power throughout this period, the active agency of workers on strike or threatening to strike, was on the pitcher's mound of the sharing.[26] There might have been postwar prosperity without all those strikes and other forms of union power, but it surely would not have been shared anywhere nearly as much as it was. What's more, even the highly institutionalized activities of American contract-based unions demonstrated the efficacy and power of organized collective action, as year after year they extracted money and time, amid much business whining and hand-wringing, from some of the biggest, most powerful organizations in the world. And the visible result was that prosperity was stronger than ever before (or since) and was more widely shared than ever before (or since).

As a further result, the "loathing of all ancient institutions" such as racial segregation, racial and ethnic hierarchies, patriarchy, and rigidly hypocritical sexual norms became more intense and acute. Each liberatory movement, including the labor movement, called forth a backlash of repression: for example, the Taft-Hartley Act of 1947, the White Citizens Councils and a revived Ku Klux Klan, the American Psychiatric Association's pathologizing of gays in the *Diagnostic and Statistical Manual of Mental Disorders*, and the all-fronts "containment strategy" to restore and keep women in their place.[27] But until at least the late 1970s the backlashes just stimulated more creative, strategically complex, and determined collective action in the streets, in the courts and legislatures, and in neighborhoods and workplaces.

These liberatory movements occurred in serial order, usually involved different groups of people, and often conflicted with each other, sometimes bitterly. There was no unified uprising of the people. But as life got better, as money and time for what you will increased, as union workers demonstrated the power of organized collective action to change not just their circumstances but also the causal forces creating those circumstances, there was by the mid-1960s what James Patterson describes as a *contagion* of "organized movements among previously marginalized groups."[28]

Patterson is unique among postwar historians in seeing rising expectations at the core of the period. For him, there is a clear causal chain: rising standards of working and living, prosperity in a word, caused "rising personal expectations [to grow] ever more grand," and these "ever-larger expectations about life" led to a contagion of organized movements, not just the largest and most visible mentioned above but also farmworkers, senior citizens, the disabled, and Native Americans, Chicanos, and other ethnic-identity groups organized to change their circumstances, both economic and cultural.[29] In Tocqueville's words, "evils, patiently endured as inevitable, seem unbearable as soon as the idea of escaping them is conceived. Then the removal of an abuse seems to cast a sharper light on those still left. . . . [People] found their situation all the more intolerable the better it became."[30]

The important thing here is not just that marginalized groups saw the gains being made by the unmarginalized and fought to be included; that's part of it but probably not the most important part. Rather, it is the experience of gains for themselves, the experience of expanding free time and money for what you will, that spurred them on—that and the availability of organizing traditions from within which they could innovate. Likewise, at a certain point even attempts at repression began to have motivating as well as repressive effects both in spurring innovation and in requiring an increase in determination, a doubling down effect. Nothing illustrates this better than the black freedom movement during the Glorious Thirty.

First, there were real gains beginning with World War II when tight labor markets opened manufacturing and other jobs to blacks, mostly in the industrial

North. There also was the exaggerated egalitarian ethos of World War II propaganda (only occasionally including blacks and then only as a result of organized protest) and the genuine unity of purpose during the war. Hypocritical rhetoric doesn't always fuel grand expectations, but in this case it did, along with the experience of interracial organizing in the Congress of Industrial Organizations unions and of the wartime sacrifices involved in forbearing white racism. The Double V campaign for freedom and democracy at home as well as abroad was carried into the immediate postwar period, where it was largely but not entirely defeated by 1950.[31] Repression of blacks and their struggles for equal rights and freedom intensified in the 1950s, but that repression was likely experienced more acutely because of the immediacy of the wartime experience of unity and the continuing rhetoric about a "century of the common man." But real gains were continuing to be made as well, and if Tocqueville's logic is right, that undoubtedly helped spur people on.

Black family incomes, for example, increased in real terms by about 40 percent from 1949 to 1959, about the same percentage as white family incomes though from a much smaller base.[32] Beginning with the sit-ins in 1960 the level, degree, intensity, and sophistication of organizing—cultivated in various forms in the 1950s—systematically increased and spread to achieve the breakthroughs of the mid-1960s. By 1969 the median black family had increased its income by 128 percent in real terms since 1947, and in the 1960s it increased even faster than the white median.[33] By 1970 black families made 61 percent of what white families did, up from 51 percent in 1949—the largest jump toward racial income equality in US history.[34] This increase in real family incomes resulted from huge increases in clerical and professional employment for black women from 1940 to 1970—from 1 percent to 23 percent and from 5 percent to 11 percent, respectively.[35] Likewise, black men gained increasing numbers of jobs in manufacturing from 1940 to 1970, by which time "black families were more dependent on manufacturing jobs than were whites."[36]

African American legal scholar Randall Kennedy calls the period from the 1950s to the 1970s the "Second Reconstruction" because during those years "the distance traveled by blacks was astonishing." Kennedy provides the following summary:

> In 1950, segregation was deemed to be consistent with federal constitutional equal protection. No federal law prevented proprietors of hotels, restaurants, and other privately owned public accommodations from engaging in racial discrimination. No federal law prohibited private employers from discriminating on a racial basis against applicants for jobs or current employees. No federal law effectively counteracted racial disenfranchisement. No federal law outlawed racial discrimination in private

housing transactions. In contrast, by 1970 federal constitutional law thoroughly repudiated the lie of separate but equal. The 1964 Civil Rights Act forbade racial discrimination in privately owned places of public accommodation and many areas of private employment. The 1965 Voting Rights Act provided the basis for strong prophylactic action against racial exclusion at the ballot box. The 1968 Fair Housing Act addressed racial exclusion in a market that had been zealously insulated against federal regulation. None of these interventions were wholly successful. All were compromised. All occasioned backlash. But the racial situation in 1970 and afterwards was dramatically better than what it had been in 1950 and before.[37]

The racial situation after 1970 would continue to be better than it had been in 1950, way better in many respects, but economically there has not been much progress since 1980. Many cultural attitudes have greatly improved; for example, 87 percent of the population now approves of black-white marriages, compared to 4 percent in 1950 and only 29 percent at the end of the Glorious Thirty.[38] But African Americans are disproportionately represented in a working class whose living standards and working conditions have been deteriorating for nearly half a century now. As incomes stagnated and declined for almost everyone, they stagnated more for black families; the ratio of black-to-white incomes has actually declined since 1980, from 61 percent of average white incomes to 56 percent.[39] The median real earnings of black male workers quadrupled from 1940 to 1980, starting from a miserably low base, but after that declined 8 percent to 2014.[40] As shown in the family-income figures in table 1.1, since the Great Recession it is getting worse, as even the slow growth of family incomes has disappeared, throwing more people into poverty, especially for black people.[41]

Likewise, in Randall Kennedy's list above, in every area except public accommodations, legal rights for blacks have been and are being pared back from whatever peak they once had reached, some of them after the Glorious Thirty but all moving in the wrong direction as I write. From the perspective of today and if you keep your eye on the trajectory, those years from 1945 to 1975 might look a bit more golden and glorious for black folks than they seemed at the time. Even expectations seem diminished today, as simply rearranging our criminal justice system so that it kills and incarcerates fewer young black men can seem like a bridge too far.

The other liberatory movements begun during the Glorious Thirty have somewhat more complicated trajectories, but like the black freedom movement itself, all are split by class with the professional middle class—whether black, women, gay, or Latinx—either continuing to progress or at least holding their own, while the working class in each group continues its steady spiral down toward living standards and working conditions that by the end of the Glorious Thirty were thought to be gone forever.[42]

The relationship between economic prosperity and liberatory movements that Tocqueville was the first to notice—that people can find "their situation all the more intolerable the better it [becomes]"—can still seem counterintuitive today. The assertion of a positive causal chain from the economic to the social psychological to the political has not attracted much social science inquiry, but a liberal economist and a conservative political scientist have subjected it to historical investigation and pretty much confirmed it as a common, though not universal, pattern. The liberal economist Benjamin M. Friedman examines the histories of the United States, Europe, and developing countries (mostly in the twentieth century) and finds the following correlation: "Economic growth—meaning a rising standard of living for the clear majority of citizens—more often than not fosters greater opportunity, tolerance of diversity, social mobility, commitment to fairness, and dedication to democracy."[43] The conservative political scientist Samuel P. Huntington, looking at much the same history with a greater emphasis on developing countries, found "an apparent association between rapid economic growth and political instability," because in many situations "economic growth increases well-being at one rate but social frustration at a faster rate."[44] Among these many situations are some pretty important ones: the Protestant Reformation and the English, American, French, Russian, and Mexican Revolutions.

Friedman and Huntington come at the same phenomenon from different angles. For Friedman, "a rising standard of living, over time . . . usually leads to the positive development of . . . a society's moral character," whereas Huntington is more concerned with the short-term consequences of economic growth leading to "social unrest" and "political instability." Both point to "enhanced aspirations and expectations," which Huntington fears will, "if unsatisfied, galvanize individuals and groups into politics," while Friedman thinks these enhanced expectations make a society more likely to be more tolerant, fair-minded, and democratic.[45] It seems to me both are right—one writing in 1968 and one in 2005—that shared prosperity is very likely to lead to social unrest and political instability *as well as* the positive development of a society's moral character.

This dynamic process is nowhere better illustrated than during the Glorious Thirty in the United States. During its first half our big thinkers were so amazed at its "unprecedented prosperity" that they declared us an "affluent society" by 1959, and then seemingly out of nowhere, its second half surely had more than its share of social unrest and political instability.[46] Huntington's side of the Tocqueville thesis surely proves out. How about Friedman's side, with its lofty proclamation about our moral character? Take 1940 as your starting point, for example, or go back for decades, centuries, or even millennia and see the strength and solidity of the taken-for-granted assumption that both blacks and women were naturally inferior to whites and men—an assumption that by now each generation of Americans finds harder and harder to believe that anybody could ever have thought.[47] Racism and sexism take on different forms today, with unendingly cunning efforts at making comebacks, but is there any doubt that we've had a bit of positive moral development or, conversely, that our declining standards of living now threaten our character as a people?

Here's the nub: Economic prosperity is good for the soul. There's a puritanical backstory that makes many Americans assume or strongly suspect the opposite—that fear of falling and profound insecurity keep us on our toes and spur us on to do better than we would if we became comfortable with ourselves. The actual history of the Glorious Thirty suggests otherwise, whether you're looking at productivity growth and innovation or at the impacts the rolling "rights revolutions" had on so many common, mediocre people's lives.[48] Once upon a time we had rising standards of living for everybody, and being fat and happy didn't lead to widely feared complacency and soul-eroding hedonism but instead to a kind of "transvaluation of all values," in Friedrich Nietzsche's memorable phrase. The removal of one injustice just caused us to notice another and another. As our burdens became lighter our sensitivities became more acute, and we found our situation all the more intolerable the better it became. I can tell you that it didn't always, or even usually, feel so great to live through all these intolerably acute sensitivities, but it was exciting and soul-expanding too. Many parts of it felt glorious at the time but not nearly as glorious as it seems now that it's gone.

When it was over, when we eventually had our falling to ground, I was relieved. As we ignominiously fled from Vietnam in 1975, I felt like I could finally relax. I didn't know that living standards had already begun their long-run declines or that the professional middle class I was still working hard to become part of would separate itself more emphatically from working-class ways. I didn't know that as economic expectations began to diminish, the class cultures I had trafficked between and among would both become narrower, less open and less supple, as they more and more lost contact with each other.

This is the final glory of the Glorious Thirty in my reckoning—the simultaneous rise of middle-class professionalism as a dominant culture and the solidification of a working-class culture craftily expanding, exploring, and enjoying the for-what-you-will parts of life.

There are two kinds of upward mobility, in many ways the very core of the so-called American Dream. Both involve "getting ahead" but in two different forms: one is simply getting ahead of where you were before, and one is getting ahead of others, advancing your position in a hierarchy of positions. Because advancing your position inevitably includes getting ahead of where you were before, the two are easily confused. Likewise, getting substantially ahead of where you were before can feel like a change of position even when it isn't, especially if you are not concerned with—or, as is quite common in the working class, even have contempt for—what others see only as hierarchy. Both kinds of upward mobility flourished during the Glorious Thirty as never before or since.[49] And because they did, they strengthened each other. To get ahead you didn't need to change your position, to transform yourself into something you were not and did not want to be. On the other hand, if you did want to transform yourself and become something or somebody you were not, there were many avenues and much encouragement for doing that. Having that choice was pretty glorious too, both at the time and looking back! In fact, for me it is a primary glory I don't want forgotten, one built on all those other glories. Shared prosperity, a taken-for-granted (if exaggerated) economic security, and small but steady expansions in time and money for what you will allowed—indeed nurtured—a freedom to either *be yourself* or *become an altogether new self* or, as I did, do a bit of each.

THE RISE OF PROFESSIONAL MIDDLE-CLASS LABOR

The less one could believe "one's own eyes"—and the new world of science continually prompted that feeling—the more receptive one became to seeing the world through the eyes of those who claimed specialized, technical knowledge, validated by communities of their peers.

Paul Starr, "The Social Origins of Professional Sovereignty"

As a rising tide lifted all boats after World War II, a new class emerged in size and power, a professional segment of free wage labor that gained power, especially cultural power, as it placed itself between (and, when it could, above) capital and labor. This middle class was initially defined by its middleness between what had been seen for a century as the two main social and economic forces of a modern capitalist society. This was not a traditional petty bourgeoisie of small businesses and shopkeepers or of independent doctors and lawyers but rather a group of wage workers who were paid salaries and were given substantial autonomy at work based on their professional credentials, knowledge, and skills—a professional middle class of people who had authority over others even as they themselves answered to bosses. This class came to have a comfortable standard of living by which it is sometimes identified, but its power was based in the way it mediated between the social and economic interests of capital and labor and, above all, by the way it advanced a meritocratic culture of knowledge, talent, and work effort, formally and informally enforced by an achievement-oriented ethic of professionalism. This is the class I worked hard to become part of at a time when it was especially easy to do so.

At the same time, the traditional part of free wage labor—the working class—was being transformed by union-won increases in wages, living standards, and working conditions. As more clerical, retail, cleaning, caring, and cooking jobs emerged as part of an expanding service economy, those workers had lower wages than factory workers but increasing standards of living as well; plus, many of them wore white collars and had relatively pleasant working conditions. Though blue-collar employment was becoming a smaller portion of the overall economy, it was still expanding its absolute number of jobs, and additional opportunities for these jobs were provided as many blue-collar workers, almost exclusively white and male, moved out of them and into the increasing levels and number of management positions where they worked.[1]

As we began to describe ourselves as a "middle-class society"—in some versions, "the world's first middle-class society"—there was a fundamental confusion of collar colors, income levels, educational attainment, and race and gender. "Middle class" often referred simply to a supposed majority of people having incomes sufficient to buy things beyond the necessities, and by the 1960s this included steelworkers, autoworkers, and many other members of both the traditional industrial working class and the emerging service-economy working class. In this usage there was no "working class." Factory workers had become "middle class" because they had the discretionary incomes that made them sought-after consumers, and clerical and retail workers, usually women, were "middle class" because they dressed up to go to work in a variety of collar colors. But just as often, especially as the period progressed, "middle class" assumed that a person had a college education and was part of the self-disciplined, forward-looking aspirational culture that was inculcated through the rapidly expanding higher education of those days—even though at the time many management jobs did not require a bachelor's degree, and neither did emerging categories of "technical" jobs that would eventually be redefined as "professional" (e.g., engineers and computer programmers). Racial and gender stereotypes further complicated things. A white woman clerical worker with business-appropriate dress and manners, for example, would be defined as undoubtedly middle class, while a black woman with the same job, dress, and manners might be suspected of being "poor" although both were paid less, often much less, than male factory workers and were expected to be informally as well as formally subordinate to their male bosses. To further complicate our class confusion, all this was changing both economically and culturally, so year to year it was not that noticeable, but decade by decade it was. The world of 1955 was very different from 1945, and by 1975 the social-class world of thirty years before was hardly recognizable, even though many of us still thought in old categories.

This class confusion, the broad amalgamation into seeing almost everybody as middle class, furthered by blacks and women demanding opportunities to be in that middle, was fostered by a general downplaying of rank and hierarchy in popular culture, especially with the emergence of rock and roll in the mid-1950s. All this was part of the glory of the time, especially after the mid-1960s successes of the civil rights movement, as it seemed like we were moving toward that general happy "Mediocrity" Benjamin Franklin had mistakenly thought had already been achieved at the beginning. But within this confusion, sometimes embracing but often resisting the erosion of rank, hierarchy, and distinction, a middle-class professionalism was emerging as the mainstream or dominant culture. At the core of that culture was a college education and its relation to the growing number of professional and managerial jobs.

Just before I was born during World War II, in the United States only 5 percent of people ages twenty-five to twenty-nine had college educations (indeed, only about 40 percent had completed high school). By the time I turned thirty that proportion had increased to about 25 percent, and I was among them.[2] Job growth stalled in the 1970s, but by then getting a bachelor's degree was a golden ticket to one of the twenty million *new* professional and managerial jobs that had grown in tandem with the rise of the college educated.[3] It took me a little longer than most, but by 1977 in my midthirties I had one of those too. Besides being another glory of the Glorious Thirty, the wild increase in college educations and professional and managerial jobs is a historical development of enormous—and mostly overlooked—significance: from one of twenty of us being college educated and one of ten having professional or managerial jobs to one of four for each.

Though this rise of a "new class" was sometimes noted at the time, it has been largely ignored by historians looking back.[4] The rise itself is usually straightforwardly reported, especially the rapid increase in higher education attainment rates, but there is seldom any attempt to assess how this changed class structures and relations. Rather, what gains attention is the rise of an "affluent" middle class that confuses absolute and relative upward mobility as, for example, both (white) accountants and (white) autoworkers moved from city to suburb, often living in the same places. The general rise in the standard of living was so unprecedented and spectacular, so widely shared, that class relations no longer seemed a relevant topic at the time or for historians looking back—especially since the stirring rise of the black freedom movement put race at center stage of US history for the first time since the American Civil War and Reconstruction. But the numbers are stunning, a sufficiently large change in quantity that we should expect it also to be a change in quality.

Though the growth of professional and managerial jobs was a long-term trend of the twentieth century, going from one of seventeen jobs in 1900 to more than one of three now, their period of greatest growth was during the Glorious Thirty, captured in table 2.1 here in census years across the four decades from just before World War II to just before the Reagan Revolution. Professional and managerial jobs tripled during the first four decades of the century, while the labor force as a whole increased by only 80 percent. But while the labor force doubled in the next four decades, professional and managerial jobs increased fivefold, from five million to twenty-five million and from 11 percent to 26 percent of all jobs. As higher education exploded during these years to try to keep pace, a college education gradually came to be seen as essential for securing one of these jobs. This in turn greatly increased the social and cultural power of the professoriate, which was itself one of the fastest-growing professional occupations. In the immediate postwar years a broad liberal education reigned, but by 1980 business schools and other more practically oriented programs such as computer science and a variety of communications programs were firmly ensconced in even the most elite universities. Though there were conflicts and divisions between and within academic disciplines, a broad professional middle-class worldview focusing life on individual achievement and personal accomplishment was purveyed both in the curriculum and in the social life of higher education, even at state universities that were growing like weeds at the time.[5]

"Professionalism" is rightly associated with early twentieth-century progressivism, its hyped commitment to empirical reasoning and its practical application in the social as well as the natural sciences—secular and virtuous but pragmatic, data-driven problem solvers. Across the century you can see the emergence of this class in the middle between capital and labor, often allying itself with the poor and laboring classes in appealing to the ruling class but in the process making a place for itself (ourselves) as the dominant class culturally, defining work as a career with professional autonomy and life as primarily a series of achievements and transformations, doing and becoming. When it saw hierarchy,

TABLE 2.1 Professionals and managers in the US labor force, 1900–present

YEAR	# LABOR FORCE	# OF PROFES-SIONALS	PROFES-SIONALS % OF LABOR FORCE	# OF MANAGERS	MANAGERS % OF LABOR FORCE	COMBINED PROFES-SIONALS AND MANAGERS #S	PROFES-SIONALS AND MANAGERS % OF LABOR FORCE
1900	27 million	1.1 million	4	592,000	2%	1.7 million	6
1940	47 million	3.4 million	7	1.7 million	4%	5.1 million	11
1980	97 million	17 million	17	8.1 million	8%	25 million	26
Now (2019)	157 million	37 million	23	27 million	17%	64 million	40

Sources: Table Ba1033–1046, "Major Occupational Groups—All Persons: 1860–1990," in *Historical Statistics of the United States*, Millennial Edition On Line, ed. Susan B. Carter, Scott Sigmund Gartner, Michael R. Haines, Alan L. Olmstead, Richard Sutch, and Gavin Wright (Cambridge: Cambridge University Press, 2006). All numbers for "now" are from Bureau of Labor Statistics, *Labor Force Statistics from the Current Population Survey*, #11, "Employed Persons by Detailed Occupation, Sex, Race, and Hispanic or Latino Ethnicity," with 2019 as the most recent year.

which it did not always embrace during the Glorious Thirty, this culture insisted it be based on merit, especially certified merit.[6]

Across the century, management itself was redefined as a profession or set of professions, with the rise of business schools and the MBA as certification of broad business knowledge as well as a pragmatic, empirical, and "well-rounded" mindset and personality. Management aspired to be "scientific" not merely in the narrow sense of the industrial engineer, with his time-and-motion studies, but more broadly as decision making driven by evidence and reasoning that revealed potentials and opportunities not only in products and markets but also in organizational process and "the human element." Being a profession required a substantial degree of autonomy from owners (capitalists and shareholders) and even from higher levels of management. This was the *managerial capitalism* that defined the Glorious Thirty, referring primarily to the authority of line managers. But staff professionals were seen to require autonomy too; within the overall direction of line management, staff had both day-to-day autonomy in executing specific functions and reasoned input into the determination of the overall direction based on their specific knowledge and expertise.[7] Line managers and staff professionals together constituted the larger group that John Kenneth Galbraith tagged as a "technostructure." While Galbraith may have overestimated its actual authority and autonomy, he surely captured the ethos of middle-class professionalism and its struggle to be the dominant force by mediating between capital and "society"—workers as both workers and consumers. Because they were seen as being in the middle, technostructure workers "saw both sides" and were not, both as individuals and as a group, that different from the workers they managed or the customers they sold to.[8] By 1960 they seemed like the natural leadership group of "general happy Mediocrity" in the United States, working their way up the corporate ladder based not on their ownership of land or capital but instead on their talent and merit as proven in documented accomplishment both in school and in the workplace.

Some in the corporate technostructure are listed by the Bureau of Labor Statistics as "managerial," but many others are listed as "professionals" because they do not supervise anybody. There are many subdivisions within the professional middle class, but this is an important one. Line managers exist as part of a formally well-defined chain of command, whereas staff professionals without managerial responsibilities are "off to the side," and though subject to the chain of command, they are not responsible for enforcing it, giving them some independence from it in both thought and action. Together, however, they constitute a *business wing* of the professional middle class, broadly reflecting a business ethos and understanding of the world. During the Glorious Thirty they were rising in power and influence within corporate structures and therefore within society, but culturally the main action in forming a distinctively professional middle-class culture was driven by a *communications/education wing*. Here the rise of the university and its Glorious Thirty insistence on autonomy provided an independent power base for the development of a professional middle-class culture, often explicitly opposing business-wing tendencies even while feeding most of its graduates into the technostucture. While the labor force as a whole doubled and the entire group of managerial and professional workers increased fivefold, higher education faculty and other professional staff grew nearly sevenfold.[9] Likewise, other culture worker jobs grew at least somewhat more rapidly than professionals and managers as a whole: for example, editors and reporters at more than fivefold, designers at fourteenfold, personnel and labor relations at twelvefold, and "therapists and healers" at tenfold. Even "authors" and "artists and art teachers" greatly outpaced general job growth, doubling and tripling their numbers.[10] Some of these occupations had large rates of increase from relatively small bases, but much larger groups of professionals such as elementary and secondary teachers nearly tripled their already large numbers, and they all had to pass through the university.[11]

For most of the Glorious Thirty, there was a glorious tension between the business and communications/education wings of this wildly emergent professional middle class. What's more, the massification of higher education combined with a consumer-driven popular culture that overwhelmed the producer-driven one with rock-and-roll music, paperback books, television, and cars and record players for almost everyone.[12] "Affluence" (i.e., the spread of discretionary income and time) was more than a necessary condition for a flood of horizon-expanding soul searching; it was a motivating factor pushing Tocqueville's logic of new expectations leading to discontent, especially for young parents and children in the emerging professional middle class. Corporate business rigorously tried to enforce a uniformity and conformism in everything from dress codes and business practices to personality types and the character of "corporate wives" even while—and possibly because—it recognized the need for professional and managerial autonomy in getting its work done. The university meanwhile was exposing its students to Leo Tolstoy and Fyodor Dostoyevsky, Jean-Paul Sartre and Albert Camus, then Norman Mailer, James Baldwin, and Allen Ginsberg and forcing even its business students to read *The Lonely Crowd* and *The Organization Man*. Just as popular culture made new strains of music and soulfulness available to wider and wider audiences—everything from Chuck Berry and Miles Davis to *West Side Story* and *La Boehme*—paperback best sellers were often what Sarah Bakewell calls "authenticity dramas" such as *Catcher in the Rye* and *The Man in the Gray Flannel Suit*. All this refers to the *intellectual ferment* of the 1950s, a time still seen as conservative, placid, conformist, and excessively normal, which is the way it was experienced by many of those who lived through it, but they also left a record of their "moral panic . . . about . . . faceless, mindless conformism" in their opposition to what they were privileged to experience as dull and meaningless.[13]

I went to college in the 1960s (off and on for the entire decade and more), by which time the relentless drive for success clashed in multiple and crazy ways with the prohibition against "selling out" and the beatnik-inspired rejection of "the bitch goddess of success." Some went determinedly in one direction, others just as determinedly in the other; some dabbled in each, while others (like me) swung back and forth and sometimes went in both directions at the same time.[14] In the 1960s the soul searching spawned by affluence met the necessity for protest and action spawned by the black freedom movement, an unjust war, a patriarchal society, and one injustice after another—all of which ended not just with a simple backlash but also in an adjustment in expectations whereby both business uniformity and communications/education free thinking gained some ground by giving some. This was the activity of a new class in formation. Free wage labor though it was, it carved out a sense of self, of self-actualization, meritocracy, and at least for a while "making a difference" that was new and powerful. We would end up with a more egalitarian and democratic society, one more firmly rooted in the power of a middle-class professionalism that officially valued critical thinking, especially if that thinking focused on the individual self and its continuous improvement.

By centering on the dialectic between a technocratic business wing and a communications/education wing during the Glorious Thirty, I'm neglecting other dramas of professional middle-class class formation—such as what was happening to the traditional middle class of doctors, lawyers, and clergy. The growth of professional and managerial jobs from 1940 to 1980 was not mostly in these traditional professions, which either merely kept pace with overall job growth (clergy), did more than a little better than overall job growth (doctors), or did only three times better (lawyers) versus the fivefold increase of professional and managerial workers as a whole.[15] But the economic, political, and cultural power of these professions persisted even as over time they lost some of their economic independence with increasing numbers joining the ranks of free wage labor. Another important group I'm neglecting is the wide variety of engineers, many of whom received trade school certifications for specific engineering tasks (heating/air-conditioning, computer hardware maintenance, etc.), while bachelor's degrees in mechanical, electrical, and civil engineering flourished as well, resulting in a sixfold increase in these occupations across those forty years. In my own observation there was (and maybe still is) a distinct engineering occupational culture, one with a kind of purity in its relations with nonnatural physical reality and the way things work and one about equally disdainful of the "know-nothing" business wing and the "artsy-fartsy" communications/education wing. But these and other growing professional jobs also illustrate how sloppily open, in flux, and dynamic a middle class in formation, or in reformation, was during the Glorious Thirty. New opportunities for professionalism proliferated, and within those opportunities autonomous spaces were as yet unsupervised or even unknown within the chains of command.

A new kind of professional middle class was being formed on the ground, so to speak, by the managers, business professionals, doctors, lawyers, and engineers, but the communications/education wing had outsized power and influence over the culture as everybody was challenged spiritually, morally, and culturally by what British social scientist Avner Offer has so richly detailed as "the challenge of affluence."[16] Living without scarcity, working without tight supervision at work you (usually or at least often) enjoyed doing, expanding your horizons, and feeling the real possibility of becoming something you were not yet—this was exhilarating, but it was not as easy or as uncomplicatedly liberating as most of us had anticipated. With discretionary time and money, how should you use it? With wider horizons, which way should you go? What could you become, and what should you if you could? In these conditions the communications/education wing spoke to and for this class in formation, with a popular culture that assumed widespread literacy routinely contesting with the supposedly free-thinking but carefully certifying culture of the university. There was excitement and anxiety, conformism and liberation, freedom and confusion, the exhilaration of doors that had been closed now being swung open and the fear of walking through one of those doors. What *is* on the other side, and what will be lost if that door closes behind me once I walk through? Writers, teachers, artists, and other producers and reproducers of culture had the new class's attention and a special role in helping us think about and eventually navigate this altogether new terrain. It was Camus versus *Playboy*, Bob Dylan versus *Father Knows Best*, Norman Mailer versus Walter Cronkite, and Betty Friedan versus Anita Bryant.[17]

From a bird's-eye view, middle-class professionals constituted a new class arising between capital and labor, a broader version of Galbraith's technostructure. But if you look at it as a transformation in the composition of free wage labor, it's also an unprecedented rise of a significant part of the proletariat—a promotion, if you will. Though some of those twenty million new free wage–labor professional and managerial jobs were taken by the children of small-hold farmers moving off the land and by doctors and lawyers giving up their own practices to be employed by larger partnerships and firms, the majority must have been people like me leaving the working class.[18] Some working-class young people were running headlong into an exciting future, others ambivalently backing into opportunities they could not afford to avoid, and still others, like me, doing some of each by turns. From that bird's-eye view we all were simply the sparks created by the explosion of higher education in the postwar United States, but for each of us as individuals it was a fraught drama full of personal turmoil—adjusting, adopting, adapting, rejecting, and holding on to one of two broad ways of living a life.

One way saw life as lived within a tangled web of relationships, valued loyalty to kith and kin, and found drama in the struggle to simply be yourself, to at least pull your own weight within your circle of family, friends, and workmates—a kind of fatalism about who you are or were "meant to be" awkwardly combined with a commitment to being strong and true, "a good person" within your personal and socially entangled limitations. The other way defined the self much more expansively and individualistically, more independent and more open to self-directed change with greater freedom from the constraints of entangled relationships. In this view you could make yourself who you wanted to be, or at least it was important to try to be somebody you were not yet. The dramatic rise of middle-class professionalism during the Glorious Thirty meant that this second way gained more and more traction as the years and decades went by. By 1975 it was something like hegemonic, the stuff of university commencement speeches for sure but also a kind of constant cultural reminder spreading out from the university to both elite and popular culture "not to sell yourself short," that all people had more potential than they were using and that each of us had a duty—or at least an opportunity—to achieve that potential. For common folks, mediocrities like me, this kind of universalizing of potential was new and "modern" and both exciting and existentially anxious. For me there was a working-class counterculture, however, that warned don't get ahead of yourself, don't be thinking you're better than others, and even don't expect too much of yourself or of life in general and above all don't try to be something you're not. As Jason Isbell's father insisted, "don't try to change who you are, boy, and don't try to be who you ain't."[19]

This working-class counter is now widely viewed as a cultural disability within a more hegemonic and elitist professional middle-class culture, and though I am ideologically opposed to that classist prejudice, within my own family I practice it anyway. The stakes were too high to allow my son and grandsons to think there might be an option to going to college, for example—it's either that or a life that is nasty, brutish, and short. I know better than that, but I'm not about to tell them. What was different when I was coming up was that both ways worked. You could be yourself tried and true, eschew the cultural washing of hearts and brains involved in going to college, and still get ahead, have a good life, including expanding your horizons, not dramatically maybe but bit by bit. Today that is less the case with each passing year, and that's not just a problem for working-class life and culture and thus for the majority of people, but for us privileged middle-class folks as well. During the Glorious Thirty an expanding professional middle class lived alongside and often against a vital cultural alternative that a prosperous and economically powerful working class provided. Whether complement or antagonist, this alternative culture enriched middle-class professionalism in those days. But now if it's true, as I think, that the power of us middle-class professionals is based on our value in mediating between a ruling class and a confidently strong and self-representing working class, then we are becoming less and less valuable as the working class is weakened economically, politically, and culturally. Especially if we're not excellent, not among the highly talented, just mediocre, our true nature as free wage labor becomes more and more apparent as working-class conditions deteriorate.

Working-class ways enriched professional middle-class culture during its period of formation, when the culture was still open, experimental, and exploratory, still trying to find its way; when middle-class professionals themselves were likely to have working-class origins in grandparents if not parents; and when middle-class culture's achievement orientation and status consciousness were actively challenged by those who scorned them as "the bitch goddess of success" and were proud to sing that they were "not sleepy and there is no place I'm going to." How to live in a world with discretionary time and money seemed like a universal problem then, and there was more than one legitimate answer to it—more troubling, soul-wrenching questions then but also more possibilities for more people than now. Now it seems our middle-class professionalism is simply a cultural shield to keep our discretion to ourselves and pass it on to our progeny. I don't want to go back to all the intellectual ferment of the 1950s or to the political and cultural turmoil of the transvaluation of all values in the 1960s, but I do want to recover that progress we were making toward a general happy mediocrity when a rising tide was lifting so many different boats.

WORKING-CLASS AGENCY IN PLACE

But isn't it a good thing that people are not all alike and don't all do spectacular things?

A self-described "ordinary housewife" in 1957 England

You might think that working-class culture would have been weakened by the Glorious Thirty's combination of affluence and the opening of working-class life to the possibility of going to college and getting a professional job, let alone by the emergence of a professional middle-class cultural hegemony at the national level. But it wasn't. Rather, shared prosperity allowed working-class ways to flourish both in their concentrated localism and in their increasing openness to being influenced by and to influence the wider world over which, for the most part, working-class people cede control to others. The more secure people felt in their jobs, homes, and lives, the more proud and sure they became of their way of doing things and living a life. And though this could have narrowing effects as well, it generally made them more open to outside influences because they felt in control of what mattered most to them. The very contention between working-class and middle-class ways during this period strengthened both.

That at least is the way I see it, but before I explain, let me clear away some underbrush, starting with the disappointment with the working class that middle-class scholars and intellectuals experienced during this period. British historian David Kynaston captured both the nub of the issue and the timing: "By the late 1950s the Labour Party's relationship with affluence was becoming increasingly tortured—theoretical acceptance of its desirability combined with visceral dislike of its manifestations."[1] For a variety of reasons, there is no analogue to our Democrats as a party, but the "tortured relationship with affluence" describes the political confusion of a generation of American intellectuals, including some from working-class backgrounds, who wrestled with contradictory inclinations to mourn the loss of the working class's "revolutionary potential" but to celebrate the achievements of a powerful contract-based unionism and a nearly bipartisan government commitment to stimulating aggregate demand. The idea of the working class came with a certain historical expectation seeded by Karl Marx, Friedrich Engels, and their progeny that was alive in people's imaginations throughout the Glorious Thirty, as either hope or fear, and this shaped (and distorted) the way both the communications/education and the business wings of the middle class viewed actually existing working-class people and their cultures. The business wing publicly affirmed "affluent workers" as evidence of the success of the capitalist system (called "free enterprise" in those days) and as more fulsome customers to whom they could sell things, while also retaining their traditional view of their own workers primarily as labor costs. The communications/education wing, on the other hand, had an element of mourning for the loss of what it had seen as (or had been told were) the noble aspects of working-class life, often a weird combination of workers' capacity to endure hardship and systematically rebel against it.

I might not have this exactly right, but I am pointing to an additional complication involved in discussing the American working class that is introduced by one class bringing its cultural predispositions to understanding a different class with quite different but mostly unstated cultural predispositions. This complication necessitates a degree of self-reflexivity that some American social scientists are just beginning to recognize. Cross-class interpretation is highly complicated even today, when class lines are more clearly marked by education. But it is especially difficult in looking back when the historical record is largely filtered through the eyes of a professional middle-class still in formation then and by a communications/education wing of that class still in cultural combat with the business wing. What's more, it did not necessarily help to be from the working class, especially if you were in the midst of abandoning it and still thrilled with the cultural capital available in the communications/education wing of the professional middle class. Indeed, Kynaston's primary literary example of a "tortured relationship with affluence" was the Leeds-bred Richard Hoggart's *The Uses of Literacy*, a 1957 book that had a large and highly sympathetic US audience in the 1960s, especially among those of us who were in the midst of crossing classes. Hoggart's poignant remembrance of working-class life in the first half of the book turns to angst in the second half as he sees workers becoming "middle class" in a "Candy-floss World" of consumerism, a spiritless choice for superficial pleasures easily manipulated by advertising.[2]

A significant part of the professional middle-class's class formation involved contrasting its culture (our culture) with that of an amoral ruling class and a passively manipulable working class. The business wing saw itself as bringing virtue to the former and material improvement to the latter, whereas the communications/education wing championed more intellectual and cosmopolitan virtues and sought to improve the working class in less material ways. As such, both wings saw working-class people as being in need of improvement, though of different kinds. As the period progressed, however, the business wing strengthened its traditional concern about workers as labor costs and also began to worry that affluence was undermining work ethics and other "spiritual" values.

The way consumerism felt from the inside was very different. After doing without and teaching your children how to do without, getting things you wanted involved more than the immediate pleasure of having them. As fulfilling needs became a recurrent pattern, it expanded your sense of possibility. And some of the things we wanted—refrigerators, washers and dryers, TVs, our own car—transformed our daily lives, making some household chores easier, thereby increasing our discretionary time and expanding our horizons on the road and through our TV screens. These bigger items required steady work, saving some part of your discretionary income for a down payment, and then regularly meeting installment payments—all of which was a relatively new experience one year and then became an embedded routine just a few years later.

Increasing incomes, less time at work, and the steadiness of income and work were new in working-class life, and as they emerged, working-class dispositions, expectations, and relationships shifted. To see this requires taking a longer view. Labor historians have usefully distinguished male workers of the late nineteenth and early twentieth centuries as either "common laborers" or "craftsmen," with the former having a "rough" and the latter a "respectable" culture of masculinity. The rough culture of the common laborer was typically that of a bachelor (even if formally married), "'a swearing, drinking, brawling, hurting, dying mass' shaped by a harsh climate, difficult toil, meager economic resources, and a social life of heavy drinking."[3] It was a culture shaped by "continuous changing of jobs," an "uninterrupted search for jobs" that required a certain unrooted geographic mobility. As Stephen Meyer has commented, "The rough work world often made these men unsuited to the tame domestic life."[4] The respectable culture of the craftsman, on the other hand, was shaped by a skill-based "control, independence, and the ability to make decisions" at work, which issued in a "manly bearing" of "dignity, respectability, defiant egalitarianism, and patriarchal male supremacy" at home and in the community.[5] The respectable male worker was inherently domestic, expecting himself to establish roots whenever possible, form a family, raise (or at least provide for) children, and establish a social and moral legacy for them. The scale and relative steadiness of postwar prosperity meant that although actual craftsmen were still a decided minority of male workers (let alone all workers), the respectable culture of masculinity gradually but overwhelmingly came to predominate. In this culture steadiness, reliability, and dependability—being someone who could be counted on at work, at home and, in the neighborhood—were what earned respect for oneself and from others. This sort of manliness was very much preferred by women, who were expected to have the same qualities of steady reliability and also cultivate and enforce them in their men.

This does not mean that the rough culture disappeared, only that it was subordinated and in many ways incorporated within respectable manliness. Where I grew up, rough manliness was an expected stage of a young man's life, sowing some wild oats before settling down and settling in to a life of work, marriage, and family. The typesetters at the newspaper where I worked in 1964, for example, tricked up a banner headline to go with the standard three-paragraph article announcing my wedding—"Metzgar Loses Freedom"—and nobody needed to have the joke explained. Episodes of rough manliness—occasional binge drinking, some push-around fights, even "meaningless" sexual infidelities—were respected among married adult men and tolerated among women so long as they did not interfere with a through line of steady work and reliable fulfillment of family responsibilities. There was, of course, no tolerance of a rough womanliness in the respectable working-class culture, though the extraordinary attention given to "honky-tonk angels" in the country music of the day confirms their existence. Much of the drama of working-class life during the Glorious Thirty involved the potential of men (not to mention adolescent boys) going off the rails with excessive drinking, uncontrolled anger, or various forms of unfaithfulness to family life. Getting laid off or losing your job entirely or getting stuck in a lowly paid job that didn't reliably pay the bills (that is, the less prosperous you were), *the greater the threat* of a man going off the rails. The more prosperity you were experiencing, on the other hand, *the higher the stakes* in these dramas and the more yoked both men and women often felt to their mortgages, installment payments, bad jobs, and even their children.

The possibility of achieving this respectable working-class culture—which some perceptive sociologists of the time called "settled-living" and "routine-seeking" in contrast to "hard-living" and "action-seeking" working-class ways—expanded pretty dramatically across the Glorious Thirty, especially in union households like mine.[6] But it was never without its opposition to rough, action-seeking ways, which paradoxically also had their attractions, especially to men but also to women in more indirect forms.

The expansion of a "craft" masculinity started at work, where the system of seniority-based access to a ladder of increasingly higher-skilled jobs established by unions in key industries came to predominate even in nonunion workplaces. Within that system, employers had to control unit labor costs based on the increased productivity that came with the lack of turnover and the steady increase in workers' knowledge and skills across their work lives. Though they seemed not to realize it, employers benefited greatly from a golden age of productivity growth based in part on this system. Workers did too, of course, but the increasing pay based on internal job mobility—and the expectation of internal job mobility—required a steadiness that many men found oppressive. Having steady work with good wages was at best a double-edged sword and at worst a trap, especially if you hated the work you did nearly every day you did it but even if you found ways, often ingenious, to make it tolerable. Changing jobs, laying out for a while, or going on a multiday bender that might put your job at risk—classic behaviors of industrial workers in earlier times—now were harder to do because they were potentially so much more costly and were no longer acceptable within respectable settled-living working-class culture. Indeed, having a good job meant you had something at risk, and therefore taking any risk, even to "better yourself," often seemed unwise.

There were a variety of responses to this situation as it emerged. Some men, such as my father, chose absolute sobriety and kept their rough working-class ways at work, where it could be expressed in fighting the boss, often but not exclusively through the bureaucratic grievance procedures that did not put your job at risk. Centering their lives on their families, these men exercised their patriarchal authority, establishing a zone of autonomy where they could control not only their own lives but also those of their wives and children. This wasn't always oppressive but usually felt that way, especially as more freedom, less insecurity, and new opportunities emerged with increasing affluence. At the other extreme were men whose relations with their families were restricted to providing a paycheck in return for meals and a place to stay while finding their zone of autonomy in tavern life or other "all-male" pursuits such as hunting, fishing, or fooling with cars, with sometimes elaborate activities planned at the bar or the gas station where they regularly hung out. While these men were more at risk of falling or running off the rails and more subject to alcoholism, most incorporated a little masculine roughness within a steady work life and reliable breadwinning for their families. There were also actual craftsmen, like one of my uncles, who enjoyed their work at work and their family life at home while never fighting the boss or challenging the matriarchal authority of their wives at home or in the neighborhood. There were numerous other varieties of working-class masculinity, including some men for whom steady reliability, whether at work or at home, just wasn't in their makeup—often likable, even lovable characters but pretty universally disdained, even by themselves.

What was common among all these varieties was the nearly absolute division between work life and real life. The better paid and more secure your job, the more time and money for what you will, and the more rewards for steadiness increased, the stronger that division became.

The relative affluence of the Glorious Thirty undoubtedly domesticated working-class men, and my impression is that this is what working-class women had long hoped for and worked for. But it was complicated. In the words of a "wild and a little crazy" Sawyer Brown character, "Some girls don't like boys like me / Ah, but some girls do." Many Glorious Thirty working-class women sought straight-up respectable and sometimes even holy men, sometimes as partners and sometimes merely as reliable providers. But other women wanted a little (or even a lot) of roughness in their men; respectable boys and men were seen as boring and even characterless. Young women were typically attracted to men with a little local charisma and expected to have to do some domesticating of the "wild and crazy" parts of the men they loved. What's more, most rough young men expected women to try and to succeed in taming them, even as they resisted the taming and resented it when it "went too far"—or when it was just temporarily inconvenient. There was, as has repeatedly been pointed out by historians and other scholars, an acceptance—indeed an embrace—of the breadwinner/homemaker division of sex roles in Glorious Thirty working-class families, something that had previously been largely unavailable outside the middle classes.[7] But this too was complicated as the ideal played out in many different actualities. Though formal patriarchy prevailed, many working-class couples established true partnerships in which a division of labor between paycheck and homemaking was a mere practical arrangement that did not conflict with joint decision making (and arguments) about renting or owning, other family purchases and activities, and above all children's upbringing. There were families like mine (and like Troy Maxson's in August Wilson's *Fences*) in which the husband and father had the final say, but there were just as many in which the wife and mother made all the decisions while barely consulting an uninvolved father. For many working-class women, the household was a zone of autonomy that they managed with very little interference from their husbands—even if they had to offer a little feigned or real deference to the "patriarch" from time to time. Many women loved "good family men" who were home most of their nonworking hours and were engaged in raising the children and other family activities. But others preferred their husbands being at a tavern or gas station after dinner (or working second shift), where they would not interfere with her household autonomy and child-rearing choices.

Though I will discuss this more in coming chapters, the emerging predominance of a respectable settled-living versus a rough hard-living working-class culture during the Glorious Thirty should not be confused with a much more status-conscious and competitive "middle-class respectability."[8] They are different, very different, in multiple ways. But to my mind, this upsurge of working-class settled living is another of the glories of those years. The magnitudes of the increases in settled living—based on steady work at decent pay—between black and white workers then were, of course, very different, as they are now. But the pattern of increase was the same, as black men greatly increased their presence in manufacturing, postal work, and public transit and black women in clerical and sales jobs.[9]

As Herbert Gans articulated, working-class life during the Glorious Thirty was broadly characterized by "routine-seeking." But once routine, steady predictability was established—or, rather, once you got used to it and came to take it for granted—your comforting daily routines could begin to seem like "ruts." Economists might call this the decreasing marginal utility of the secure "settled-living" lives so many working-class men and women had worked so hard to achieve, an instance of the law of diminishing returns. Gans focused on "action-seeking" men who relieved their settled-living lives with "adventurous episode[s], in which heights of activity and feeling are reached through exciting and sometimes riotous behavior," such as "a card game, a fight, a sexual interlude, a drinking bout, a gambling session, or . . . a fast and furious exchange of wisecracks and insults."[10] But there were also men, like my father, who found creative outlets in elaborate hobbies (often involving hunting, fishing, and automobiles) or in being active in their unions, churches, or ethnic lodges. Women did too, but they had a different rhythm to their lives. After all the children were securely settled in school, they had "time on their hands" they needed to "fill." It was quite common for these women to take part-time jobs as my mother did, which sometimes evolved into full-time ones as their children matured, as was also the case with my mother. There were men, as many scholars emphasize, who rigidly resisted this phenomenon, seeing working wives as a challenge to their manly provider role. But in my experience these men were routinely seen as weird, impractical, and even insecure (though that word was almost never used), as the practical benefits of an additional paycheck far outweighed any Victorian-style breadwinner ideology, which I doubt was ever very strong in working-class life. Working outside the home and contributing to the breadwinning, however, inevitably changed gender power relations within the household, whether women maintained separate control of their earnings (as my mother did) or merely contributed to the household pot, control of which often belonged to women anyway.

There are numerous variations in how this played out, not all of them with happy endings, but the point here is about the dynamism of shared prosperity. Routine-seeking, respectable settled living in the working class of those days can look like embourgeoisement or as just plain boring, as indeed it often seemed to us teenagers at the time. But it was a hard-won achievement paid for with a culture of steady reliability, one that required self-discipline and sacrifice, with lots of drama and struggle to stay on the straight and narrow. The drama mostly focused on keeping men steady, with women seldom being in doubt themselves but

nonetheless responsible for keeping their men in line and managing the consequences when they weren't. What's more, settled living once achieved was a base,
a foundation, and a spur for creative endeavors of various sorts, only some of
which involved either consumerism or Gans's potentially destructive "adventurous episodes." Others included increasing civic engagement through a union or
a church and various kinds of self-improvement activities, from learning to read
blueprints or struggling to achieve sobriety to taking your household management
and people skills into the workplace. What Arthur McIvor in his history of the
postwar British working class calls "incremental emancipation" didn't end with
increased time and money for what you will.[11] It began there, with the what-you-
will parts of working-class life issuing in a riot of various directions and opportunities, including for my generation the somewhat forbidding option of going
to college.

I graduated from high school in 1961, near the midpoint of the Glorious Thirty.
I was on the college track my last two years of high school and was diligently preparing my self for college (or for what I thought college would be), and I was
excited to embark on that adventure. But I was an outlier in my working-class
world. Though many more of us were on the college track than the vocational
track, the largest group was probably on the commercial track, like Judie, and not
many on the college track were actually hoping, wanting, or preparing to go to
college. In fact, it was disdained. Even most of us who went vowed before we left
not to "turn into college boys."

That disdain, I think, exhibited a class consciousness of sorts—an awareness
of important cultural differences within different kinds of free wage labor. Part
of it was just about what kind of clothes and shoes you wore, the haircut you had,
and other lifestyle stuff like that. And some of that part was simply about their
being different from the way we were. But the disdain went deeper than that. Some
of it was resentment at the college-educated thinking they were better than us,
but in many ways we were willing to grant their superiority on a whole range of
things without, however, accepting their simplistic and exaggerated sense of hierarchy.[12] Though different people described it differently, our sense was that college made people stiff and formal and turned them into phonies who thought they
knew more than they did while actually lacking common sense. As a result, they
seemed anxiously unsure of themselves and looked to others in the chain of command for both direction and affirmation. I now think it was this last part that was
most important—going to college put you in danger of losing your real self and
then having to be or to seem to be somebody you were not. This seemed like it
would be a very uncomfortable way to live a life and completely undesirable in itself, but the way it seemed to lead middle-class people to seek affirmation and personal direction from those higher in formal hierarchies seemed not only unwise

(since so many higher-ups were neither competent nor trustworthy) but also pathetic in its abject abandonment of self-respect.[13]

This disdain for the college-educated was widespread, shared by some teachers, small businesspeople, and even bosses in the mill, but it was also recognized that we didn't actually know many of these people and that things were changing. My mother and father, who in very different ways strongly encouraged me to go to college, shared the disdain, for example, but counseled that "things are opening up" and that going to college didn't mean "you had to be like that." My mother's own experience of college (her last year at the University of Pittsburgh in Pittsburgh itself) was painfully lonely and isolated, but she felt she hadn't "really given it a chance" and "it didn't need to be that bad." Because I was so inept at all things mechanical and pretty good at school, there was not much of an option for me. Besides, like Dad I had some craftiness to me, and I aspired to be a newspaper reporter, hopefully a sportswriter, which seemed like an occupation where I could avoid "becoming like that." So even an outlier like me, one who would both initially and then in the long-term succumb, started out disdaining the culture of the professional middle class.[14]

For boys, that disdain made a lot of sense during the Glorious Thirty. The things they were learning as boys, above all the handyman mechanical skills but also hunting, fishing, and the outdoor arts, would be useful and usefully improving all their lives. The things where I was at least up to par—sports and (mostly verbal) fighting—were only tangentially useful in indirectly teaching you team skills and cultivating an attitude of standing up for yourself, but their practical value diminished in adulthood. Though the mills were not hiring in the late 1950s and early 1960s, there were still lots of well-paying jobs in the crafts, including in printing and auto mechanics, and this is what most boys who wanted to be real men aspired to. Though the last two years of high school were geared for the college kids and there was lots of propaganda about how important it was to further your education, most of my male contemporaries scarcely gave it a thought. For girls too, the homemaking and family-organizing skills they were learning from their mothers, aunts, and sisters were of lifelong value in a way that most of what they (often enthusiastically) learned at school was not. Even the bookkeeping and other business skills girls like Judie learned in the commercial track were seen as immediately useful but not nearly as interesting, as intellectually and morally compelling, as the management of family life. College, though it seemed like it might be fun, seemed both a waste of time and not nearly interesting enough to justify an extended delay in starting real life by going to work right after high school. Most parents, it seemed, pretty much agreed if they thought about it. Earning a decent living did not require a bachelor's degree in those days, and going to college could seem like a risky adventure that put your true self at risk. What's more, parents routinely worried about whether their children could buckle down to the daily grind of working and, as a result, were eager, for both financial and moral reasons, for their kids to get started earning their own living.

By 1961, a year I remember in great detail, there was both a disdain for going to college or becoming a "college joe" and an appreciation of the expanding opportunities for pursuing higher education. In some measure this was simply a matter of different people and groups of people having different points of view, but as working-class ways seemed strong and sure at the time, there was a wider tolerance then, as going to college seemed merely an additional option, not a forced choice or a threat. The trade-off between good pay and good jobs was widely recognized (and often exaggerated). Industrial workers had bad jobs with good pay, while teachers and administrators, jobs increasingly requiring a bachelor's degree, had good jobs with bad pay. Though these white-collar jobs were highly gendered (which seemed perfectly just at the time!), their proliferation attracted increasing numbers and proportions of men. They were a great outlet for guys like me without the mechanical aptitude and/or with a doubtful capacity for "taking it"—that is, enduring the hard physical labor and daily grind of industrial work. But pursuing white-collar work was an understandable choice for easier work even for guys who could have been real men, especially if they were smart or at least didn't mind school. I have been part of hundreds of conversations comparing the pluses and minuses of blue- and white-collar jobs across multiple decades in a variety of contexts. Though I have witnessed many different points of view—including aggressive blue-collar disdain for teachers who "can't do" and white-collar folks who exude a sure sense of their own superiority even as they express sympathetic sentiments of equality—what I am nostalgic for is the standard working-class generosity that "it takes all kinds." I can remember a time when these conversations usually tended toward a mutual recognition and acceptance that someone "just wasn't cut out for real work" and someone else "was never really college material." I can remember a time when the judgment made by others or by yourself that you were not college material did not seem like a death sentence, just a recognition of who you were and how you fit into the larger scheme of things. That's what a New York University English professor with a Bronx accent asked me to consider in 1965—there was no judgment to his suggestion that I might not be college material, just a genuine concern that I find a proper place for myself. That, not the Bronx accent, is why I'm sure that guy was from a working-class background.

Today nobody would dare ask a prospective college student, let alone one who had already been admitted as a transfer student, to consider that he or she might not be college material. First, such a question is a major violation of professional middle-class aspirational ideology, especially in universities. Everybody is college material because all they need to do is work hard to become that material. Second, given the way our economy and labor markets work today, for a person to be judged or to decide on one's own that he/she is not college material means the person will likely be consigned to a hard life of low wages and unsteady, precarious work. But worst of all, in university settings today to not be college material pretty much means you are not a worthwhile human being, entitled to equal legal and other human rights for sure and maybe even some empathy or sympathy but not worth much respect because you did not work hard enough to become the necessary and desired material.

This is what has been lost and needs to be restored. Today, from every corner of our society except in the most isolated working-class and poor precincts and often even there with No Child Left Behind–style "school reform," megaphones blare at children and their parents that you must start at an early age to transform yourself into college material. Once upon a time when college was merely an option and not necessarily the most desirable one, you did not need to transform yourself and spend your entire young life doing it. You could if you wanted to, and there were increasing opportunities and tons of encouragement for doing that, but you didn't have to. There was not just one right way to live a life, to be a good and productive person. You didn't have to act like us, learn to speak and think like us, and eventually become like us. You could be yourself and still earn a good living.

Because going to college, adopting middle-class ways, and getting a professional middle-class job was an option for working-class kids like me and not a morally freighted necessity for everybody, it strengthened working-class culture in a number of ways. For one thing, it weeded out those not fully equipped for working-class life. This made the culture more consistent and coherent within itself, which could have had only a narrowing effect, but the emergence of an increasingly pervasive middle-class professionalism on the outside actually worked to expand working-class horizons. You could adopt certain middle-class ways that were being promoted at the time, such as reading paperback books or using time-outs instead of spanking, while your neighbor didn't adopt those ways but maybe some others in modified forms. Having these choices was itself enriching, but as middle-class ways became more culturally dominant nationally, this also made working-class people more aware of their own path and direction. The increasingly official preference for the professional middle-class way made the working-class way clearer and more proudly defended and lived both on the ground and within and around an emerging middle-class cultural hegemony.

As a national middle-class culture emerged through the communicative arts, it was infused with working-class characters and ways of seeing and expressing— nowhere more than in popular music, as working-class young people transformed R&B and country into rock and roll, but also on TV and in movies and other entertainments.[15] Though popular culture was overseen by capitalists and middle-class professionals, if it was to get its chunk of expanding discretionary income, the culture industry had to appeal to working-class tastes and sensibilities, and talented people from working-class backgrounds were especially good at divining those. As culture worker jobs of high-, low, and middlebrow varieties proliferated, there were careers open to talent for working-class young people with an artistic bent. Though this dissipated rather dramatically as the Glorious Thirty matured, working-class ways enriched and helped shape a more egalitarian national middle-class culture during its period of class formation.

What's more, to a considerable extent middle-class professionals championed workers and their institutions against the Big Money remnants of the robber barons. Middle managers and professional workers gradually but steadily built their technocracy, increasingly (if never exclusively) based on merit and on their relationship between capital and labor. Especially in the workplace but also in the broader society, a meritocratic middle gained power as it simultaneously represented the ways of capital to workers and consumers and the ways of workers and consumers to capitalists, shareholders, and higher levels of management. Thus, the rise of a new class of professional free wage labor in the middle strengthened working-class culture both in immediate practical ways and in indirectly legitimating it as a vital, if not wholly desirable, alternative to itself.

Finally, just as young working-class migrants enriched middle-class life in the aggregate as we crossed over to a new class, many of us retained strong connections to our working-class families of origin, bringing back certain middle-class ways and perspectives. Some of this in youth was "breaking away," arrogant proselytizing, of which I did more than my share and that didn't enrich anybody. But mostly it was just our being there in our new form of being, our sense of becoming, and our different sense of the future, among other things. I imagine now that it was like a person from a foreign country coming to stay in your home for a while. You may not like the person's foreign ways, but it's interesting how different people can be, and, after all, "it takes all kinds" and he or she will be leaving before long. This has a lingering, broadening effect. As long as there was a rough cultural equality, as long as neither of us thought "they" should become more like "us" or at least did not push that notion too hard, a lot of shared learning occurred as the cultures influenced each other over time. Many settled-living working-class extended families had middle-class professionals in them by the 1960s and 1970s, and middle-class ways didn't seem so objectionable or foreign if they were exhibited by people you had known since they were children. Besides, most of us crossovers were not fully assimilated as real middle-class people yet, and many of us spontaneously code-switched back to working-class ways without even thinking about it.

At this point I may be indulging in some of that bad nostalgia, screening out all that nowhere-at-home alienation and wrenching cognitive dissonance I felt at the time while yearning for a past that is irretrievable because it was never really like that. But looking back, it is one thing to report how you felt and quite another to recognize after the fact the processes that were occurring in and around you. This distinction seems natural to me, since the two worst things that ever happened to me (so far)—getting kicked out of college in the early 1960s and being unemployable in my chosen profession in the 1970s—turned out to be the second and third best things that ever happened to me. I felt depressed and miserable at the time, but I can see now how the process shaped my life for the better. What's more, from the perspective of the more recent past and the future we are heading toward, the lived past undoubtedly looks better than it actually was. But there is a comparative effect to this nostalgia that is productively orienting, not simply false. For those who think they see social reality—past, present, or future—exactly as it was, is, or will be, this may seem distortive, but my argument is that reality is so dauntingly complex that we need simplifying frames to orient ourselves toward acting on the future, and this nostalgic framing is valuable and necessary for our moment.

The rewards for steady reliability are no longer what they were, and this has weakened working-class culture even though it persists, often heroically, against more than one grain. Restoring those rewards is economically more feasible now than it was then. Harking back to the Glorious Thirty means recognizing the potential of working-class agency in place—the value of a working class seeking not to abolish capitalism to achieve a classless society but instead simply using organized collective action to demand and achieve *more*, specifically more time and money for what you will. A democratic socialism is more necessary and feasible now than it was then, not as a completely different system from capitalism, as I and many others once (vaguely) envisioned, but rather as a more social and egalitarian form of it. What needs to be valued and remembered is the way increasing incomes and free time for what you will gave both working-class and middle-class people so much more agency, thus checking the power of capital without doing away with it. Though this increased agency could sometimes counter and reduce alienation at work, it left the basic structure of free wage labor in place. But working-class organization—labor unions aided by democratic government—recast power relations at work and in the economy and in doing so extracted discretionary income from capital. This extra income gave free wage labor of both classes a certain consumer sovereignty, a concept that postwar economics textbooks famously exaggerated but nonetheless gave workers real power in shaping capitalist enterprise to suit their wants and needs. "Please us, and you'll make profits" is not exactly a stirring revolutionary demand, but it played a vital political economic role in reinforcing an ethos that valued the common medio-cre mass of humanity not only for their work, but also for their spending power.

This was not exactly what Eugene Debs meant when he insisted that workers "rise with your class, not out of it," but it was that kind of rising.[16] There *were* more options for individuals to get out of the working class, but there was also much more rising based on organized collective action and increased spending power, rising that opened up new, if sometimes pretty narrow autonomous spaces where working-class people were free to enjoy themselves and develop whatever capacities might move their passions. They did not change their class positions, but the Glorious Thirty was especially glorious because working-class people could and did rise with their class and not just struggle to get out of it.

"AT LEAST WE OUGHT TO BE ABLE TO"

The future ain't what it used to be.

Yogi Berra

Old folks like me love to reminisce, especially when we're with people who have experienced the same things. Oldies but goodies now form an entire branch of the music industry, and what is called nostalgia is part of many marketing strategies for selling things to people like us. But reminiscing is not nostalgia. Reminiscing is pleasurable, even when what is remembered was awful at the time or so wonderful that it can be bittersweet to recall. Nostalgia, on the other hand, is a condition, an emotional state that is hard to shake off once it has taken hold. Modern usage of the term "nostalgia," from a Greek root meaning a "painful longing for home" that motivated Odysseus, originally denoted a psychological condition of homesickness (*Heimweh* in German), an uncontrollable aching for something that's been lost. Reminiscence is a relaxed indulgence. Nostalgia hurts and is demanding.

Some of my relatives like to reminisce about the smell of hot oil in a factory or the whiff of sulfur mixed with dead leaves in the autumn air, and I still take pleasure in remembering nights sitting on the first-base side of Point Stadium watching the blue-orange flame from the Lower Cambria Works dance behind the third-base side. Judie and her sisters love to recount the fear they experienced as their father drove drunk on Sunday evenings from their grandparents' house to their home thirty miles away; what terrified them at the time makes them giggle now as they swap remembrances of things well past. By my lights, none of that is nostalgia because it does not hurt enough to want to avoid it. In Johnstown both men and women will sometimes evoke the good times "when the mills were working," but there is an active effort to avoid wallowing in it. Typically, some-

one will say "yeah, those were the days" as a signal to move on to another subject, and amazingly, with a collective sigh, everybody does, with nobody giggling.
That's nostalgia, and you can feel its power to get away from you like a coal truck
losing its brakes coming down a hill.

Nostalgia, like grief, loses some of its power over time. But we can't help looking back, telling younger and younger people that it doesn't have to be this way,
that once upon a time life was open and exploratory for almost everybody in a
way that it is not for them. Typically the young find our nostalgia irrelevant, either
because they don't believe us or because they're convinced that whatever good
times we experienced cannot be repeated. And in truth, we tend to be sloppy in
mixing our reminiscences with what could be a rational, restorative nostalgia.

It's true the mills are not coming back. Nor can the exciting period of class
formation of a new kind of professional middle class be repeated, as we're already
well formed and rather fixed in our ways. Besides, we would not want to restore
most of the Glorious Thirty with its taken-for-granted racism and sexism and its
other forms of backwardness compared to the present. What we should want to
restore from those days seems much more abstract than the sights, sounds, and
smells that trigger our reminiscences. I have argued that what needs to be restored
is simply those steady across-the-board increases in money and time, increases
in discretionary income and time for what you will. These seem abstract because
society-wide trajectories are revealed only through statistical measurement, but
they have social and psychological, political and cultural impacts that are real and
immediate, that move hearts and minds and allow us to be more generous and
adventuresome. Like any kind of freedom, discretionary time and money bring
out both the more devilish and the better angels of our nature, but the limited
record we have supports Benjamin Friedman's worldwide conclusion that the
through line of good times leads to more open hearts and stronger, more supple
minds.

Though clearly desirable, is it possible to restore the Glorious Thirty's sustained
upward trajectories of discretionary money and time? Just because something
happened once does not mean it can happen again. Former *Economist* editor Marc
Levinson argues that the Glorious Thirty was an "economic miracle" that far ex-
ceeded "reasonable expectations," the result of the convergence of an extraordinary set of economic circumstances that can never occur again; it was not
"normal," and we need to lower our expectations for the future.[1] Historian Jefferson Cowie doesn't buy that economic argument but contends that the political circumstances that allowed the creation and development of a New Deal order
from 1935 to 1965 are highly unlikely to ever occur again.[2]

The economic argument against a glorious restoration is much less formidable than the political one, as a wide array of solid evidence and argument has

established the renewed viability of New Deal–style economic remedies. As referenced earlier, this policy literature is explicitly nostalgic in the restorative way I advocate: it looks back to the Glorious Thirty not for inspiration but instead for evidence of what worked and could work again in our very different circumstances. Though I have nothing to add to it, I want to highlight two foundational policy goals derived from looking back to our golden age—sharing the gains from productivity growth and restoring steeply progressive taxes—as ways of reducing our growing inequality of income and wealth and funding a greatly expanded social wage.

During the Glorious Thirty the top 10 percent of taxpayers got about one-third of all gross (or market) income, and I remember thinking how unfair that was without ever asking myself what level of unequal incomes would be fair. Today, the top 10 percent get about half of all income before taxes, with the bottom 90 percent sharing the other half. It's funny how that old-time two-thirds share for the bottom 90 percent now seems so just and fair and what should be normal![3] Today, what was is a good benchmark for what could and should be. Getting back to a Glorious Thirty distribution of market income would provide nearly $3 trillion every year to be distributed among about 142 million full- and part-time workers in that bottom 90 percent—that's nearly $20,000 a year for each and every one of them.[4] Someone earning $60,000 now would instead make $80,000, someone making $15,000 now would make $35,000, and so on. That's a simplistic illustration, but it should give you an idea of how much discretionary income—and the freedom that goes with it—would be available to the vast majority of people if we could just go back to the good old days of 1945–1975.

The reasons for our growing inequality of income and wealth are complex, highly contested, and, of course, politically charged. But one of the candidates for the primary cause seems particularly compelling: the financial gains from the growth of productivity (output per hour) were shared with production and non-supervisory workers during the Glorious Thirty, and they have not been shared since, as indicated in figure 4.1.

The rise in real hourly compensation from 1948 into the 1970s is, of course, what I've been arguing is the core glory of the Glorious Thirty. The fact that it tracked pretty closely to the growth in economy-wide productivity means that this unprecedented rise in living standards did not threaten inflation and thus economic growth. In fact, it sustained and even supercharged historically high levels of economic growth, as detailed in chapter 1. The 1970s economy had its problems with "stagflation," possibly caused in part by a "profit squeeze" and resulting "capital shortages."[5] It might have been justified back then to decouple the growth of wages from productivity for a while in order to beat back the inflation part of stagflation so the economy could grow healthily again. But whatever justification

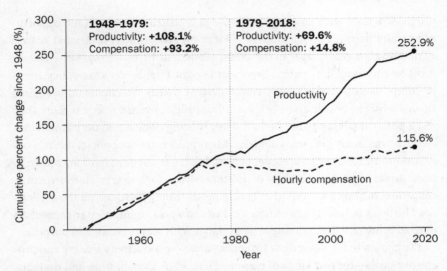

FIGURE 4.1. Productivity and earnings growth in the United States, 1948–2018

Source: Economic Policy Institute, https://www.epi.org/productivity-pay-gap/.

there might have been for such a pause has long since vanished. Today there is a capital surplus and a wage squeeze. If compensation had caught up with the gains from productivity growth, production and nonsupervisory workers would share about $2 trillion more each year than they did in 2018, or about $21,000 a year each.[6] Thus, the disappearance of productivity sharing can account for most of the enormous growth in the inequality of market incomes since the 1970s.

Market income is income before taxes, and while federal income taxes are still mildly progressive, payroll, state, and local taxes are not. In general, combining all taxes, each income group now pays about the same percentage in taxes as their share of all income. The top 1 percent, for example, now gets about 22 percent of all income and pays an average of about 23 percent of that income in taxes of every sort.[7] It was very different during the Glorious Thirty, as corporations paid much more and the richest of the rich got truly soaked. Federal income taxes were steeply progressive, requiring those with the highest incomes to pay much larger percentages of their incomes than those at the bottom and in the middle. The top marginal rate, for example, was over 80 percent (twice what it is now), and inherited wealth of more than $10 million was taxed at 77 percent for the entirety of the period.[8] These very high top rates, which Thomas Piketty admiringly calls "confiscatory," were not intended to raise a lot of revenue; rather, they were quite explicitly meant to discourage the highest market incomes and thereby leave more money available to be gained by workers in their wages and other compensation.[9] According to Sam Pizzigati's history of US tax policy, a wide array of steeply progressive taxes were amazingly effective in equalizing incomes (and opportunities), and these tax policies deserve a lot of the credit for creating what he calls a "middle-class golden age" in the 1950s, 1960s, and 1970s.[10] Progressive economists love to recall how radical President Dwight Eisenhower's tax policy seems in comparison to today's jerry-rigged system that is systematically weighted against working people and work itself. But progressive tax policy is more than just a political talking point. Serious work is being done based on historical research across many different countries. Many golden age tax policies didn't work or had unintended negative consequences, but it has not been hard for researchers to locate hundreds of billions of dollars available to fund green infrastructure, education, health care, and other crying needs simply by restoring those Glorious Thirty tax policies that we know worked and whose unintended consequences were all positive.[11] This is restorative nostalgia with scope, point, and purpose.

I've chosen to highlight these two policy areas—productivity sharing and progressive taxes—for two kinds of reasons. First, while globalization and dramatic technological change do indeed, as so often claimed, make it impossible to restore many of the glories of the Glorious Thirty (including some nonglories we would not wish to restore), there is nothing in our current economic circumstances that restricts us from restoring productivity sharing and progressive taxes like we had back in the day—nothing, that is, but our politics, and that's my second reason. Jeff Cowie's historical argument against a glorious restoration is based in showing how the New Deal order that created the first Glorious Thirty was forged in economic depressions and wars as well as within some other contingent circumstances that allowed us to temporarily (as it turned out) break with our long history of oligarchic rule indirectly supported by a deep culture of radical individualism. It is the solidity of that oligarchic rule today, an oligarchy of wealth that appears to be strengthening its hold on our politics as I write, that makes it so very difficult to insert either productivity sharing or progressive tax policy into our public discourse, let alone into law.

I very much fear that Cowie may be right—that the Glorious Thirty was a great onetime exception to the mainstream of American history and culture. But I also know there are other streams in addition to the main one, that middle-class culture is not the only one available. What's more, there are contradictions within both middle-class and working-class cultures, contradictions that if brought into interaction with each other, as has happened in the past, could create new circumstances and new possibilities. I'm not sure how this might play out in our politics, but as in many other areas of life, the increasing isolation of these class cultures and the characteristic middle-class dismissal of working-class ways as a deficit culture rob us of prospects and possibilities that might otherwise be there. As a people, we are not realizing our potential.

The beginning of wisdom in this regard is for the mainstream, dominant culture to simply recognize that there is an alternative class culture that it dominates, possibly unintentionally. That should be the easy part and is the basic task of chapter 5. More difficult is recognizing how different ways of doing things, different ways of seeing and being in the world, not only challenge your own way but also complement and enhance it by being ready-to-hand to draw on when necessary or even just for the hell of it. Hopefully, the rest of the book will suggest numerous such possibilities.

I want to end this chapter with a broad characterization of the Glorious Thirty's zeitgeist, glimmers of which appear from time to time in our own political and other public discourse still today. Henry Wallace's "century of the common man" was never as popular and widespread a guideline for understanding and living in the post–World War II period as Henry Luce's "American century" meme. But as Joshua Freeman points out, Wallace's guideline did have quite a run during the Cold War even as the "man" part (and his whiteness) were being decisively challenged.[12] Tony Judt, looking more broadly at both the United States and Europe, saw the Glorious Thirty as a "social democratic moment" when "the hitherto neglected interests of large sections of the population would now be addressed."[13] Well, yes, there was that, but in the United States the all-too-brief century of the common was a lot more robust than simply "addressing" the interests of large sections of the population. It had a cultural punch that affected politics and social life. As Pizzagati details,

> The squeeze on the midcentury rich wouldn't be just financial. The wealthy . . . felt a growing middle class invading ever more of their physical and cultural space. The rich were losing their social preeminence. . . . [T]he chattering class . . . no longer fawned over the lifestyles of the rich and famous. They explored instead the interests and exploits of average-income men and women. The rich had lost their role as cultural pacesetters.[14]

There was a robust "cultural disdain for great wealth" and a healthy fear of its economic and political power. And there was a strong prejudice that "average people mattered most," a consensus that the goal should be to achieve that general happy Mediocrity Benjamin Franklin had prematurely admired so much.[15]

The "middle class" crowding the wealthy's physical and cultural space back then was a diverse, complicated, and ill-defined bunch—not just middle managers but also autoworkers and postal clerks, secretaries and nurses, teachers and professors, truck drivers, social workers, carpenters, therapists, and more middle managers, some of them executive secretaries. We were all pretty average in those days, days when steelworkers could earn more than professors. Compared to the malefactors of great wealth, we were all pretty common, the vast majority of us simply free wage labor as of old but with more time and money and better working conditions. There were important cultural differences among us—regional, religious, racial/ethnic, and gender and sexual differences—but also a broad class difference. Part of us became those "cultural pacesetters" the rich used to be, a communications/education wing of the professional middle class, a chattering group if not exactly a class of our own. We have cultural power—not just the stars and superstars among us but also us rank-and-file mediocrities—that can be politically powerful if we know how to use it. One insufficient but necessary condition is to become much more class conscious than we have been, more conscious of ourselves and others of how we can and do complement each other and of how we could be stronger together if we recognized and appreciated our different ways of seeing and being in the world.

Part II

FREE WAGE LABOR AND THE CULTURES OF CLASS

Karl Marx struck out on a lot of his confident predictions about the future of capitalism but none more so than this: "The various interests and conditions of life within the ranks of the proletariat are more and more equalized, . . . and [this equalization] nearly everywhere reduces wages to the same low level."[1] Marx accurately traced the dynamics that led in this direction, but many other factors, including organized worker resistance, intervened to cause a different and happier result.

The dynamic of downward equalizations was there, however, and still is. Though it was greatly restrained and even undermined for nearly half a century around the Glorious Thirty, it has more recently reasserted itself in large parts of the workforce, resulting in what some scholars call a "precariat." In one industry or economic sector after another, whether meatpacking, warehousing, trucking, retail work, computer coding, or home health care, you can see this equalizing down of wages and conditions. Likewise, you can see it within many professions, for example, health maintenance organization general practitioners and the dependence of universities on contingent faculty. But when you look at the workforce as a whole, there is a great range of incomes and conditions, none greater than the differences between managerial and professional workers and the rest of the workforce. This is what I have been calling "the professional middle class" and "the working class."

Still, almost everybody in the Bureau of Labor Statistics' breakdown of the workforce—whether middle or working class—is what Marx called free wage labor, a form of work and of sustenance that was just beginning to become predominant in his time.[2] It's important to realize that the vast majority of middle-class professionals today, including most managerial professionals, are what in Marx's time would have been unambiguously seen as proletarians. Both "free" and "wage" had very specific meanings that differentiated them from earlier predominant forms.[3] Wage workers were neither independent farmers producing for themselves as well as for the market, artisans selling the products of their labor (shoes or cloth, for example), nor independent professionals such as doctors and lawyers. Wage workers merely sell a portion of their time in return for a wage, and during that time they do what their employer tells them to do. At the end of their workday, they are free in the sense that they owe the employer nothing more and that the employer owes them nothing at all beyond the wage. This contrasted with feudal lords who had formally recognized moral and legal obligations to their vassals and to whom vassals had similar more strictly enforced obligations. Likewise, it was the opposite of the slaveholder who needed to feed, clothe, and shelter slaves in order to protect his investment in human property. Being free, neither vassal nor slave, was a double-edged sword. The indifference of the wage employer outside of the workplace freed the worker from being controlled in all aspects of life. But it also meant that the worker was entirely dependent on having a job and one with a decent wage. With such a job, a worker had some free time for what you will. But without one, wage workers had nothing to sustain themselves, no means by which to exercise their wills other than to seek employment. They were "wage slaves," bound by necessity to having a job.

Class struggle over the last two hundred years has established a web of economic safety nets and social wages to partially protect wage workers from unlimited subjection to finding and keeping a job. As productivity and therefore wealth systematically increased in advanced forms of capitalism, workers also won increased wages and reduced hours, weeks, and years of work. But despite the wide range of incomes and conditions, despite the wages-and-hours distinction between salaried and wage workers, almost all of us in twenty-first-century America are proletarians, dependent on wages from employment to sustain ourselves. The wide range among our incomes and our wealth makes us more or less dependent on that wage, but anyone who could not sustain themselves without working for a wage is free wage labor, whether manager or janitor, professor or administrative assistant. Today a prime-age worker in the bottom 80 percent of the income distribution could get by without a paycheck for from six days to six months, and the majority of the top 20 percent could not last more than a year.[4] By this measure, the person who could last a year without a job lives in a different world than someone who could last only a week, but both are still wage slaves dependent on having a job to sustain themselves or their families.

As proletarians all, though we have conflicting interests, we have an overriding common interest in protecting wage work in general from unrestricted vulnerability to the vicissitudes of the market. The variability of wages and conditions, rather than a downward equalization, strengthens capitalism by creating a hierarchy of life conditions, life chances, and life prospects that divide us in a way Marx could never have anticipated, and each of the various steps in that hierarchy is well worth fighting to maintain or achieve. Today most occupations that pay well and offer a decent level of job and life security are professional jobs, including management, that operate within a professional ethos cultivated through various kinds of higher education.

It is important to see our shared class interests, our unity as free wage labor, because together the professional and working classes are the vast majority, and coalitions among us are vital for representative democracy to positively transform the current and developing system. But it's also important to see the differences in life circumstances that tend to produce different class cultures. These different cultures often, even usually, cause us to misunderstand each other because we fail to meet each other's expectations. These misinterpretations of each other, in turn, are part of what keeps us from seeing our common interest and effectively working to reconcile our conflicting interests.

In chapter 5, I show that much in professional middle-class culture encourages professionals to ignore or deny the existence of any other class culture. Middle-class culture has a distinct tendency to see itself as the one right way, as the one and only worthwhile culture that other cultures should be measured against and that all people should aspire to achieve. Given our cultural power to shape public frames, agendas, and discourse, this hegemonic tendency creates additional distances and conflicts between us and the working class. Chapter 6 will then present a systematic portrayal of what I see as the categorical differences in the cultures that lead to common misinterpretations while also arguing that the cultures can and often do complement each other at both societal and individual levels.

In this discussion, however, it is important to remember that though I am ignoring it, there is a ruling class, whether you call it the capitalist or owning class or the 1 percent (which may actually be the top 2 or 3 percent). Through their economic power, both in the workplace and in the ways they mobilize their wealth, this class rules a lot of our lives directly—on the ground, so to speak—though not necessarily in a unified, coordinated way. In addition, through their ownership of most means of communication and their increasingly important role in funding higher education, not to mention their enormous power in bankrolling politicians, they exercise substantial cultural power as well. But most of this power is exercised indirectly through us middle-class professionals; by shaping our basic economic and political parameters, they influence our sense of realism on what can be productively thought and done. Still, though this is now deteriorating, as waged professionals we have a historically huge degree of freedom of thought and action. Within that realm, my argument is that we can both better protect ourselves as a class and advance the common good by opening a more nuanced and equal dialogue with working-class people and their cultures.

THERE IS A GENUINE WORKING-CLASS CULTURE

Nothing epic. Just the small heroics of getting through the day when the day doesn't give a shit.

Philip Levine

If I'm not what the white man thinks I am, then he has to find out what *he* is.

James Baldwin

In the summer of 1999 in Youngstown, Ohio, I attended my first working-class studies conference. I had just finished *Striking Steel*, and a tangential part of that book articulated what I saw as core differences between professional middle-class and working-class cultures. For the conference, I planned to read a twelve-minute passage from the book describing how weird and unproductive it felt to displaced steelworkers to be taught to write résumés in the 1980s. To account for this phenomenon, I boldly explained that in contrast to middle-class culture, "working-class culture emphasizes being and *belonging*, not achieving and *becoming*."[1]

I was nervous about reading this passage because I had never heard anybody articulate the idea that there were distinct class cultures, let alone sum up their differences in a sentence. What's more, my favorite sociology book at the time, *Habits of the Heart: Individualism and Commitment in American Life*, firmly declared that for the past century "the middle class . . . has so dominated our culture that neither a genuinely upper-class nor a genuinely working-class culture has fully appeared. Everyone in the United States thinks largely in middle-class categories, even when they are inappropriate."[2] Though I knew this was wrong, *Habits of the Heart* is such a rich appreciation and critique of middle-class Americanism by a team of five authors who seemed to know everything that it seemed preposterous that I could be so firmly right and they so terribly wrong.

At the conference, however, counseling psychologist Barbara Jensen delivered a paper including references to the exciting potentials of middle-class *becoming* and the warm advantages of working-class *belonging*.[3] What's more, in the question-and-answer period, a room of some thirty people argued with Jensen about this or that, but they all seemed to assume that becoming and belonging marked core differences between the class cultures. Through a wave of vertigo, I went from "how could I be the only one who knows this" to "geez, everybody here knows this, and I have nothing to say."

Maybe you have to be an academic to realize what an existential panic this can put people like us in. But that panic passed quickly into a sense of both relief and excitement. I realized what a burden I had been carrying around trying to think through on my own what I saw as an impenetrable middle-class misunderstanding of working-class people and therefore of themselves/ourselves *and* of our society and its social, political, and economic prospects. I quickly made friends with Jensen and her cohort of mostly women academics and for four days soaked up stories about how fucked-up the middle class was contrasted with warm though often troubled remembrances of working-class pasts. I learned about imposter syndrome, survivor guilt, and code-switching, common phenomena among people who cross over from working-class families of origin to professional-middle-class jobs, especially in academia. I had known lots of middle-class people from working-class backgrounds, of course, but what was distinctive about this group was their fiercely stated preference for working-class ways and their ability to articulate what they liked and disliked about each way of life. Many of them loved their jobs but felt stressed and uncomfortable around their colleagues while also no longer feeling quite at home with their parents, siblings, and old friends. I found myself sharing stories I could tell briefly and easily because I didn't have to explain context and insist on nuance; instead, I got knowing looks, nodding heads, and yes-but responses. I was joining a conversation they had begun a few years before, so there was an intellectual seriousness to their discussion that went beyond a support group experience. But for me it was something like therapeutic.

I discovered, however, that others from working-class backgrounds were less positive about their culture of origin, especially if they were from hard-living or poverty-class families, including both those who were and were not comfortable in their current middle-class environments. They had made great efforts to wean themselves from that culture and were eager to help others do the same, but they were not interested in defending or preserving a culture they did not see as separable from poor living standards and bad working conditions. Other crossovers didn't like our "essentializing" or "stereotyping" the two class cultures, which seemed to them to ride roughshod over the complex individuals they knew in each class. Often these were folks who identified themselves as working-class academics, proudly coming out on their campuses as committed to working-class ways (especially an egalitarian antistatus ethic) and actively resisting the impulse to code-switch or see themselves as imposters in a professional middle-class world. Working-class academics also saw aspects of working-class culture as positive, but they tended toward the specific aspects of lifestyle, tastes, and manners of speaking rather than the kind of more universal characteristics Jensen had asserted. Meanwhile, those from middle-class backgrounds often express frustration with our navel-gazing penchant for autobiographical thinking, and they fear that romanticizing the working class and its ways might undermine the broader project of transforming workers' living standards and working conditions.

What many of us from working-class origins share at these conferences, however, is an ability to relax and just be our complete selves. Since midlife I haven't felt alienated from either middle-class or working-class worlds, fancying that I can move back and forth with relative ease, being a little working class in middle-class environments and a lot middle-class in working-class ones. But the emotional power of that first encounter—a feeling of finally being at home that had me uncontrollably weeping when I had my first quiet moment at the end of that 1999 conference—suggests that I had been more alienated than I realized. Others have told me about similar experiences, including people now in their twenties and thirties. Swapping poignant stories about our first encounters with working-class studies is now a standard part of evening socializing at these conferences.

This experience of class cultural clash and of how deeply it is felt has been thoroughly documented over the past thirty years. Anthologies such as *Strangers in Paradise, This Fine Place So Far from Home,* and *Working-Class Women in the Academy* have gathered poignant accounts of how difficult and complicated college can be for students from working-class families.[4] Class-culture differences are widely recognized today in academia, with many universities paying increasing attention to the specific problems of first-in-family (or first-generation) college students, including criticism of how middle-class biases exacerbate the obstacles these working-class students typically face.[5]

Cultures cannot clash unless there are more than one of them and their differences are substantial. But this does not mean that the clashing cultures are both genuine and of roughly equal value. Working-class culture could be, as often envisioned, merely a *deficit culture*—one characterized by the absence of mainstream values, skills, and ways of thinking and doing, a culture that is best understood as deficient in the kinds of things necessary to be a fully developed human being. A deficit culture is not genuine in the sense that it is just a backward version of the mainstream, a culturally lagging receptacle of another culture that it is gradually, perhaps all too slowly, adopting. Or working-class culture might be a *dominated culture*—one shaped, indeed deformed, by the material, social, and psychological conditions of its domination. A dominated culture is not genuine either. Since it is merely a result of its domination and exploitation by others, it does not fashion its own way of doing and seeing things but instead is a series of programmed responses to stimuli manipulated by someone else. Finally, working-class culture might be a *residual culture*—one destined to fade away.[6] A residual culture is genuine and may once have been (and for some still be) valuable, but it no longer suits current circumstances.

My argument is that working-class culture is genuine in the sense that it has an internal coherence that is separate and distinct from middle-class culture, has positive value both in itself and for US society, and vitally contributes to the shaping of middle-class life and culture even as it forms itself within and around that dominant culture. Working-class culture does indeed have some deficits, some of which I have spent my life as a teacher trying to fill, and it has been formed in conditions of domination. But professional middle-class culture has some deficits too and is not without its conditions of domination either, even if not as severe and if weighted more toward the social psychological than the economic and material. Finally, I suggest that the working class's deep culture—as distinct from lifestyles, tastes, and changing norms—is not merely residual but instead is shared by the majority of Americans of all ethnicities and colors, including many standard-issue middle-class professionals as they reach midlife. Working-class culture embodies what some labor historians have called a "making do" or a "getting-through-the-day" culture and what Jensen calls "a roomier sense of now."[7] It is more reactive than proactive and thus can benefit from exposure to the more ambitious and aspirational character of middle-class professionalism. But its greater agility within the force of circumstance and its narrowing of life to the immediacy of being and belonging have a lot to offer in filling those empty spaces in middle-class life, with its relentless pursuit of status and achievement. If the working class is not what we think it is, then we middle-class professionals may have a valuable opportunity to get a better sense of who we are.

Class Blindness and the One Right Way of Middle-Class Life

Habits of the Heart is unique in declaring outright that there is no genuine working-class culture. But the book was merely being explicit about what is still conventional scholarly practice more than three decades later: casting arguments about American society as a whole by focusing on its "main element," the ubiquitous but nevertheless elite middle-class—meaning people with a college education, a professional or managerial occupation, and a healthy family income. Today this practice can seem quaint amid the array of sociological studies of ethnic/racial, gender, and, to a lesser extent, class differences. But that habit of mind that thinks it's okay to take the professional middle-class part as if it were the whole of American culture and society is still the predominant one among the education-communications wing of the professional middle class. It's a combination of a relatively superficial but widely accepted intellectual convention supported by a deep class insularity and prejudice.

The claim that there is only one genuine culture in the United States was made in *Habits of the Heart*'s original preface and was neither developed nor supported there or later in the book. We are not told what the authors think constitutes a genuine culture. Nor are we told why they think middle-class culture is genuine and working-class culture is not. The bald statement in the preface is merely a dismissive gesture that allows them to conflate "middle class" with "American" for the rest of the book.

This is common practice. Books such as *American Manhood* and *American Cool* make similar claims, often admitting a certain narrowness in their prefaces but then proceeding to treat their version of middle-class culture as synonymous with American culture. Peter Stearns, for example, not only admits a middle-class narrowness in his introduction to *American Cool* but furthermore lets the cat out of the bag by granting that "like many studies of the middle class, it is biased toward evidence from Protestants in the North and West."[8] Likewise, Claude Fischer's *Made in America: A Social History of American Culture and Character* grants in his first chapter that his sense of a singular American culture "originated among Northeastern Protestants and then spread and gained power over time."[9]

I can see why authors and publishers would not want more descriptive but unwieldy titles such as "American Middle-Class Protestant Manhood in the North and West," but this is more than a matter of deceptive marketing. The practice of excluding working-class and other cultures from the discussion and of assuming "people like us" are the singular norm is what Benjamin DeMott has called "middle-class imperialism."[10] It is not direct economic or political domination but supports that domination. It also is unlikely to be conscious and intentional, since it is hard for any culture *not* to take itself as the norm, experience its ways as appropriate and natural, and assume that the way it understands things is the correct way. It is convenient to assume that other cultures are best understood simply by what they lack in comparison with the dominant mainstream one. But what if that understanding is simply false? What if working-class culture has a coherent but different set of values and norms that fit into and around the dominant mainstream culture? If that were true, then the mainstream culture, though dominant, would be subject to a series of mistakes and illusions about the society it culturally dominates. It would also be likely to misunderstand itself as a culture.

The professional middle class in America *is* culturally dominant, even though we are economically subordinate to a ruling class and somewhat less politically subordinate but in a more complicated way. But the concept of a dominant culture presumes that there are other cultures different from the dominant one, for example, Protestants in Italy, Slovaks in the former Czechoslovakia, Kurds in Iraq, or new and recent immigrants in all countries. A dominant culture cannot be understood by excluding reference to the ones it dominates, how and why it predominates, and how it influences—and is influenced by—other cultures.

Claude Fischer's *Made in America* marshals a wonderful combination of statistics, survey research, and insightful historical interpretation to demonstrate that across the nineteenth and twentieth centuries, "increasing proportions of women, youth, ethnic minorities, and the working class adopted [middle-class] culture, even after sometimes resisting it." Fischer is undoubtedly right that today "the American middle class lives and promulgates the distinctive and dominant character of the society" and that across the twentieth century "more and more Americans joined the mainstream culture."[11] But "increasing proportions" and "more and more," like "dominant," don't mean that middle-class professionalism is the one and only culture or the only valuable one. Nor does it mean that even after all the increasing proportions, it is the culture that is lived and promulgated by the majority of Americans. It just means it is dominant.

A dominant culture does not need to dominate. It can be predominant, the preferred culture, first among equals, if you will. But when it construes itself as the one and only right way, it cannot help but dominate other cultures and the people who live within those cultures, whether it consciously intends to or not. Black studies and women's studies as academic fields have decisively shown how narrow-minded and harmful construing white maleness as the norm has been. Likewise, those whose regional cultures differ from northeastern Protestantism often resent how their differences are routinely seen as mere backwardness. Indeed, Colin Woodard has cogently argued that there are no less than eleven "American nations" with not just different regional cultures but also "rival" ones.[12]

When you consider how diverse we actually are by race, ethnicity, gender, sexuality, religion, region, and life stage, it can make your head spin. And spinning heads naturally desire some mainstream unity among this potentially explosive diversity. To a large extent, a rough unity can be productively provided by middle-class professionalism but only if we don't lose sight of our middleness, our ability to see and live our positioning between a ruling class (whether you call it capitalist, owning class, or an oligarchy of wealth) and a working class that have genuinely different ways of living a life. Superficial conventions that allow and indeed encourage us to talk among ourselves, to mistake our part for the whole, let alone dismiss other classes as uninteresting, backward, and not genuine, blind us to fundamental realities of the society we are trying to understand. *Habits of the Heart*'s more fundamental intellectual flaw derives from this simple but blinding convention. The convention allows a rather spectacular lack of curiosity about working-class life and how it must be distinct from middle-class ways—

just logically, without any empirical investigation let alone daily experience of working-class people.

Habits of the Heart poignantly bemoans a narrowing of middle-class life as now centered on a *career* rather than a *calling*. Once upon a time "to enter a profession meant to take up a definite function in a community and to operate within the civic and civil order of that community." A calling was less individualistic, less focused on developing one's self, and more focused on fulfilling a social role that functioned to benefit one's community and a broader social good. A career, by contrast, "was no longer oriented to any face-to-face community but to impersonal standards of excellence, operating in the context of a national occupational system. Rather than embedding one in a community, following a profession came to mean, quite literally, 'to move *up* and away.' The goal was no longer the fulfillment of a commonly understood form of life but the attainment of 'success,' and . . . whatever 'success' one had obtained, one could always obtain more."[13] For the authors of *Habits*, this constant urging to self-improvement, to achieving higher and higher levels of success, led to "unprecedented psychic demands," resulting in a "therapeutic culture" that has come to define the dominant middle-class and thus American culture.[14] They called for a more civic form of professionalism, restoring a sense of calling and a greater sense of social vision and mission.

This is still a powerful critique of "American life" that has engaged subsequent generations of social scientists and other thinkers.[15] But how could it not occur to these authors that there are lots of people, probably an overwhelming majority, who do not have careers and have never thought of their lives that way—people who have "just a job," neither a calling nor a career but merely a way to *earn a living*? How could these people not have a culture, a way of living a life, that is very different from one built around a career?

Let me start with that relatively uncommon group of people who hate their jobs and are willing to tell you that even if you haven't asked. People such as my father and also Joan C. Williams's father-in-law, who dropped out of school in the eighth grade to help support his family and eventually "got a good, steady [factory] job he truly hated . . . for 38 years."[16] I've always admired people like this. Most people who hate their jobs find ways to tolerate them. They enjoy the workplace social life of the people they work with. Or they value the work they do even though they don't like doing it. Or they find ways to create little spaces within their work that they like living in. And above all, they avoid calling attention to how much they hate their jobs, especially to others but also to themselves. "It's not so bad" or "it could be worse," they tell me. On the other hand, those who can flat out say "I hate what I do every day" and keep it in front of them have a special strength of will that may not be good for their mental health but is an extreme form of the dignity and self-respect working-class people win with the unadulterated grit of sticking with a bad job, taking it, and hanging in there. Their job complaining is often a back-handed form of bragging. My boss is worse than your boss, all the people I work with are assholes, what I do is worthless, and my job is dirtier, scarier, or more tedious than yours, but I get up every day and get the job done. I've witnessed these "my job is worse than your job" competitions dozens of times in working-class settings, albeit mostly among men with some alcohol in them but also less dramatically among sober working-class women. I have yet to witness, and cannot imagine, a middle-class professional describing their job as so bad they deserve respect, even a round of applause, for simply enduring it.

Many working-class people don't hate their jobs, of course. Even though, like the job haters, they take pride in showing up every day and doing a good job, they genuinely enjoy enough aspects of their work to keep them satisfied at the level job surveys ask about.[17] Many have intrinsically interesting and satisfying work, from skilled building trades workers at the high end of wages (when there is work) to personal care workers at the low end. But even this varies a lot across a work life, as supervisors vary from great to awful, as work is deskilled or sped up, and as the aches, pains, and injuries of aging accumulate to make lifting or standing all day more difficult and painful. Still, they *take it*.

If you have a *career*, it makes sense to view life as a journey, one where you constantly strive to see what you can achieve and who you can yet become. But if you have a *job*, especially one that pays decently, it makes more sense to see life as a daily cycle of punishment and reward, of their time and my time, of necessity and freedom, of earning a living and living. People with jobs invest much less of their selves in their jobs than people with careers. As a result, what they do to earn a living has less of a hold on them than people with careers from which they are never quite free. I've been part of hundreds of conversations in which people debate the relative merits of "leaving the job behind when I walk out the door" versus "being engaged with it more or less all the time." As a middle-class professional with no fixed workday, I could see how much freer people with jobs were when not working than I was or could ever be, even though I was so much freer at work. I've always felt like they were more present in the present than I was, as my mind could never quite empty itself of the schedule of tasks ahead of me. I cannot remember a time when I did not appreciate their way even as I realized I could never live that way.

How could having a job rather than a career not result in and require a different kind of culture, a different set of predispositions and expectations, norms and values, and ways of living a life? This different culture could not simply be the absence of dispositions required to have a career, norms, and values that could eventually be handed down like secondhand clothes to cultural laggards. The culture needs to be different to accommodate different circumstances. Nor could this different culture be merely residual, a leftover from the past that will eventually disappear, so long as our economy still produces more jobs than careers, which it does and will go on doing.[18] And who is more dominated, those of us who invest so much of ourselves in our careers that inevitably tie us into larger systems of command and control or those who keep the biggest part of themselves free of responsibility for those systems?

Middle-class observers, even the newer class-aware generation of sociologists, often assume that professional middle-class careers are objectively better not just as jobs but also as ways of life. That's why even the most empathetic observers—from Paul Willis to Julie Bettie—focus on the irony and tragedy of working-class young people reproducing their class positions with the cultural choices they make within educational and societal systems in which they are "unpreferred," at best.[19] The best of these sociologists, such as Willis and Bettie, appreciate the immediate logic of working-class antischool cultures among young people but see only the long-term hardship, the absence of broader choices, and a future without becoming that seems only negative and unfortunate in reproducing a system of inequality. The presumption that careers are always and everywhere better than jobs blinds them to the preservation of self and the choice for a simple integrity that are often at the core of working-class young people's rejection of middle-class ways. An aspiration to get a good job, defined as one that is decently well paid and steady, can seem like no aspiration at all unless you see it as an affirmative choice to avoid the selling of one's soul that seems to them involved in pursuing careers that are highly structured by others and that can dig deep into your self and your relationships with friends and family.

As an exercise, let's say you could get the same pay and benefits for being either an advertising executive or a personal care worker. Would it be irrational to choose the latter because you thought advertising was mostly a form of lying to people, whereas you found everyday satisfaction in helping people who need help (as one of my middle-aged nephews does)? That, of course, is not the way it works. These are not the kinds of choices any American actually has. But what about the choice between being an operations manager getting $81,000 a year versus a union-protected but highly monitored UPS delivery driver getting $66,000.[20] As an operations manager, the perception is that "you can't be your own man," "you're simply a tool of upper management," "you're cut off from the people you work with," and "you no longer own yourself." Might not the sense of independence you get from simply being bossed, being scheduled and monitored by others but not having responsibility to enforce and reproduce the system, and not being responsible to force, cajole, and intimidate others—might not that be worth earning $15,000 less? I have talked with scores of people who think so, including some UPS drivers, and it has never occurred to me to argue with them.

Advertising executives and operations managers may take offense at this way of stereotyping them and their jobs, but such perceptions and evaluations of middle- and upper-class people are widespread among the working class, as documented in numerous social science investigations.[21] Working-class people with just jobs could be too simplistic or outright wrong in their assessment of middle-class professionals and the way our careers can twist us into inauthenticity in our interpersonal rela- tions. But this does not mean there is nothing in these assessments but "class envy" and the "healing of class injuries" or a merely "reactive identity" that compensates for the shame they are thought to feel for not being successful.[22] Instead, they may be making an affirmative choice for simple integrity, because either they value integrity more than we do or are cynical about the more complex integrity we middle-class professionals think we can achieve, especially when we're young. In my judgment, their cynicism about complex integrity is usually too sweeping, but it's not as if there's no evidence for their view. I have known and read about ad- vertising executives, operations managers, and even sociologists who were either a little or a lot twisted by careerism. Indeed, a 2012 study in the *Proceedings of the National Academy of Sciences* found that "higher social class predicts increased un- ethical behavior."[23] As in gymnastics, we middle-class professionals should get some points for attempting the more complex, but we should at least be aware that there is more than one right way to live a life; that there are advantages and disad- vantages to any culture, even ours; and that there may be profoundly legitimate reasons for folks to choose a different culture than the one we know and love.

Today the disadvantages of choosing eight hours for work, eight hours for sleep, and eight hours for what you will instead of a career are larger and stronger and getting more so. Because I graduated from high school smack in the middle of thirty years of rising wages and expanding opportunities, I was especially aware of the value of a choice for simple integrity and preservation of self because we talked about it as working-class teens and young adults and because my working- adult students often brought that discussion into my classrooms in later years. In current conditions I can't be sure that the choice between a job culture and a career culture is still as palpable and affirmative as it was for my generation. Log- ically it would seem unlikely, as steady jobs with decent wages and benefits are so much less readily available now. But I still see working adults with sturdy job cul- tures all around me. I think they often exaggerate how terribly corrupting having a career can be, but I still often witness the same ingenuity in living a job life even as the work is less steady and not paid as well as it used to be.

Of one thing I'm sure. Careers are not as readily available today as most middle- class professionals think, and forcing, cajoling, and scaring all young people into college tracks and college is a fool's errand. Barely more than one of five jobs today require at least a bachelor's degree, the document required for entry into most careers. And while that proportion is growing, there will only be one of four such jobs twenty years from now.[24] By this measure, the vast majority will still have jobs, not careers. For them, a "taking it" job culture that frees up the rest of life for what you will makes a lot of sense if and only if we can get back to the kind of steadily increasing wages and decreasing work time the United States had for the thirty years after World War II when unions were strong and productivity gains were shared with workers.

But as conditions in the working class are steadily eroding, dramatically increased by periodic economic collapses such as those in the early 1980s, late 2000s, and 2020, the professional middle class is not untouched. Those deteriorating conditions are coming our way, and some have already arrived, as we can see with the rise of contingent academic labor and other forms of short-term contract work for even the most highly skilled professionals.[25] And it's not just economics. As the gap continues to widen between their and our life conditions and life chances, our middle-class fear of falling intensifies as the fall becomes steeper and scarier, if not for us then for our children and grandchildren.[26] As more of us are forced into defensive crouches, middle-class professionalism can turn into its opposite— less and less about achieving and becoming and more and more about preserving our privileges so we can pass them on to our progeny. My guess is that jobs and careers—the waged and the salaried—stand and fall together, not all at the same time but like erosion followed by an avalanche.

It is an act of generosity that so many of our professional big thinkers seek to share our cultural capital with the poor and working classes by using that great equalizer, education at all levels, to help them and especially their children become more like us.[27] Despite this generous impulse, however, such approaches cannot work for two big reasons. First, there are not and will not be enough jobs requiring our kinds of social and cultural capital, not enough professional jobs with possibilities for careers. Most of the work that needs done in our society— cleaning, cooking, caring, clerking, moving and making things, selling, waiting, and guarding—does not require much education, and people who do that work generally do it simply to earn a living.[28] What they most need is not our cultural capital but rather steady work, much more income, and increasing amounts of free time for what you will. Second, they have their own cultural capital and, though open to and often hungry for education, they have a strong tendency to resent and resist the kinds of cultural capital we're trying to sell them. Sometimes this resistance is irrational and unproductive, especially from a professional perspective that tends to see the potential of only one individual at a time, but mostly it is based on a strong attachment to the culture they already have, a realistic appreciation of how it works in their lives, what they value more than we seem to, and a gut-level wish not to be like us.

If free wage labor has divided itself, or been divided, into jobs and careers with distinct class cultures, as I have come to believe, then it would be important to recognize this. If middle-class professionals go on treating working people as if they are just underdeveloped versions of ourselves, it will just continue to piss them off, often mixed with dangerous levels of ethnic, racial, and nativist resentments as economic conditions worsen. But if we realize how much we depend on them and how much they depend on cultural dispositions different from ours, we might just recognize how much a job culture of being and belonging might offer us, especially in midlife as most of us run out of potential to achieve and become. We might also come to political accommodations that would enable us, together, to mount the kind of strong countervailing force to our ruling class that would provide the economic base for both class cultures to flourish once again.

Class Identity: A Journey from Principled Crossover to Unintentional Straddler

As I was writing *Striking Steel* in the 1990s, clearly identifying myself as decisively middle class was helpful in order to explain and appreciate the union-drenched, working-class culture of my steelworker father. "Othering" him and his class was essential to presenting him and his kind in an appreciative way without having to directly challenge middle-class ways that tend to disdain or dismiss people like him. But it was more than just a rhetorical tactic. It helped me think through how I was so very different from him. I was in my fifties then, and I had long identified as working class, referring to both my roots and my Marxist faith but also to certain leftover manners, mores, and behaviors that I either couldn't or didn't want to overcome. It was psychologically hard for me to admit to being middle class, but once I did, so many streams of observation and thought opened up that I got pretty rigid about defining myself and people like me as class *crossovers*.

When Alfred Lubrano showed up at a working-class studies conference in 2002 to try out his notion of being a class *straddler*, I was immediately and argumentatively dismissive of the concept. Lubrano, the son of a bricklayer, had worked his way up from street reporting to feature writing at the *Philadelphia Inquirer*. His going to college had involved leaving his family's home in the Bensonhurst neighborhood of Brooklyn every day to commute on the subway to an entirely different world at Columbia University in Manhattan. When I met him, however, he and his wife had a healthy six-figure income and lived on a farm with horses in the Philadelphia countryside; he dressed pretty fancy and spoke with the polish you'd expect from an Ivy League grad. "Hell, Al," I told him, "you're no 'straddler,' you've crossed over even more than I have!" Lubrano insightfully developed his notion of class straddling in *Limbo: Blue-Collar Roots and White-Collar Dreams*, based on a moving account of his own experience and poignant stories from his interviews with other crossovers, many of them from that working-class studies conference.[29] The book and the concept of class straddling resonated in a fully compelling way with most working-class academics, but not me. As long as our feet were planted in professional middle-class jobs with professional middle-class incomes, it didn't matter that parts of our minds and hearts were still working class, straddling the cultures. What mattered was where our feet were planted, and not to admit that we were middle class bordered on bad faith. Over time our minds and hearts were bound to catch up with where our feet were.

I was already dug into this notion before I met Lubrano based on sporadic discussions with other working-class academics, most especially David Greene, a psychology professor at Ramapo College in New Jersey. David had grown up working class in West New York, New Jersey, and even though he was a tenured professor who had served a stint as the dean of arts and sciences at Ramapo, he fiercely identified as still working class, rejecting not only my designation of class crossovers but even Lubrano's concept of straddling. In our conversations he was fine with my identifying as a crossover, but I couldn't abide his thinking that he was still working class. Our lives and careers were so similar. David was born in 1945, and his formative years were during the entirety of the Glorious Thirty, including political radicalization as a student. He had married young and had one child, and he had a twelve-semester-hour teaching load at a fourth-tier university, as I had. He taught mixed-class kids, not working adults, but like me he loved working there. Even our sense of working-class life and what we thought was valuable about it were more than simpatico.[30] I unmercifully picked on his having been a dean, as I had twice turned down that horrifying opportunity. Our argument never concluded, but over time I came to the conclusion that David had indeed led pretty much the same life as I had but had lived it very differently. He had stayed working class culturally in a way I had not. Where he lived, how he dressed, and how he acted, evidently even as a college dean, were working class. He didn't have a full, if flawed, middle-class mode he could slip into like the one I had and was pretty comfortable with. Even though we had the same class position and the same appreciation of working-class life, we did not have the same values that guided the way we lived. Though we had the very same *class position* as middle-class professionals, that position did not come with a ready-made *class identity* for folks like us.

There is an irreducible element of subjective choice amid the drift of our spontaneous reactions to the specific people and situations we encounter as we move from one class position to another. The specifics of where we come from in the working class determines some of the identity we end up embracing to guide us into and through a middle-class profession, not just rural, small town, or city or region and religion, let alone race, sexuality, and gender, but above all how hard or settled our growing up working class had been and specifically how our parents had handled their life situations and us as their offspring. Some hard-living working-class young people have such destabilizing and loveless (or inconsistently loving) family lives that once they see a way out, they run into it as hard and fast as they can, closing doors in their minds and hearts behind them, intentionally or accidentally, and not looking back—at least not until they feel like they have arrived at a safe place with a secure identity as a self-sufficient middle-class professional.[31] These folks, in my observation, tend to be more culturally middle class than even generationally middle-class people, and they are unlikely to show up at working-class studies conferences. Others from hard-living families had at least one parent whose unconditional love for them and whose street-level ingenuity in managing difficult circumstances keep them tied to their working-class roots even as they negotiate middle-class life without any help from their parents. These folks tend toward fierce family loyalties even as they flee into "another country," and they can hardly help but be straddlers. Settled-living working-class people such as me, on the other hand, were "damned near middle class" (as a friend told me) when we started out; especially during a time of expanding opportunities, we can just sort of drift into the middle class without being fully aware of the valleys and borders we're crossing. For me I didn't realize I had crossed over until it was too late to go back, even if I had wanted to. Still, within the play of circumstances, patterns, and tendencies, there is individual agency. What is a meaningless event for one is an epiphany for another, and the effect of a particular epiphany may last for a week for one of us and a lifetime for another. In there somewhere we are deciding, choosing which way to go, going with the flow or resisting it a little or a lot.

So, while even a college dean may have an authentic working-class identity and while there are multitudes of straddlers among us, it was important and helpful for me to define myself—or recognize myself—as a crossover, to fully adopt a professional middle-class identity consistent with my class position. Sure, I had lingering working-class loyalties and some leftover stylistic differences, and I was weirdly uncomfortable with a middle-class identity, but Judie and I were a professional middle-class couple living in a distinctively middle-class suburb with a professional middle-class son, daughter-in-law, and grandsons who would grow up with the social and cultural capital of the educated middle-class. This did not just happen to me. I had chosen it, not all at once but instead by degrees and pretty consistently across several formative decades. What's more, I didn't want to change it. Though it had not been inevitable, my head and heart had chosen to live near my feet.

Writing *Striking Steel* helped me reconcile and become comfortable with my middle-classness and actually spurred me to double down on my commitment to working-class causes, mostly through union educational activities, and to be more professionally productive. With a less complicated definition of myself, I was able to focus more steadily on the world outside.

But it didn't last. The consistency of my identity and position and the clarity it brought me blew up some years later in a single afternoon as I read the first hundred pages of Annette Lareau's *Unequal Childhoods*.[32]

Lareau is one of those sociologists who hangs around a family at home and on the road, taking careful notes about what everybody says and does. Most of the book consists of case studies of the various middle-class, working-class, and poor families she (and her research assistants) hung out with in an unnamed northeastern city, probably Philadelphia. Using this exhaustive approach with twelve families chosen from extensive interviews with eighty-eight families of different classes and races, Lareau found a categorical difference between middle-class and working-class child-rearing approaches but relatively small differences between working-class and poor families or between blacks and whites of the same social class.

Lareau's first two case studies, of fourth-graders Garrett Tallinger and Tyrec Taylor, present strongly positive examples of each of the categories. Garrett had two very dedicated parents with professional jobs who are highly engaged with their three children, with lots of challenging dialogue and with a demanding schedule of activities their children enjoy but are also educational in one way or another. This *concerted cultivation*, Lareau says, is characteristic of a middle-class child-centered approach. Tyrec has loving, though separated, working-class parents who see their parental duties as providing food, shelter, and moral guidance but otherwise leaving their children free to find their own way in life through the *accomplishment of natural growth*.

Whereas Garrett spends little time outside of adult-structured activities with children exactly his own age, Tyrec is much more free "to make his own fun" with children of different ages, both within a large extended family and in his neighborhood, and mostly outside direct supervision by adults. Tyrec lives in an adult-centered world where the adults are busy with other things as they provide him with broad directives, which he generally follows, and so long as he does, he has an enormous amount of freedom for himself. Garrett, on the other hand, is encouraged to challenge adult authority, including doctors and teachers as well as his parents, by asking questions and probing for the reasoning behind adult directives. As a result, Garrett is much more comfortable in the presence of adults than Tyrec, but Tyrec learns to manage a wider range of peers in being part of organizing their self-generated activities. Because school and related organized activities share the middle-class ethos of concerted cultivation, Garrett lives in a continuous lifeworld that reinforces his commitment to constant and continuous improvement of himself. Tyrec, on the other hand, crosses back and forth between two worlds—the adult one of family and school, where he is compliant, and the one among peers, where he is sometimes the leader and sometimes the led and is always free to withdraw from any given activity and initiate one of his own.

I immediately recognized that as middle class as Judie and I had become, we had raised our son Judd with the working-class natural-growth approach but without the advantage of an immediate extended family. As I read Lareau's first case study on the Tallingers, I was existentially thunderstruck at what lousy parents we had been. Don and Louise Tallinger both had professional jobs that required regular travel; Judie's and my jobs required no travel. The Tallingers had three kids; we had only one. And yet as they advanced in their demanding careers, they managed their children's lives through a daunting array of activities in a way that I could not imagine Judie and I being capable of. Though I had an unusually flexible job, working at home a lot of the time, our son Judd was necessarily a sometime latch-key kid—letting himself into our apartment, walking the dog, and then being on his own until Judie got home from work on the nights I was teaching. What's more, the Tallingers, like other middle-class parents in Lareau's study, were actively involved with teachers and other school activities, which is what the school expected of parents. Judie and I, on the other hand, relied on the school professionals to have our child's best interests at heart and to make the right decisions about his academic direction. Like the working-class and poor parents in Lareau's study, we relied almost exclusively on Judd's reports of what was going on at school, giving him directives from time to time but mostly expecting him to manage his school life, both the formal classroom work and the informal social life with his peers. We had moved to Oak Park for its good schools, and once we did, we rarely "interfered." We did involve him in some after-school activities, but more to provide some adult supervision when we could not be home and to involve him in various sports we thought were natural for a boy. The Tallingers, on the other hand, carefully cultivated any interest each of their three children expressed by providing ballet and piano lessons or enrolling them in soccer and gymnastics and then regularly taking them to and attending their events. Judd naturally ended up hanging out with other kids who were not involved in a lot of activities, all of them with working-class parents, mostly settled living. In retrospect, as Judd was in his early thirties and married with children when I was reading Lareau's study, I realized that the troubles he'd had with the police and initially with college had been the result not of his bad choices but instead of my poor parenting. As highly educated as I was, I had not known any better!

The Tallingers should not be confused with helicopter parents or tiger moms who are manically obsessed with their children's achievement, but even parents like them are practicing a historically extreme form of concerted cultivation. Middle-class-origin contemporaries of mine report having considerably more free time to run than the middle-class families studied by Lareau. In their day, with such dramatically expanding professional jobs, middle-class parents could be more relaxed even as they tended to be child-centered and very attentive to their children's intellectual and psychological development in a way working-class parents usually were not. The extreme economic differences between professional and working-class lives today have sped up middle-class children's concerted cultivation, reducing their free time and bringing the stress and anxiety of passing tests into their lives earlier and with much more intensity.

Though I initially read Lareau's case studies as revealing how deficient working-class child rearing could be, she did not see it that way. Lareau is a cultural sociologist who thinks her job is to describe child-rearing practices and the class cultures they reflect with an understanding that any practice or culture has both advantages and disadvantages. Among the advantages she found in working-class families were less stress and exhaustion for both parents and children, less sibling rivalry and more of a connection between siblings, less boredom and impatience among children who were more creative in using unstructured time in a satisfying way, and a faster route to adult self-sufficiency. She also observed an emerging sense of entitlement among middle-class youngsters that would serve them well in school and an emerging sense of constraint among working-class kids that hurt them in school and in dealing with other middle-class institutions but also might tend them toward greater cooperation with others. Recognizing how a sense of entitlement generates a more proactive approach toward life that is more likely to lead to success in a career, Lareau puts this latter difference in context:

> Nor are the actions of children who display an emerging sense of entitlement intrinsically more valuable or desirable than those of children who display an emerging sense of constraint. In a society less dominated by individualism than the United States, with more of an emphasis on the group, the sense of constraint displayed by working-class and poor children might be interpreted as healthy and appropriate. But in this society, the strategies of the working-class and poor families are generally denigrated and seen as unhelpful or even harmful to children's life chances.[33]

As I read the second case study on Tyrec Taylor, it made me recall how happy I was as a child just running the neighborhood, and as Judie and I discussed it, she had the same reaction: "Mom just opened the door and let us run." Likewise, we remembered how happily independent Judd seemed running the urban streets of Oak Park and how happy we were that he was having a free childhood exploring what we then overestimated as reasonably safe streets. And we loved his friends, every one of them down-to-earth, decent, lively kids of many colors who respected us and our rules as they were in and out of our apartment. Would we have done it differently if we could? It's hard to decide. When Judd was eighteen to twenty-two years of age, we would have jumped at the chance. In his early thirties, when I was reading *Unequal Childhoods*, I was ambivalent and confused. Now that he is in his forties, though there are specific things I wish we had done differently, I wouldn't change the basic approach even if we could have, and we probably couldn't have. He, however, without ever reading Lareau, steadfastly adopted a concerted cultivation approach with his two sons, partly because it was the most readily available cultural repertoire in his adult world but mostly as a reaction to the mistakes he thought we had made with him. Now, however, he worries that his college-graduate sons may be "much too entitled."

That's the way it is with genuine cultures. They give us guidance or put pressure on us to behave in certain ways and not others, to expect certain things and not others of ourselves and of other people, to feel natural and comfortable in some situations and awkward and want to get away in others. But they are not like recipes, specifying exact amounts of this or that. No matter how measured we are, the bad just comes along with the good, and what's more, even as we adopt certain well thought-out strategies, other ways of doing things just occur within us without our choosing them. As I see it, a culture is a collective entity outside an individual, and individuals can wholeheartedly imbibe it or wholeheartedly resist it or anything in between. That's why there is so much individual variation, even within the most unified cultures. But some parts of a culture just get embedded in us without our being able to consciously imbibe or resist them. Sometimes we don't even know they're there. Just taking them for granted, they seem as natural as breathing.[34] Judd consciously adopted a child-rearing strategy. Judie and I just breathed ours in, like air.

It turns out that I am more of a class straddler than I'd thought. Class cultures exert their influence over us even when we're not looking. The severe divisions between Tyrec Taylor's adult and peer worlds—the one with accepted constraints, the other with free-floating activity—prepared him for a job culture, where you give away part of your day in order to have free time for what you will with the rest. And indeed, I remember countless adults telling me and others countless times to enjoy our childhoods because adult life was a grind of work and family responsibilities, yet again cuing us to understand life as time blocks of freedom and necessity, the one paid for with the other. It is a limited and limiting view of life, even tragic in some versions of it, but there's also a space for creativity and enjoyment in it, a way to preserve your true self and a simple integrity by giving a large piece of your time to the bosses without giving up who and what you really are. The proletarian wager is that there will be enough left of you at the end of a workday, a workweek, and a work life to be able to create and enjoy a life of your own. Some do, some don't, but how could that wager not be genuine?

The Complex Half-Lives of Class and Culture

Both class and culture are complicated in a way that race and gender are not. Even though societal definitions and expectations may change around you, as they have for race, gender, and sexuality, and though there are lots of exceptions to the rule, race and gender are relatively fixed and clearly defined. Class, on the other hand, has no even illusory biological component any more. It is a social position that can change across a lifetime. In American culture at least, working-class people are expected to want to change and assumed to have the power to change their class position. And yet the class position of your family of origin, which may itself have been changing during your childhood and adolescence, affects both your formative experiences and the taken-for-granted cultural repertoires you use to interpret that experience. Many of those cultural repertoires tend to go with you as you change class positions, and as I've noted, there is an irreducible element of subjective choice to one's class identity and thus to which cultural parts get consciously brought into the future as is, which get modified, and which get abandoned altogether. Some of it is conscious, and some of it is not. I thought I had been unusually conscious, for example, but in retrospect I relied a lot more on a job culture as I pursued a career than it seemed at the time.

Betsy Leondar-Wright, on the other hand, has shown in her exhaustive study of social justice activists that *class trajectory* matters as much as class origin in determining what predispositions, expectations, and assumptions people bring into their behaviors. Not only where you come from but also where you're going matters. Leondar-Wright produces one of those graphs with boxes and arrows that social scientists sometimes use to portray both structure and dynamism. As you'd expect, there are *lifelong* poor, working-class, professional middle-class, and upper-class people with continuity between where they're from and where they're going, and Leondar-Wright shows how they routinely misunderstand or otherwise rub each other the wrong way based on different class cultural dispositions and predispositions. But there are a variety of class straddlers as well, not just the upwardly mobile professionals from working-class backgrounds for which straddling has been documented and reflected upon but also the downwardly mobile, both involuntarily and voluntarily downwardly mobile. This wider variety of people with internal experience of more than one class position and culture should help lifelong members of the various classes bridge cultural gaps, but Leondar-Wright's observations show it doesn't often happen that way. The *voluntarily downwardly mobile* are an especially interesting group. Though they tend to show up more readily among the kinds of activists Leondar-Wright studied as purpose-driven people on a mission to reject their own class privilege, they may also reflect a broader and more instinctive dissatisfaction with the pressures to achieve and become within professional middle-class cultures. This kind of reverse class straddling was especially prominent in the late 1960s and into the 1970s—as illustrated by Leondar-Wright's own trajectory as a community and economic justice organizer and by the scores of labor "colonizers" who were my contemporaries in the labor movement—but as Leondar-Wright documents, downward class straddling is still alive and well and crucially important for progressive social movements today.[35]

The reasons upward and downward class straddlers don't often act as cultural bridgers are complicated (and Leondar-Wright provides guidelines for how they more readily could), but the broad takeaway is that the cognitive dissonance involved in mixing and crossing classes is either blinding or disorienting, especially when you lack a class cultural vocabulary to help you make sense of it. The broader takeaway is that there could not be such cross-class misunderstanding or such strongly felt cognitive dissonance if there were but one genuine mainstream culture that everybody could or should live up to.

No matter which way you're going in changing your class position, there is a kind of half-life to the culture of one's original social class. And this means that working-class ways have been and are being infiltrated into middle-class professionalism, just as some middle-class ways get adopted in and adapted to working-class life. Jessi Streib has shown the continuity in what she calls class sensibilities among professional middle-class couples from different class backgrounds. Though the couples themselves see their differences as strictly related to their individual personalities, Streib found clear correlations between class backgrounds and the couples' differences not only in parenting styles but also in feeling rules and in how the individual spouses manage money, balance work and play, and share housework and family time. Streib concludes that unlike professional middle-class couples in which both partners are from middle-class backgrounds, the presence of unassimilated upwardly mobile class crossovers "injects new sensibilities into middle-class spaces" and that "a culturally diverse middle class is more favorable for those striving for upward mobility than a culturally homogenous one."[36]

There cannot be a "culturally diverse middle class" if there is but one and only one genuine class culture. In fact, as documented in part 1, when people of working-class origin flooded into an expanding professional middle class during its period of class formation, there was much give and take between the cultures. There is undoubtedly less today, as professional-managerial occupations are growing more slowly, while middle-class professionals have increasingly isolated themselves in where they live and with whom they interact.[37] It is the possible loss of this class-cultural dialectic, whereby one culture helps balance and enrich the other, that I'm warning against. Professional middle-class isolation breeds both hubris and ignorance, a dangerous combination in any situation but especially if you are the dominant culture responsible for explaining the ways of the world to everybody else.

There is another way that working-class culture might influence middle-class life across the life stages of professional careers. As *Habits of the Heart* itself points out, professional careers inevitably flatten out for most of us, as "the grade grows steeper at the peak of a professional field, the ledges narrower at the top of the corporate pyramid."[38] This often occurs in midlife when our family responsibilities become more demanding and, if we have children, more interesting and potentially fulfilling. What was a career with its aspiring, striving, achieving, and exciting sense of individual becoming slowly morphs into a job, mostly a means toward another end, no longer much of an end in itself. It might be helpful at that point to know that there is an alternative job culture that has already worked out some ways of living with a job rather than inside a career. Those of us from working-class backgrounds may have an advantage in falling back to a job culture we've always known was there, though we may also tend to flatten out prematurely without testing our full potential. But this flattening-out moment is so common and widespread within middle-class lives that there are likely internal resources among more purely, less mixed-up middle-class cultures as well. As the authors of *Habits of the Heart* observe, "For the fortunate among the career-weary, the private world of family and friends grows brighter, and a more expressive self comes to the fore."[39] Still, most middle-class professionals would benefit in this moment from knowing and interacting with some working-class people who have long favored belonging over becoming and being over achieving.

Paul Osterman's study of middle managers who had experienced waves of restructuring and downsizing during the 1990s, as Judie had, observed a common reaction among managers who had either plateaued or been downgraded. Many redefined (or perhaps recognized) themselves as craft workers rather than professionals. This involved a shift in focus from their own individual development to the work itself, which they found more intrinsically interesting and worthwhile as they used their existing skills to address constantly changing problems and to better handle the ever-recurring ones day by day. In doing so, they developed a craft pride whereby the work itself, neither a career nor a calling, became "an end as well as a means."[40] Such a craft pride is very common within working-class life and not just among craft workers such as those in the building trades. Even so-called low-skilled work that may not seem intrinsically interesting is often ingeniously made so by workers who mindfully attend to the work itself as if they were Michelangelo carving a statue. Sociologists Tim Strangleman and Tracey Warren use a Jim Daniels poem about a short-order cook handling a rush of orders at a diner to introduce how common craft pride is among workers in a variety of jobs that are not considered crafts.[41] Personal care workers, among the lowest paid of the proliferating low-wage workforce in the United States, love to tell me about the various situations they've faced with clients and how creatively they've handled them. There is craft pride with or without such bragging, and while it is not nearly universal within a working-class job culture, it is very common. It requires a strict focus on the work itself in the moment, undiluted by any attempt to meet external professional standards of excellence or by any long-term planning for career development.

It would be interesting to know how many of Osterman's middle managers or other standard-issue professionals who find a satisfying job culture in midlife are from working-class backgrounds or otherwise learned from interaction with people who make a sharper distinction between living and earning a living. My idea is not that every professional middle-class person lives a career culture and every working-class one a job culture. It's much messier than that. Rather, the two broad class cultures with various ethnic, regional, and other variations are socially available within our society: middle-class professionalism with a much louder megaphone and also a working-class culture passed along from hand to hand through generations in families and communities without megaphones but with a powerfully realistic logic that, for all its limitations, may be more sustainable across a lifetime. In any case, the availability of both cultures enriches and strengthens us as individuals and as a society. A middle-class professionalism that either through ignorance or imperial arrogance sees only one right way and doesn't recognize a valuable alternative culture ready-to-hand is likely to misunderstand itself and the society it becomes, achieves, and lives in.

The Value of Having Two Class Cultures

What I most like about professional middle-class life, besides the income and working conditions, is its openness to evidence and reasoning and a general willingness, when not obsessive about it, to constantly improve whoever or whatever we currently are. There is a basic stream of reasonableness and decency in our manners and morals that we share with the working class, but we have a broader willingness to change and adjust ourselves to changing circumstances. That willingness may tend to make us less rooted in people and places as well as in core principles. But our rational suspicion of eternal laws of life, such as those expressed in a litany of folk sayings repeated much more commonly among the working class, leaves us generally more open to alternative points of view—or at least we have a stated commitment to doing that. That openness and commitment is what I'm appealing to. My wager is that the absence of a class cultural vocabulary is some part of why middle-class life has been narrowing for the past few decades.

As numerous scholars, including Annette Lareau, have pointed out, our educational efforts at all levels could be greatly improved if we educators understood that working-class young people come to us not with an empty cultural bucket or with one full of only bad habits but instead with a genuine culture that has strengths and weaknesses intimately related to one another, just as any culture does. But equally as important for us middle-class professionals is that working-class strengths could complement or offset some of our weaknesses, just as we could offset some of theirs if we understood their culture and how it productively contrasts with ours.

The next chapter will try to explain what I and some others see as those contrasts. I'm not convinced that I have everything lined up in exactly the right way, as I rely a lot on my own direct observation and experience, which is pretty limited to that of a white guy in the Rust Belt. But the oppositions I develop should be suggestive, even if not precisely accurate, for all regions of working-class life. For the time being, I hope I've shown that there is both logic and evidence that there is a genuine working-class culture, one that is not simply deficient, dominated, or residual. Built around having a job rather than a career, it is a culture that can and has worked on its own, contributes mightily to our society as a whole, and has helped shape our dominant mainstream culture, mostly for the better, and could do so again if good times for them should ever return.

CATEGORICAL DIFFERENCES IN CLASS CULTURES

I am what I am and what the world has made me.

Herman Melville, *Billy Budd*

Becoming isn't about arriving somewhere or achieving a certain aim. I see it instead as forward motion, a means of evolving, a way to reach continuously toward a better self.

Michele Obama, *Becoming*

Sociologists have a concept of *feeling rules* that most people have experienced and that perfectly illustrates how culture works. Feeling rules are "social guidelines about what individuals should feel and how they should express their feelings in a given situation."[1]

A feeling rule is both outside us as what "society" expects and inside us as our "conscience." We can feel it putting pressure on us to think or feel a certain way that we may not actually think or feel—not feeling sad at a funeral, for example. We can attempt to conform our feeling to how we're expected to feel, or we can stick with how we actually feel and disdain the rule. Whether we do the one or the other is probably influenced by other cultural rules—a sense that we should generally fit in as best we can so as not to disrupt others, for example, or a sense that we should always be independent or authentic. With remarks, looks, and other behavior, other people enforce the feeling rules that influence us, but we nonetheless can feel our freedom to decide how to react.

This is the way culture is. It provides rules for what to expect of ourselves and others—guidelines but also pressures. And though culture rules are experienced as being in the social world outside us, what others expect, they are internalized in one way or another, sometimes consciously but mostly not. How we internalize a set of culture rules is somewhat different for each of us, as some rules inevitably have more weight than others.

Jessi Streib's study of cross-class marriages suggests that feeling rules vary substantially by one's class of origin. Those from professional families are taught to manage their feelings, whereas working-class families encourage spontaneous expressions of feeling—including both anger and laughter—as "signs of authenticity and integrity." Spouses of middle-class origin are less likely to allow themselves to feel intensely, especially around anger and conflict, and according to Streib, this often makes the working-class spouse the "emotional leader" in the marriage because both "feelings and discussion of feelings were . . . not threatening or uncomfortable to them but normal parts of relationships." Streib found the following oppositions. Working-class rules "called for feeling and expressing emotions intensely and quickly," while middle-class ones "called for feeling and expressing emotions calmly and slowly." Likewise, working-class rules encourage one to "express a wide range of emotions spontaneously," while middle-class rules favor expressing "a narrow range of emotions after processing them."[2]

I think Streib's interpretation is both insightful and broadly correct, but the difference between feeling rules and actual feeling—and therefore the need for individual human agency to reconcile them, at least on occasion—suggests that there is great room for variation among different individuals within the same class culture. There are introverted and extroverted people in all classes, for example, and Italian Americans are generally more emotionally expressive than Anglo or German Americans, regardless of class. Likewise, there are stoics (or people attempting to be stoics) in all classes. Other things affect culture rules besides class. *Culture is about the rules, not the way each and every individual actually thinks, feels, or acts but rather the kind of social guidelines or pressures predominant in the social world within which individuals live and make choices.* One of the core dispositions a college education typically acculturates, for example, is a reliance on evidence and reasoning versus emotion. In the educated middle class, people are often told that being "too emotional" is "unprofessional." In the working class, emotion is much more likely to be responded to with equal and sometimes opposite emotion. Emotions are not only respected more in working-class life than in middle-class professionalism but they are also *expected* even when not respected and are experienced as "normal parts of relationships," not as disruptions in those relationships. This doesn't mean that middle-class people are never emotional or that working-class people always are. It means that they live largely in different social worlds, with different kinds and degrees of social guidelines and cultural pressures, most of which they have internalized, however imperfectly.

Different cultures deeply affect the way people live their lives, but they don't determine them. Some cultural rules (such as Judie's and my child-rearing approach) are so deeply embedded as to be invisible, but others are readily apparent and articulated in various sayings and rules of thumb. Because cultures are both implicit and explicit, both tacit and expressed, and because they can be and are internalized in different ways and shape and frame the very way we see and act in the world, cultures are slippery things to describe and interpret.

Class crossovers like me often experience the cultures of class as conflicting and envision them as opposites, either/or binaries, social guidelines that pull us in different directions. And that is how I present them in this chapter—as categorical differences. But this does not mean I am unaware that actual living, breathing human beings are living within a daunting variety of cultural proclivities based on how they have been socialized within families and other social institutions and, importantly, by their own individual agency. Rather, my claim is that there are distinct class cultures that play central, though not exclusive, roles in shaping people's lives and that you can best see the differences when they are or appear to be in conflict with each other. Thus, this chapter presents a binary interpretation of two broad class cultures, an interpretation of what the way-of-life rules are for each of these cultures and how they are different from one another. The basic conception here is that they are conflicting human proclivities that prioritize different aspects of and goals for human life.

Though I try to be even-handed in presenting and evaluating the two class cultures, that attempt is complicated by the fact that professional middle-class culture takes itself to be mainstream, the best and most appropriate culture, or even the only genuine culture. This requires me, as I read it, to be more critical of middle-class culture while defending working-class culture against what I see as middle-class prejudices and misunderstandings. On the other hand, while I am not uncritical of working-class ways, I am generally indulgent of both cultures, thinking that both have positives and negatives, advantages and disadvantages, like most cultures across the world in human history.

The Lineup of Categorical Differences

Nearly twenty years ago I developed with Barbara Jensen a version of the table of class characteristics presented in table 6.1.[3] I have refined this table somewhat for myself, starting with the notion, as explained in chapter 5, that middle-class professionals pursue careers (at least for the first half to two-thirds of their lives) while working-class people generally have "just jobs" that cause and allow them to make a stronger distinction between living and earning a living. Still my lineup of the categorical differences in class cultures is simply suggestive, not so much fully developed ideas as observations and notions that have helped me map my social realities and that I think might be insightful for others.

The basic conception here is that working-class cultural rules prioritize *being and belonging*, while middle-class professionalism gives greatest weight to *doing and becoming*. From these different orientations, several different cultural characteristics derive. Though I'm not always sure of the causal connections, my claim

TABLE 6.1 Categorical class-culture differences

PROFESSIONAL MIDDLE CLASS *PEOPLE WITH CAREERS*	WORKING CLASS *PEOPLE WITH JOBS*
Doing and Becoming	**Being and belonging**
• achievement-oriented	• character-oriented
• life as transformative	• life as a tangled web of relationships
• future-oriented	• present-oriented
• high expectations, preference for pursuing dreams, aspirations, and some idealism	• moderate to low expectations, with preference for realism
• status concerns	• antistatus
• individualistic	• solidaristic
More cosmopolitan	**More parochial**
• broader links to persons, places, groups, and institutional affiliations	• stronger loyalties to persons, places, groups, and institutional affiliations
• unintended homogeneity	• unavoidable diversity
Likely best result:	**Likely best result:**
• Individual achievement has a positive human impact.	• A secure community with some form of collective efficacy
Likely worst result:	**Likely worst result:**
• the lonely individual	• unachieved potential

is that these characteristics have a logical and psychological coherence that makes them genuine cultures that guide life in different, if not opposite, directions.

Being versus Doing

Being and doing are opposing emphases for living a life, as are *belonging and becoming.* Though many of us try to achieve both or a balance between them, what is valuable about a culture is that it tells us which is more important than the other. It nudges or outright shoves us in one direction rather than another. I'll begin with the being/doing opposition because it is likely the most counterintuitive.

The "doing" in the being/doing opposition goes counter to a common usage. Working-class and especially blue-collar people often see themselves as doers, while middle-class professionals are merely talkers or pencil pushers. Likewise, middle-class professionals, especially managers, most often see themselves as conceiving and planning, while workers merely do the work to execute the plan. In both these usages, the working-class person is conceived as the doer, more committed to actual doing than to thinking stuff up or, alternatively, restricted to doing the work others plan and direct. No matter how you say it, this separation of planning from execution is a key class reality, but it contrasts doing with creative thinking or decision making rather than with being.

An opposition of doing and being is about how you think of yourself and others. Do you define and evaluate yourself by what you *do*—by your achievements and accomplishments—or by the kind of person you *are* as a friend, a worker, a parent, a sister, or a neighbor? My observation is that middle-class professionalism is dominated by an achievement orientation that emphasizes what you do over the kind of person you are. It is not that professionals don't want to be good people, however that is defined, but rather that we worry less about it, often taking it for granted, than about achieving some goal, often one with special distinction involving money, prestige, or power. We are ambitious to do something significant, to leave our mark on the world, to accomplish something important or valuable, especially something that gains wide recognition. Middle-class professionalism encourages and reinforces this aspiration, not always monomaniacally but very strongly and with a great deal of certainty.

Working-class culture counsels somewhat the opposite of this. Life is not about a list of singular accomplishments on a résumé but instead is about the kind of person you are day in and day out, often your steadiness or, though nobody would use the word, your "consistency" over time: being consistent with your own true self, for example, as well as being consistently a hard worker and a good parent, workmate, friend, or spouse. The working-class focus is on character, not accomplishment, and the intensity of that focus can be hard to see from a middle-class doer perspective.

There is, for example, a common fatalism about character in working-class life, as people are inclined to take themselves as they are and envision themselves as having a true self, a ready-made character to which they need to be true while also striving to be good. Being true to one's self is important for both moral and practical reasons. Morally, being a phony, trying to be something you're not, "putting on the dog," and "putting yourself above others" are moral failings. Practically, it is unwise "to get outside yourself," to try to go beyond your limits, to try to be something you're not, because in doing so you're likely to do something foolish or at least "look like a fool" or make potentially fatal mistakes, or become a phony "in over your head" in more ways than one. The idea of trying to become some other, some better self—which to my mind is at the heart of middle-class culture—seems both unnatural and unwise in a working-class world. It is better to try to fit into groups where your ingrained weaknesses are accepted because they are offset by others' strengths just as your strengths, whatever they are, offset others' weaknesses.

To middle-class eyes such as mine, the working-class way can seem merely passive acceptance, a disabling complacency, and a view that severely limits horizons and encourages low expectations. In my view, all of that is true but only part of the story. In a being culture focused on character, character building is a vital aspect of life even if within the limits of your own given character. There are external cultural pressures to be a good person. Though the specifics of what constitutes such a person vary by time and place, a common one is simply being tough enough to handle life's inevitable difficulties, often including lousy, dirty, tedious, and/or dangerous jobs, but in any case tough enough not to be broken by the hardships that are an expected part of everybody's life.[4] How tough life actually is varies by circumstance, but the culture never envisions being tough enough as something that is easy to achieve. Likewise, working hard and having personal integrity (again defined differently by time and place) are usually core working-class values, as is being a good parent, workmate, friend, neighbor, or spouse (or at least some of these). The point, however, is that none of these are experienced as easy to live up to, easy to be, because one's own true self is experienced as flawed and limited, and as a result life is often lived as a daily drama of reconciling your own limits with what is expected of you and what you expect of yourself.

For example, British historian Allison Light reviewed a number of Victorian workers' memoirs and focused on that of William Swan, a London bricklayer in the 1840s whom she sees as typical. Swan lived in truly terrible and worsening conditions, "never having funds," but his memoir's primary focus was on "a cosmic struggle within himself" between his Baptist conception of what a good man should be and "his own failings, his need for strong drink and his longing to let off steam in swearing or womanizing." This "inwardly strong life," according to Light, would have been and might still be a surprise for middle- and upper-class readers had they read these memoirs, but she finds them impressive in the strength of "the conviction that getting on in the world was not what mattered most" and "that every human being was capable of 'heartwork,' and of fellowship with others."[5] More than a century and a half later, these commitments to pursuing good character, including fellowship if not always religious salvation, rather than achieving success still seem apt to me.

In contrast, in the middle-class we do not generally see life as requiring much endurance and toughness and are therefore much less likely to tolerate unfavorable conditions. We tend to act to change those conditions rather than adjust ourselves to be capable of enduring them, which is what working-class cultivation of "toughness" is. In pursuing our goals we must overcome obstacles, whether through hard work, intelligence, or scheming. As we often say about ourselves, we are or should be proactive, not reactive. Even though we have a more dynamic sense of self, we try, or should try, to adjust the world to our needs even as we try to mold ourselves to become ever more effective in the world. A middle-class sense of character is centered around agency, both in improving ourselves and in better adjusting the world to our needs and goals; thus, our sense of character includes becoming in order to *do* more and better. Our character building is in the service of doing. Working-class character is about *being* good in and for itself or at least persistently trying to be.

As a middle-class professional, I generally favor the middle-class way. I've lived my life that way, and both as a general education teacher and within the labor movement, I have spent a lot of my doing in trying to cultivate larger senses of individual and collective agency among working adults. But there is a compelling logic to working-class ways, given the dramatic differences between our life circumstances and theirs.

Working-class people are often seen as undermining their own interests by blaming themselves for their misfortunes, whatever they are, and it is true that this often undermines both their will to oppose their circumstances and their own self-worth—and in some situations to a degree that is psychologically disabling.[6] But it is quite clear from even the simplest conversation that working-class people are well aware of the socioeconomic and political circumstances that undermine their and their families' well-being, even if some are inclined toward misleading scapegoats. They will often eloquently complain and denounce those injustices, but most of the time they see no way to effectively change them—and most of the time they are right. The well-worn counsel of middle-class people like me encouraging working-class people to be more like us would make sense (and actually did make a lot more sense during the Glorious Thirty) if there were wall-to-wall jobs that support careers. But there aren't, and there won't be in the future. And while many middle-class people seem not to see that, most working-class people do if for no other reason than they and most everybody they know are doing the just-jobs work that needs to be done. The working-class strategy is to focus on controlling those things you can control, and that often turns out to be your own character and behavior. It's not that they don't want to change the world, and there is probably a tenth of them who work all or a good part of their lives doing things to change it or to prepare for changing it, but rather that they see so few opportunities for doing so. And those opportunities, both individual and collective, have been diminishing for more than forty years now.

Working-class culture is founded on the necessity of giving away part of your day or week, and thus part of yourself, in order to earn a living. In my observation—which occurred during the thirty best years for working people in US history, followed by four decades of decline resulting in conditions that are still not as bad as what preceded those thirty years—a founding working-class strategy of life involves *ceding control in order to gain control*. This strategy is embedded in the wage relationship. In the classical formulation, you trade eight hours of toil, eight hours of being told what to do, of suspending or at least limiting your freedom of action, in order to have the means to have eight hours for what you will. As I argue in chapter 7, this pattern of ceding control in one area to gain or enhance your control in another is repeated in various aspects of working-class life. Those eight hours where you get bossed around, for example, include some minutes and places where you gain control by ceding it during other parts of the workday. If I'm right about how core this strategy is, then the emphasis on personal character as well as on fellowship or belonging is part of steeling oneself for the day-to-day grind of (mostly) distasteful work, the earning part that gains the means for the living part.

The necessity of earning a living is, of course, shared with most middle-class professionals, but pursuing a career puts your self-worth completely at stake at work, whereas the working-class division of work and living is looking to have good—or at least tolerable—relationships in both parts of their lives. Workers want to *be* and be perceived as good workers. Professionals want to *do* and be perceived as doing excellent or outstanding work.

It is, of course, not so clear-cut in most people's lives, but the cultural emphases, the direction of the nudges, should be recognizable. I'd say there is a continuum, with one end being what Yale professor William Deresiewicz sees as "an extreme version of upper-middle-class practice—the unrelenting pressure . . . to excel, the willful disregard of everything except 'achievement.'"[7] On the other end are those working-class types (mostly male) who are comfortable, even perversely proud, of being lazy workers and irresponsible parents. In between there is a lot of shared territory in wanting both to do good and to be good but with distinctly different emphases.

These differences have profound consequences for how working-class people and their culture are perceived and misperceived by middle-class interpreters. For example, social scientists have widely observed that working-class parents counsel their children to be obedient, particularly in school but also to all adults. Jessica Calarco, however, calls this a "strategy of deference" that contrasts with middle-class parents' instructing their children to adopt a "strategy of influence," speaking up for themselves and negotiating with teachers and parents for special arrangements. For Andrew Cherlin, on the other hand, obedience is not a strategy but instead is a simple working-class value that dates back to the beginnings of the industrial revolution, when working-class parents "placed much less emphasis on self-reliance and more on respecting and observing authority."[8] For Cherlin, there have been two centuries of simple working-class obedience. What Calarco observed in her long-term ethnography of third-, fourth-, and fifth-graders is a school strategy that includes working out things for yourself (what some might call "self-reliance") rather than bothering the teacher, with working-class parents emphasizing character (primarily, working hard and taking responsibility for your actions) versus middle-class parents' emphasis on the importance of individual agency in achieving academic success.[9] Likewise, Krista Soria refers to "the values of humility and invisibility taught in working-class families" and how these contrast with middle-class expectations of "self-promotion, self-assurance, and visibility."[10]

There is simple obedience in working-class life, but there is also strategy. Outside the criminal underground, parents typically want their kids to stay out of trouble and have the strength of character to steadily endure hard work for almost all of their lives. This begins in school, and it does involve obedience to authority. But working-class parents also are much more likely to let their kids run loose for great parts of the day and week when they're not in school and also tend to tolerate disobedient behavior by their children as long as it occurs outside their observation and does not involve active mouthing back. Thus, the stated culture of obedience is supplemented by an implicit culture of freedom and autonomy in "making your own fun." To working-class kids in this context, humility and invisibility can seem like tactics to avoid authority's notice so you can do whatever you want. Paul Willis's "lads" are one particular manifestation of this, one that is especially conscious of how out of sync they are and how rebellious they can be even while deferring to authority most of the time.[11] Working-class obedience is not simple passivity. It's not even always simple obedience. It is quite often just one part of a more complicated strategy for living a life when you expect a good part of it to be somewhere between difficult and miserable.

Middle-class interpreters are very keen to point out (convincingly) how both simple obedience and ingenious lad-like strategies reproduce the class positions and inequalities of working-class life. Many working-class people in my experience do indeed "sell themselves short," but many more accurately calculate not only their chances for but also the undesirability of middle-class careers, and they adjust accordingly. There is not one culture that will work for everybody, and our middle-class tendency to think there is devalues and misunderstands other ways of doing things.

Given their actually existing circumstances, it is understandable why so many working-class people adopt strategies of deference, with an emphasis on their own character and behavior rather than on success in the wider world or, for the most part, collective action—an emphasis on being rather than doing. But either on its own terms or even in middle-class ones, is there any comparative value to the working-class way? I think there is.

I've argued in the previous chapter that integrity is more valued in working-class life than among middle-class professionals. Being good, trustworthy, and faithful to one's friends and family and being true to who or what you are, these are the characteristics of working-class integrity. Though by no means unknown in middle-class life, these proclivities are subject to being undermined by that culture's steady push toward achievement and success. It would not be surprising that a culture that cares more about integrity should have more of it. Likewise, it should not be surprising that a culture that emphasizes character over achievement is generally more ethical and trustworthy. Though dealing with somewhat different class terms, an important social science investigation has found exactly that. Paul K. Piff and his colleagues contend that "higher social class predicts increased unethical behavior."[12] Across seven different studies, they found that "relative to lower-class individuals, individuals from upper-class backgrounds behaved more unethically in both naturalistic and laboratory studies." And among the reasons for this, they cite other research demonstrating that "upper-class individuals have been shown to be less cognizant of others and worse at identifying the emotions that others feel" and are "more disengaged during social interactions" and "less generous and altruistic." As a result, higher-class people have a tendency to have "feelings of entitlement," "a reduced concern for others' evaluations," and "increased goal-focus." This seems a little cruel when applied to the broad spectrum of middle-class professionals, but Piff and his colleagues assert that in the aggregate there is a continuum that as income/wealth, education, and occupational status increase, so does unethical behavior.

A final note about authenticity in working-class culture. It's true, as is often noted, that working-class people strongly value authenticity, even though they seldom use that word. But not using the word is an important part of achieving authenticity, which like "sincerity" tends to disappear the more explicitly you proclaim and pursue it.[13] Working-class authenticity as we observe it from the outside is a result of a culture that emphasizes being, character, and integrity. It is a very positive characteristic of working-class life, but it has its downsides in limiting horizons and lowering expectations.

And this points to the most positive aspects of professionalism's doing culture, its emphasis on achievement and accomplishment. We are more willing to pretend, to struggle to become something we are not yet—and may never be—in order to do something possibly spectacular but at least significant for ourselves and for others. With our higher expectations of ourselves and of the world, we are indeed more proactive most of the time, and it should not be surprising that an achievement culture achieves more, both individually and collectively. The professions, after all, have developed procedures and practices, from law and medicine to teaching and management, that have accomplished great good on net. The common working-class critique of us as having "poor quality [in our] interpersonal relations," or being "fakes" and "phonies," may be correct from their standpoint, but they fail to recognize that we are subjecting ourselves to a more complicated (and potentially compromising) interaction with the world not only as it is but also as both it and we might be.[14] What's more, inscribed to a large degree in the trajectory of professional middle-class life is an eventual transition from dead-ahead achievement and becoming to a greater emphasis on being adequate or good. As our family life becomes more interesting as our children grow and/or as our careers plateau, we feel the tug of being over doing. We're not as bad as they think we are. But then, neither are they as bad as we, usually quite thoughtlessly, think they are.

Belonging versus Becoming

The opposition of working-class *belonging* and middle-class *becoming* is much better established, especially among working-class studies scholars, largely due to the pioneering work of counseling psychologist Barbara Jensen.[15] But with different terminology and somewhat different emphases, more standard forms of social science investigation have substantiated the differences in class cultures on this score.

The contrast goes way back.[16] William Foote Whyte, for example, in his 1943 classic *Street Corner Society* made a strong contrast between "college boys" and "corner boys":

> Chick and Doc . . . had conflicting attitudes toward social mobility. Chick [the college boy] judged men according to their capacity for advancing themselves. Doc [the corner boy] judged them according to their loyalty to their friends and their behavior in their personal relations. . . . Both the college boy and the corner boy want to get ahead. The difference between them is that the college boy either does not tie himself to a group of close friends or else is willing to sacrifice his friendship with those who do not advance as fast as he does. The corner boy is tied to his group by a network of reciprocal obligations from which he is either unwilling or unable to break away.[17]

This is the world in which I grew up and eventually became a college boy, and I like the neutral way Whyte formulates it. Doc's priority for belonging is likely some combination of being "unwilling or unable to break away" from a tangled web of relationships that are typically experienced both as a burden or duty ("obligations") and as support and security (the "reciprocal" part). As I've documented, in my day Doc could reasonably expect to "get ahead" without going to college and thereby abandoning his friends and family, just as Chick could in "breaking away."

Doc and Chick, however, were working-class young men with much better prospects coming out of the Great Depression than the "Brothers" and "Hallway

Hangers" Jay MacLeod studied in the late 1980s and 1990s in *Ain't No Makin' It: Aspirations & Attainment in a Low-Income Neighborhood*. But the contrary directions chosen are the same—with the Brothers conventionally following the dictates of middle-class–oriented schooling in hopes of becoming some new and better self, while the Hallway Hangers hung together in their "reciprocal obligations," sometimes involving criminal activity.[18]

Young people raised in more purely professional middle-class environments today, where nearly everybody goes to college after high school, are unlikely to have experienced the sense of belonging that has long been core to working-class life. They very often have a sense of reciprocal obligations to their parents and a desire to keep in touch with old friends, but they are moving forward—and being pushed forward by family and friends—in ways that will undermine those bonds and distance them from previous relationships. In middle-class life, becoming successful (however that is defined) is recognized as more important than maintaining relationships, and though commonly envisioned as not incompatible with sustaining relationships, becoming necessarily involves some distancing from them. The expectation is that young people will go away (not break away) to college and then pursue a professional career in a national labor market, which is also likely to require them to move. Distancing oneself from family and friends, though not desirable, is seen as a natural and normal part of life in the middle class. What's important is to develop individual self-sufficiency that will allow you to properly mature and establish a life of your own making—at best visiting family and old friends once in a while.

Working-class commitment to belonging is born of need. With fewer financial resources and opportunities for advancement, and now with less steady and secure work, reciprocal obligations within a circle of family, friends, and workmates are often necessary for survival—for help, financial and otherwise, during the rough patches that are an expected part of life. But the fellowship of belonging is also a source of pleasure, even simple joy. Simply hanging out with people who know you exactly as you are, with no need or possibility for pretense or performance, who accept you warts and all, even if they might constantly rag on those warts, is among the rewards of living you earn by working for somebody else. Hanging out is less expensive than other forms of entertainment that enhance one's cultural and social capital, but make no mistake, other kinds of cultural and social capital are being acquired in hanging out, and these are the kinds that are most often valued in working-class life.

This does not mean that working-class relationships are all peaches and cream. They are often filled with long-standing tensions and feuds, especially within families, and belonging includes many obligated tasks and behaviors against which you may chafe. Belonging also includes many instances of people not fulfilling their obligations, even some folks who regularly disappoint with their unreliability or unfaithfulness, sometimes fueled by alcohol or drugs. But there is an inexplicable reluctance to cast off even the worst offenders and a willingness to tolerate their weaknesses or draw protective boundaries around them. Repetitive cycles of forgiveness for even the worst behaviors in a belonging culture can be seen as pathological by a culture that most values individual becoming and independence. But as frustrating as it is for loyal and reliable members, it is comforting even for them, maybe especially for them, to experience the strength of bonds among those around them that cannot be broken, no matter how frayed or temporarily out of order they might be. This steadfast acceptance is more common within extended families than among friends, as the bonds are tighter, but they are both a desideratum and a general characteristic within working-class life. My settled-living family and Judie's hard-living one were nothing like the rough, so-called dysfunctional extended families portrayed in *Hillbilly Elegy* and *Heartland* because we had many more steady and reliable adults around us, including mothers who loved us and were paying attention as J. D. Vance's and Sarah Smarsh's mothers were so heartbreakingly not.[19] But even within the struggling, unsettled families portrayed by Vance and Smarsh, there are thick and intense bonds, especially with grandparents but also with other relatives. Smarsh, for example, was only periodically in the same household as her younger brother Matt, but when she finally breaks away from what she sees as the pathologies of her family, she feels an overwhelming sense of guilt and betrayal for not being there to protect him from those pathologies, even though she could only occasionally protect and comfort him when she was there. This is a sense of belonging that I suspect is rarer in middle-class life with its steadier but less intense relationships. Though working-class people are less likely to leave the bonds of family, neighborhood, or region because they value belonging more than becoming, when they do they are more likely to take some of the belonging with them, if only as heartache.

The opposition of belonging and becoming can be stated in more ways than one, and some social scientists have captured the class difference with the less evocative terms "independence" and "interdependence."[20]

Management professors Nicole Stephens and Sarah Townsend study "the dysfunctional behaviors and physiological costs that can result when individuals' cultural beliefs collide with the dominant cultural beliefs of organizations."[21] They state the working-class/middle-class contrast like this:

> Our body of ongoing research shows that people from working-class backgrounds tend to understand themselves as interdependent with and highly connected to others. Parents teach their children the importance of following the rules and adjusting to the needs of others, in part because

there is no economic safety net to fall back on. Common sayings include "You can't always get what you want" and "It's not all about you"; values such as solidarity, humility, and loyalty take precedence.

In contrast, people from middle- and upper-class contexts tend to understand themselves as independent and separate from others. Parents teach kids the importance of cultivating their personal preferences, needs, and interests. Common sayings include "The world is your oyster" and "Your voice matters"; values such as uniqueness, self-expression, and influence take precedence.[22]

Stephens and Townsend state this differently than I would, but among their findings is that middle-class culture encourages us to individuate ourselves, what they call a "preference for difference from others," while working-class culture has "a normative preference for similarity to others."[23]

This research supports the notion that the class cultures are starkly different in their values of solidarity and individualism. But I doubt that a "preference for similarity" captures the character of working-class belonging, because it misses the phenomenon of *fitting in* among working-class groups, a process that actually allows and expects a lot more difference than is typical in middle-class life, where everybody is expected to be an individual. This may seem paradoxical, but in a belonging culture that sees relationships within a group as sources of strength and support, the expectation and acceptance of differences in people's strengths and weaknesses are in fact sources of not only strength but also self-relaxation and pleasure. Differences in strengths and weaknesses are seen as potentially complementing each other if individuals are willing to take on reciprocal obligations. What Stephens and Townsend see as a preference for similarity is more likely a process of mutual fitting in with the other individuals in their group. It is a process of seeking or maintaining group cohesion and solidarity that requires a kind of effortless work to make differences complementary rather than conflicting. This should count as both social and cultural capital. English working-class academic Lynsey Hanley was dismissive of kids who did not take an interest in school and who seemed addicted to hanging out, but though a striver herself, she recognized that "it was another way of learning and being, most importantly a way of learning just how to be with other people without making a conscious activity out of doing it."[24]

There is not an articulated working-class ideology of belonging as there is with middle-class individualism, and it is not unusual for people within both class cultures to rhetorically exaggerate the degree to which they are self-reliant. But because working-class belonging is based in the everyday practical need for others, it has developed an array of stratagems for maintaining group cohesion and individual relationships within the group. Belonging gives that maintenance much more time and attention than is common in middle-class life, as people seek to fit in while also working to maintain their own (semifated) individuality within the group. The difference for middle-class culture is that sense of becoming, that striving for individual achievement and success; folks surely want recognition and acceptance by larger groups, but they expect to get that not so much by fitting in as by doing something outstanding and exceptional. It is not that relationships are seen as unimportant in middle-class life but that they usually demand and get less attention and sometimes come into conflict with our individual goals and larger prospects.

I like that Stephens and Townsend use the word "solidarity" in describing working-class values, but that word can be misleading if it conjures images of collective action, as in strikes and protests. I have written about strikes, and I grew up in a family that participated in massive nationwide strikes every three years until I was seventeen.[25] These are great feats of organization and solidarity, but that is not what I mean by everyday working-class culture being *solidaristic* (or what I take Stephens and Townsend to mean by "solidarity"). Rather, solidarity is practiced—and expected—on a daily basis in managing relationships within small circles of family, friends, and workmates and helping and supporting each other. It's more like personal loyalty, but "solidaristic" points to the tendency of these personal loyalties to get extended to other working people to whom you do not have personal loyalties (especially those of one's own race, ethnicity, or occupation), an extension that only once in a while results in organized collective action. Everyday working-class solidarity may be the soil in which to grow organized collective action, but in the first instance it probably works against that broader sense of unity. In any case, a broader sense of occupational or class solidarity is not natural to the working class but its everyday solidarity provides a seed that can be cultivated depending on the circumstance.

Another way that a belonging culture contrasts with a becoming one is what Robert Putnam identified as two forms of social capital: bonding and bridging. As Barbara Jensen pointed out, in working-class life "deep, loyal, we-are-part-of-one-another bonding" is more common, whereas bridging is more middle-class, and though "less personal" and with "weaker ties," it "can unite many people across wide differences."[26] Networking is a LinkedIn form of bridging capital as well as a skill that is now routinely taught to budding professionals, who sometimes make a distinction between network friends and real friends. Network friends are friendly but instrumental relationships, and the danger for professionals is that our striving for goals, our purpose-driven lives, may instrumentalize all our relationships. Becoming requires more focus on ourselves rather than on others, and our ideology of individualism and our expectation of self-acting independence can hardly help but deemphasize those real relationships. This is much less likely in a working-class world where belonging is more important than becoming or achieving. But it also means that working-class groups, circles of family and friends, can become "in-turned tribes" that both exclude others outside their tribe and may have difficulties dealing with them honestly and directly.[27]

Everybody both bonds and bridges with friends and acquaintances, but the different cultural emphases on what is most important shape different results, different lives. As Jensen quotes Xavier de Sousa, "Bonding social capital is good for 'getting by,' and bridging social capital is good for 'getting ahead.'"[28] This formulation, however, may understate how much working-class belonging is experienced as a given and an end in itself, not just a means to get by and make do. As a given, one's circle is experienced as a tangled web of relationships from which you are not free to exit, at least not in an uncomplicated way; what Danish philosopher Svend Brinkmann calls "the pre-existing relationships in our lives" are burdens of obligation, not all of them healthy, as well as sources of support and pleasure, also not necessarily healthy.[29] The sense of being trapped or suffocated in your preexisting relationships is not uncommon in working-class life, with its urge to break away, occasionally resulting in actual breaking away. Belonging is something you endure as well as enjoy, and as in all things, the working class is usually better at enduring than the middle class.

Many today see the economic decline of the American working class in the last forty years as undermining this culture of belonging. They point both to the decline of labor unions and other community-level institutions such as churches and ethnic lodges and to the decline of marriage unions and the greatly increased absence of fathers in both white and black working-class families.[30] I have observed this deterioration within younger generations of my own extended family. I see worsening conditions challenging the culture, eroding it slowly over time, but I also see the strengthening of it as the need becomes greater. My guess is that there is a significant gender difference here, with working-class men increasingly detached from family life and other social connections and with women increasingly dependent on those connections. Indeed, some young women save themselves through their gritty mothering of their children, usually with a little help from grandparents and other relatives and friends.[31]

My impression is that the working-class culture I grew with is not as strong or as self-confident today as it was in my time, though I am perhaps too influenced by having an extended family in a deindustrialized place, one that saw the best of the good times during the Glorious Thirty and among the worst of the bad times since. There is plenty of evidence, however, that the contrast between working-class and middle-class cultures persists and may be even wider today. Likewise, there is no evidence for what Robert Putnam and others have called the "collapse of the working-class family" and with it the culture of belonging. Comparing men with college degrees against those with only high school or less, for example,

Putnam is able to show a big and growing class difference in the percentages of fathers who are not living with their children—4 percent among the college-educated versus 16 percent among the less educated working class. This may indeed, and probably does, indicate a weakening of family ties among men, but even discounting the role of mothers, it's hard to see how the 84 percent of working-class fathers who live with and ostensibly take responsibility for their children evidences a "collapse."[32] And it is a very different story among women.

Laura Delgado is presented as an example of "downscaling for survival" in Marianne Cooper's *Cut Adrift: Families in Insecure Times*.[33] From a settled-living working-class family, Delgado has experienced a downward economic spiral since her husband lost his job. She has three children, ages ten to sixteen, and in Cooper's portrait Delgado consistently doubles down on belonging the worse things get. Cooper sees this merely as a strategy Delgado uses for controlling emotions and expectations by using positive thinking to both mask and deal with her declining circumstances. It is undoubtedly that too, but Delgado is a philosopher of working-class belonging, articulating all manner of its common characteristics as labeled in table 6.1. Cooper, however, sees merely downscaling to "nothing more than being close to family and being present for her children," not a different approach to living a life whose utility actually increases during hard times. When her electricity is shut off, Delgado makes a game out of it for her children—"We use candles at night, like we're camping"—and instructs them in how their being together (and healthy) is more important than having electricity for the TV and refrigerator, telling them how her grandmother taught her that "having nothing isn't always a bad thing." At one point, she tells Cooper, "I'm blessed with a beautiful kid, and I live in California [surrounded by extended family], and I have a great family and friends." Cooper calls this "repression work" masking Delgado's increasingly desperate circumstances. But what *is* more important—having electricity or a tightly knit family that works with and supports each other? Claiming the latter might be an effective strategy for holding yourself together, having a mental attitude that helps you cope from day to day, but it is not merely that. It is, more fundamentally, a choice for the value of being and belonging over becoming and achieving. And though it may not be a good choice in all circumstances, I can't help thinking that in the long run it's generally the better, more human choice and that in Delgado's circumstances it's especially valuable.

Status and Social Class

It is natural for one culture to discount and misunderstand a different culture, but of all the ways this happens, projection of one's own onto other cultures may be the most distorting. Such projection happens routinely in the professional middle class concerning status. The middle class naively assumes that everybody is as concerned with status and rank as they are and that there is a singular and uniform hierarchy that everyone recognizes. Neither assumption is accurate. Status is not as important for working-class people, and insofar as they rank others, it is on criteria of being and belonging, not on socioeconomic position or achievement.

I'd go so far as to say that working-class culture is ideologically antistatus, as so many aspects of it involve sanctioning people for putting themselves above or thinking they are better than others. This is very commonly experienced by class crossovers like me, as friends and relatives seem very hasty to find our using "big words," for example, to be efforts at putting ourselves above rather than using more precise and accurate terms. I have never met a class crossover who did not find this constant effort to bring us back down to earth both irritating and sad— irritating because it seems unfairly judgmental and sad both because we're not sure how true it might be and because it points to a certain can't-go-home-again distance between our new and old worlds.

Working-class life is full of various practices and sayings that express contempt for any system of status, let alone any empathy for the status anxiety that is so widespread in the daily life of the middle class. Working people are simultaneously defensive about and contemptuous of people looking down on them. Though there are moments when they are cowed by it, as in middle-class institutions such as college or a doctor's office, and plenty of places where they need to show deference to a hierarchy of power and authority, as in most workplaces, the culture counsels them to be inwardly dismissive of it, actively but effortlessly resisting any fundamental acceptance of middle-class appraisals of them. When this inner dismissiveness works, and it often does, the potential pain and humiliation of being seen as of lesser importance and worth cannot touch them—it's just the way some people think, people you don't like much, and you shouldn't care what they think of you. Still, it's always hard to face people you can tell think you're inferior, especially if you recognize that as the world goes, they probably are more valued than you are.

"You're no better than anybody else, and nobody is better than you" was the officially articulated ideology in my family, and I heard it repeatedly as I was growing up, particularly when I seemed to be especially good at something. Many of my working-class students in Chicago recognized the saying, and most others agreed that their families had that moral attitude if not that exact saying. Though perhaps not universally present in the working class, this antistatus attitude is very widespread among them and is much less common, though not nonexistent, among middle-class professionals. This does not mean, of course, that working-class people always or even usually live up to that injunction. Some workers, especially men, are delighted to look down on what they see as the undeserving poor, and there is a long history of working-class whites psychologically enjoying their "wages of whiteness" in relation to working-class blacks.[34] Cultures tell you what you should do, not necessarily what you actually do.

Working-class people do rank themselves and others, but they do it based on a different set of criteria for evaluation, values of character and personal relationships: for example, whether they and others work hard and are honest and whether they are dependable family members and faithful to their friends (and/or religion). As I've documented above, they typically judge middle-class professionals harshly based on character deficiencies in the way we treat other people and the exaggerated view we often have of ourselves. Likewise, there is often a settled-living prejudice against "the poor," often shared among the hard-living working class mostly around perceived lazy work habits and insufficient reliability as a family member, friend, or workmate. Still, both evaluations are complicated in practice and style. Working-class people are often effusively appreciative of bosses, doctors, lawyers, and teachers who do not look down on them, for example. Likewise, among people they know, they make nuanced distinctions between the undeserving and deserving poor that are based on their reading of the evidence, not prejudice. And they will most often provide help and support even for those they judge undeserving, especially if a family member or longtime friend. However, among people they do not know, most are inclined to attribute bad economic circumstances to bad character traits, and among whites this can be explicitly racist. In my observation, working-class people greatly exaggerate the number and proportion of the undeserving poor (by their definitions) among people they do *not* know. But they find much higher proportions of deserving poor among people they *do* know. Regardless, this *is* a status system but one that uses moral criteria to divide people into something like good guys, bad guys, and okay guys. The complication in style is that some people are inclined to stern and dismissive judgmentalism, while others express a sad frustration that so-and-so is lazy, dishonest, and unreliable (or addicted to one substance or another). The latter group is always open to the possibility of redemption, the former generally not.

Most middle-class interpreters, including social scientists, fail to see this class-cultural difference. They assume that working-class people have both the same intense concern with status and the same status system that middle-class professionals have. Based on this assumption, they cannot help but interpret working-class antistatus attitudes as involving "class envy," the "healing of class injuries," or a merely "reactive identity" based on working people's recognition and resentment of their low standing in an agreed-upon hierarchy.[35]

As justifiably esteemed a set of social scientists as Richard Wilkinson and Kate Pickett construct a whole book around this false assumption. Wilkinson's and Pickett's earlier *The Spirit Level* had shown conclusively how large degrees of income and wealth inequality correlate with poor health and wellness in a wide variety of countries. But they then went on to argue, in *The Inner Level*, that poor health is caused not by economic inequality itself but by how the experience of these inequalities creates increased status anxieties and what they call "heightened social evaluative threat."[36] Rife with examples from upper-middle-class life such as "dinner party anxiety" and plastic surgery and with a liberal use of the middle-class "imperial we,"[37] Wilkinson and Pickett assume that statements such as the following cover all people: "Signs of our concern for social appearance are everywhere. It is as if most of us fear being seen for what we are, as if acceptance depended on hiding some awful truth about ourselves."[38] It's clear from this unintended satirical gloss on middle-class professionalism that their research did not include the Conemaugh PNA, the Tire Hill VFW, or millions of other working-class settings where there is no concern for social appearance and there are very low levels of social evaluative threat and lots of taken-for-granted acceptance. Wilkinson and Pickett make what in working-class studies seems like a rookie mistake but is actually widespread among social scientists: using the word "status" to indicate hierarchies of power, of money, and of worth and self-esteem as if they were all the same thing, assuming that more power and money is coincident with more societal worth and self-esteem. It just doesn't work that way in the working class, not usually and not often.

Working-class people almost uniformly recognize that they have less power and authority and less income and wealth than others.[39] And though in a variety of ways they consistently seek more control of their lives, which requires more money and more power, they generally accept their position in society. But while there are those who do, most do not accept the middle-class version of their personal and social worth, and the culture actively disdains such acceptance. They have their own criteria for ranking people, and it is heavily weighted toward moral criteria of character and relationships that they see as out of sync with the values of higher-class positions. Beginning in adolescence if not before, many actively disdain middle-class ways and choose to remain working class. It is not uncommon for adults to regret their adolescent choices, especially nowadays, but the regret is almost always about their lack of money and power over their own lives, not about status, not about how their betters see them or, except in the direst of circumstances, their self-esteem. They feel they should have tried harder and done better in school in order to have better jobs today, but they still don't want to be people like us—that is, they might envy the kinds of wages, working conditions, and living standards we have but not the kinds of people we are. This a very common, if not universal, way of looking at things in the working class, and the fact that sophisticated social scientists can't see or even guess at it reflects their own social and cultural class isolation.

Scholars with long experience of working people, however, are well aware of the antistatus ethos and working-class pride. Historian Alison Light, for example, found the slum neighborhood where she had family roots to be "a close-knit, hard-working community forging a pride in itself out of suffering and generosity" in the early twentieth century, when conditions were much worse than they are today:

> Where critics saw the factory worker as coarse and common, the girls themselves often pitied their sheltered contemporaries, those "daughters of educated men," immured at home, unable to fend for themselves and constantly chaperoned. . . . The reports on health and housing expose appalling conditions and invite our sympathy, but the testimonies of the residents themselves resist their victimization, insisting on a way of life they often reckoned better than their "betters": communal values over individual possessiveness, work as a means to relish life's pleasures rather than a means to accumulate.[40]

Likewise, in this century sociologist Jeff Torlina's interviews with blue-collar workers found a nearly uniform pride in their work and an alternative status system that often put their own "prestige" above that of white-collar and professional workers.[41] Oral histories are full of people such as the coal miner who compared his life favorably to the millionaire CEO of Massey Energy: "I'll tell you what I do have that he'll never have and that's respect and appreciation from the people I live with. And that makes me a hell of a lot richer."[42] And labor historian James Barrett describes his mother: "She was . . . class conscious in a vague sort of way, full of aphorisms that reflected poorly on rich people: 'Money comes to money'; 'If you need something, go to poor people for help.'"[43]

It's not impossible that these attitudes toward their own and others' status might sometimes be "compensatory," attempts to put a positive spin on their own perceived inferiority. But it is nonetheless part of the culture in working-class life, and it is highly suspicious that those who are so sure there's nothing here but "reactive identities," not a genuine culture, are themselves class isolates. There ought to be a rule that before social scientists are permitted to speculate on the deep sources of working-class thoughts and feelings, they should have known at least ten working-class people from adolescence into adulthood or have interviewed more than a hundred of them for more than fifteen minutes.

Parochial and Cosmopolitan

Chicago journalist Mike Royko used to tell the story of a Chinese immigrant who established a laundry in the predominately Polish neighborhood where Royko grew up. The Chinese immigrant learned the language of his customers, was well liked, and had a thriving business. After several years, the immigrant laundry owner had to go to City Hall for some business, where he was perplexed to find everybody speaking a foreign language he did not understand. He had learned Polish, the language of the neighborhood, not English.

The story, probably apocryphal, is told and retold to illustrate the parochial nature of Chicago's immigrant working-class neighborhoods, "urban villages" where some people might spend decades without ever leaving, according to the folklore. But told that way, the story misses many aspects of working-class parochialism. As Jonathan Haidt points out, "The word 'parochial' means, literally, concerned with matters of the local parish, rather than the larger world. But as it is commonly used, the word is an insult."[44] Indeed, Google's dictionary defines parochial as "having a limited or narrow outlook or scope," which is not necessarily pejorative, but then lists as synonyms "narrow-minded," "petty," "illiberal," "hidebound," and "intolerant," among other insulting terms.

Staying within the story, it is worth noting that both the Chinese and the Polish were immigrants, with direct knowledge of two very different cultures in their old and new countries. Though they chose to narrow their lifeworlds in order to have intimate control of their immediate circumstances, they were likely cosmopolitan in a potentially deeper way than middle-class professionals like me who have never left their country except as tourists (often in the company of large groups of other Americans). And as labor historian Jim Barrett has written about his own Chicago neighborhood not far from Royko's, the street-level racial and ethnic boundaries meant that a child growing up there needed to know about other cultures in order to either avoid or manage them.[45] Likewise, it was the rare Chicago neighborhood where most people worked within the neighborhood; working-class men and women most often had to leave to work, and in most working-class jobs there was a wild mix of different ethnicities and races. What's more, the second generation of immigrants often is bilingual and highly skilled in mediating between the cultures of their parents and those of their new country—again potentially more cosmopolitan than children growing up in ethnically indistinct but white suburbs where almost everybody goes to college after high school.

Still, if we stick with the meaning of the term, more like "localist" or indeed "villager" rather than all those negative synonyms, I think it is right to say that working-class culture is more parochial and middle-class professionalism more cosmopolitan. The working-class strategy of ceding control to gain control seeks to control small and therefore more manageable spaces (niches) together with a relatively small group of people (typically circles of family, friends, neighbors, and workmates). It is a strategy that for the most part cedes the larger world to others but attempts to establish deep, long-lasting relationships as part of a rooted life whereby one can have detailed knowledge of past and present that nurtures an easygoing, if often tangled, social trust. It's what Michael Ignatieff calls "ordinary virtue":

> Ordinary virtue is . . . a strategy for making do, for getting on with life, for bracketing larger questions that do not admit of answers. From the ordinary-virtues perspective it is enough to do your job, to give your neighbor a lift when her car breaks down, to loan the renter across the hall your hair dryer or take in her package, to mix in the streets with people from a hundred different lands, to join in your neighbors' festivals, to make sure your own kids do their homework and do your best to maintain a marriage or relationship through good times and bad. . . . [T]hose who live by the ordinary virtues seek, to the best of their ability, to reproduce the moral order [immediately] around them, without which their lives would no longer make sense.[46]

This localistic ordinary virtue has its downsides. As Richard Pipes said of Russians, "The lives of the great majority of Russians are uncommonly personal, which makes them excellent friends and poor citizens."[47] I wouldn't push this analogy too far, as many working-class Americans are very good citizens, but it is not unusual for them to be politically shrewd, generous, and nuanced in their everyday local worlds while having distorted caricatures of others in national, let alone international, politics. But Ignatieff rightly argues, I think, that latent racism and xenophobia remain latent until they get expanded into larger tribal conflicts. Writing from Bosnia, he says:

> Every local battle between faiths, creeds, or races can be fanned into an international fire once someone claims that what is at stake are ultimate questions of global, not simply local, identity.[48]
>
> [But] as long as it was only "me" and "you," people could live together, side by side, difference abutting difference, each in its terrain of ritual and certainty, not making claims on the other, living together *and* side by side, all at once. They came to your christening, you went to their funerals. Respect was shown. . . . This is the deep logic of ordinary virtue, the tolerance that comes from taking people as they come and taking life one day at a time.[49]

So, just as the cosmopolitan middle class often assumes, working-class parochialism can be fertile soil for xenophobia of various sorts—"in-turned tribes" or even hate groups—but if Ignatieff is right, this is likely only if that soil is seeded and watered from the outside. Working-class "live and let live" and "it takes all kinds" attitudes are antidotes in local worlds. But when middle-class professionals see themselves as cosmopolitan elites and are intolerant of local loyalties some seeding occurs, and when the spate of synonyms for parochialism get hurled at them—as often happens in various forms of public discourse, not just national politics—defensive resentments often result.

Since the Donald Trump presidency and Brexit shocks and other forms of right-wing populisms, the conflicts and misunderstandings between parochials and cosmopolitans have received some attention in political commentary.[50] Though much political discussion focuses on whites with and without bachelor's degrees, seldom is this divide seen in explicit class terms across race and ethnicity. Putting it in those terms shows that the cultural divide goes deeper than mere electoral politics, where people are very much affected by conditions in their own lives and the policies and personas politicians present. In class terms, it is legitimately suggested that the cosmopolitan middle class has much to offer a working class that needs its horizons expanded, its vision of moral order broadened. The whole history of public education, including higher education, has been a process of exposing young people to nonlocal knowledge and, where funds are available, to experiences their families couldn't provide. The class-culture clash this often sets up has been well studied in the sociology of education.[51] But a complementary process occurs nearly as often, one where students do learn and even like to learn nonlocal knowledge and where long-serving middle-class teachers become embedded in working-class communities. This complementarity unfortunately lessens in higher education, but it is not rare in community colleges or even fourth- and third-tier universities such as the one where I taught. I enjoyed presenting what they called "big picture stuff," and my working-adult students were often hungry for it, but I also respected their local experiential knowledge, and we worked together to try to reconcile my big picture with their often conflicting local knowledges. In the process they became more cosmopolitan, and over time I became more parochial, more appreciative of and comfortable with the intimacy embedded in my own local knowledge.

In any case, except among the international elite, American cosmopolitanism is only skin deep among standard-issue professionals; the ideological commitment to the descriptor and its string of honorific synonyms—"worldly, well-traveled, cultivated, sophisticated, refined" in Google's dictionary—is stronger than the way people actually live their lives.

In class terms, parochial and cosmo are results of different cultural emphases—guidelines, pressures, and nudges—that impel different ways of life by encouraging people to either stay engaged in what is immediately before them or distance themselves from the immediate so they can understand and experience a larger world. While both are present in every human life, we middle-class professionals need to understand that each emphasis produces different kinds of knowledge, both of which are valuable in different ways but will inevitably lead to conflicts between us. Envisioning our set of guidelines and pressures as the one right way, the only genuine culture opposed to a deficit or backward culture, makes managing those conflicts and appreciating the potential value in them more difficult.

There is enormous good, I believe, in our professional fostering of cosmopolitanism when it's not just snobbery. We are the class that is most committed to universal human rights, not just those of our own tribe, and to the impersonal character of institutions of law and bureaucracy because the impersonality of treating everybody the same is more just and fair in the long run. And among the education-communications wing, we are the ones who foster a broader sense of knowledge, vision, and empathy. But it's not very cosmopolitan if we see our own culture as the only good one, as the one to which everyone should aspire, and believe that everyone should try harder to be like us.

English journalist David Goodhart divides modern Western populations into "people who see the world from Anywhere and people who see it from Somewhere." As "the exam-passing classes," Anywheres have "portable achieved identities, based on educational and career success," whereas Somewheres are "more rooted and usually have ascribed identities . . . based on group belonging and particular places." The Somewheres are the much larger group, but the Anywheres dominate in most parts of society, especially culturally.[52] Politically, Somewheres are more negative toward free trade, globalization, and immigration, and Anywheres are quick to ascribe backward, racist, and xenophobic motives to those views. The Somewheres don't want to rule the world, according to Goodhart. They just want their concerns taken into account, to have their voices heard as part of a democratic discourse, and Goodhart sees the twenty-first-century populist revolt as rooted in the fact that Anywheres seem incapable of allowing that. It's an insightful if incomplete view of current populisms, but I think it is instructive that as an Anywhere liberal himself, Goodhart does not advocate a rigorous reform of Anywhereism but instead simply "a less headstrong Anywhere liberalism."[53]

Middle-class professionalism is a good and strong culture that makes a large positive contribution to our society and world, but it does damage when we are headstrong, so certain of our own virtue and preferability. We *do* have a lot to offer working-class people, from medicine to education to business, but they have something to offer us as well, and even when they don't, we have a vested interest in their culture being strong and vital enough to suit their circumstances, to foster their agency and pursue their happiness.

One of the ironies of middle-class cosmopolitanism is that in our middle-class lives, especially in our professional lives, there is a lot of unintended homogeneity as professionals. Though we often pride ourselves on our ability to meet, effectively deal with, and befriend people from diverse races, regions, countries, and religions, there is a shared professionalism in our ways of seeing, being, and acting that allows us to accept and enjoy people from diverse places and backgrounds. Especially at professional conferences we can delight in the variety of our colleagues from Nigeria, Germany, and China precisely because we share more among ourselves than we do with people outside the conference. But even in broader middle-class settings, there are professional manners and mores, shared attitudes and perspectives, that we are pretty rigorous in enforcing among ourselves. Often it goes under the moniker of "civility." As a result, there seems to be a narrower set of personalities and behaviors among us than in most working-class settings. Indeed, we are generally not that good at dealing with class or even occupational differences, such as the way many professionals treat wait staff and other "menials" and the awkwardly different professionalisms in the business and education-communications wings.

The working class, on the other hand, probably values diversity less but actually experiences more of it in their daily lives. In most working-class circles, there is a wild mélange of personalities, including people who are quite limited intellectually alongside stand-up comics and others of great wit, plus a wide range of emotional styles from the steadily mild to volatile hotheads. In middle-class settings, not being smart or being a hothead will exclude you from many activities and conversations, whereas "dumbbells" and hotheads are expected and accepted in working-class ones. Likewise, introverts are common and accepted in a way that they are not among middle-class professionals, who often feel impelled to try to "tear down walls" and "bring people out of their shells." My observation is that a working-class group where everybody belongs in one way or another is more diverse in personal styles and even manners and mores than in middle-class groupings, especially those whose primary or secondary purpose is networking, not friendship.

What's more, people in a belonging culture, with its tendency to become an "in-turned tribe," experience more diversity because they are more awkward with differences in people outside their circle, differences often tied to race, ethnicity, and religion when they are noticeable but also to class in their daily experience. Because they value belonging more, they are more likely to experience others as Other, but they are also less likely to be able to avoid and dismiss them. Just as there are strategies to defer to those with more power and authority, there are ways to deal with others who have different ethnicities and religions, different ways of doing, being, and seeing. Outright hostility is one of these (especially among young men), but it is not the only one. In daily life, for both objective and subjective reasons, working-class parochialism undoubtedly experiences more unavoidable diversity than we middle-class professionals do. And for the most part, though always a potential witch's brew, they deal with it generously and effectively with what Ignatieff calls ordinary but highly local virtues.

The Uses of Binaries

"There are two kinds of people in the world, and I don't like either one of them much," Monty Python actor Eric Idle quipped in his "sortabiography."[54] The joke is funny, because dividing people into two opposite groups is so common a way for human beings to map basic social realities even though we know these kinds of oppositions are too simple. That simplicity is a good part of the explanatory power of conceptual binaries. But if rigidly adopted as labels to define individuals, "to put us all in boxes," we know such binaries can do harm by nurturing animosities on the most extreme end or simply encouraging avoidance and distance on the soft end. I learned a corollary of this teaching Barbara Jensen's *Reading Classes* to a group of traditional-aged college students after I had retired as an adult educator. Whereas in teaching working adults there was recognition of some aspects but considerable resistance to others in my list of class characteristics from Jensen, younger students just copied down the list and then started applying it as if it were scientific truth—while also routinely asking what was going to be on the test.

Oppositional binaries should open study and discussion, not close it. If they are insightful, there are all sorts of further analysis, modifications, qualifications, and internal disagreements that should ensue, including empirical studies in the ingenuous ways social scientists have devised in the past several decades. This chapter is simply meant to outline and suggest cultural poles that pull us in different directions based on social class. Many other things—race, gender, sexuality, etc.—matter for people's experience and how they interpret that experience, but I have been rigorously nonintersectional in order to draw attention to broad class misunderstandings that have consequences for how we live, including but not limited to what is still allowed of democratic politics within our current economic oligarchy.

We'd need a lot of boxes if we were to classify each individual, so many that it may not be worth the effort. I have suggested additional binaries within each class—hard living and settled living in the working class and the business and education-communications wings of the professional middle class as well as a distinction between elite and standard-issue middle-class professionals—but so many more distinctions would have to made to allow us to properly classify individuals. I'm not interested in labeling everybody one by one. But I do hope that people will recognize parts of themselves in my notion of class divisions within free wage labor and will recognize how we all experience the human tensions between belonging and becoming and being and doing but with different guidelines and pressures within the culture that has affected us most.

And as I demonstrated in chapter 5, it is not always easy to determine which culture or cultures have affected us most. Jean Boucher has explored the difference between *mono-class* people and *class hybrids*, finding that growing groups of hybrids differ substantially from one another.[55] There are class crossovers like me, but there are also people who maintain their class position and identity while being highly influenced by the culture of the other class. This commonly happens among college professors of middle-class origin who end up teaching at universities that are primarily working class. It also happens among labor union staff who rise from the ranks of their union. But even people who have experienced the same class trajectory *together*, like Judie and I, retain and embrace different parts of the two cultures while sharing other parts both intentionally and unintentionally.

As in other forms of diversity, cross-class experience expands our horizons and our understanding of the range of what is lived as proper, normal, or natural in human life. But there is also utility and value in living one and only one culture to the full, experiencing little or no opposition that might undermine your conscious dedication or barely conscious commitment. I and my family of origin benefited from living in a steel town where we had little direct interaction with people of other classes. Protected by a powerful union during the Glorious Thirty, we could elaborate our way of life on our own without much interference. Likewise, I fancy that upper-middle-class young people who go to high school and college almost exclusively with people from their own social class have advantages for achieving and becoming precisely because of the purity of their local culture and how it meshes so well with the official national culture. The problem is that we must live with one another in a society that officially and genuinely prizes democracy and democratic discourse. As the dominant culture that influences all others, middle-class professionals—especially those of us in the education-communications wing—must foster mutual understanding across class divides. I believe that we can most effectively do that by correcting our own class misunderstandings and stepping back from our jumped-to conclusions and assumptions about people and cultures that operate with different rules, goals, and aspirations.

My final three chapters will not be about more categorical differences in the class cultures but instead will explore certain aspects of working-class life and culture that middle-class scholars have neglected and/or misunderstood, many of which have filtered into broader professional misconceptions and devaluations.

Part III
STRATEGIES AND ASPECTS OF WORKING-CLASS CULTURE

In midlife after a decades-long attempt to become and achieve, I started half-consciously to revert to working-class ways. As a teacher, first in my labor classes and then in my regular classrooms, I devolved into using what I thought was instructive teasing to reinforce flaws I had pointed out in students' writing and thinking. I'm not sure how this happened, and it certainly was not consciously intentional, but I suspect they started it—by teasing me as "the professor," which nearly always meant that I was someone who might be out of touch with real life, and in other references to my being white bread, or liberal, or shilling for the university. Their teasing was both good-natured and pointed, meant to put me on my back foot but also an expression of friendship and belonging. I read their teasing as a kind of accepting me warts and all by referring to a particular wart to make a point or put me in perspective. This is how since childhood I have experienced the phenomenon of "ranking," "busting," or "the dozens" in working-class life, which by others' accounts is not always as good-natured as I experienced it or as I think I practiced it. My guess is that even the meaner forms of this kind of teasing, when they are not just comical exaggeration but instead are based on flaws perceived by the teaser and recognized by the teased, are gestures of inclusion that invite belonging through insults that you would never use except among friends. When I called a student "Ms. Sentence Fragment" or used the phrase "kind of Nazi," referring to serious criticisms I had made of them, I was saying that they were appreciated despite those flaws, accepted as belonging to and making contributions to our group even while they should be working on overcoming those flaws. My instructive teasing was not always taken in the way I intended it, and I could recount a list of times I wish I hadn't done it, but the amazing thing to me, looking back, is how rare these instances of failed teasing were and how much edgy, risky, smart-ass banter I not only got away with but was appreciated for.

This kind of teasing is a somewhat strange phenomena that occurs often in working-class groups but is wildly inappropriate in middle-class ones. The French sociologist Pierre Bourdieu associated this teasing with peasants and defined it as "ritual mockery or insults" that are "in fact tokens of attention or affection, ways of building up while seeming to run down, of accepting while seeming to condemn."[1] British sociologist Tim Strangleman's examination of many different UK workplaces found "banter which reveal a sense of care . . . in wanting to integrate through seeming rejection."[2] This is the way I experienced it as a lad and the way I think I used it as a teacher of working adults. My own experience of "busting balls" as a lad never seemed simply mean to me but instead was a pulling-down that functioned to reinforce working-class realism—to "keep it real" and to manage aspirations and expectations. Busting balls enforced group belonging both by pulling back in and by accepting you as part of an "it takes all kinds" fellowship regardless of whether you were too short or too big, had bad breath or a nasty temper, had an oversized nose or funny ears, or even if you seemed too perfect. But I do remember kids who didn't seem to take it that way and later some more middle-class adult students to whom I had to explain myself when they, in a telling phrase, "took it the wrong way."[3]

The following chapters are about what I see as general working-class ways that I found myself reverting to in my midlife mediocrity as a standard-issue middle-class professional. They are my interpretive notions of what I see as crucial aspects of working-class life based on my direct observation and experience, including of myself over a lifetime. I know these aspects are not universal among working-class people, but I believe they are widespread in many varied forms across gender, racial, and other differences. Likewise, many of them are not unknown among middle-class professionals, especially among crossovers like me who discover them operating within our lives decades after we have been living as middle-class professionals but also among less hybrid standard-issue professionals who have learned from working-class ways. I feel free in these coming chapters to simply try to develop my views clearly without trying to prove them. Rather, I hope they will resonate with others' experiences across a spectrum from the thrill of recognition to "yes, but" to "what the hell are you talking about?" In these various ways I hope readers will be driven to reflect on their own class cultural experience, even as in the process my own parochial narrowness will likely be more clearly revealed.

The three aspects I've chosen are the strategy of *ceding control to gain control*, the extraordinary value given to *taking it*, and what has been called *working-class realism.* These are interrelated and may form a larger whole that I have yet to grasp, but in each case I take my cues from middle-class misunderstandings of these phenomena, and though focused on working-class life and culture, they should also illuminate some middle-class strengths and weaknesses.

CEDING CONTROL TO GAIN CONTROL

Let her be. So all that is in her will not bloom—but in how many does it? There is still enough left to live by.

Tillie Olsen, *Tell Me a Riddle*

They created a sense of belonging and tried to make do with the way they found each other.

Toni Morrison, *The Bluest Eye*

In Johnstown there are six or seven houses on Ohio Street I noticed for years driving by, wondering if anybody lived there because their front porches and facades were blackened with coal dust from trucks that released fine dust as their drivers upshifted to descend the grade. Just driving by, there never seemed to be a light on in what would have been the living rooms. The houses have no front yards, just a narrow sidewalk separating them from the street, and are right next to each other, like row houses but wood-framed and with a slender passage between them. I had thought they might be abandoned because sweeping dust from porches was almost as common in Johnstown as getting up in the morning, though most of us were sweeping reddish brown mill dust, not the black stuff. Why would people not sweep their front porches if they still lived there?

One spring day after I was grown up and just visiting, I was given the task of walking my mother-in-law's dog up the path in the wooded hills behind these coal-stained houses. Far from being abandoned, each had an elaborate back porch or deck reaching out into a small fenced-off backyard festooned with bushes, flowers, and small patches of well-ordered rows of vegetables. Each had the distinctive marks of the home-built and home-grown, with religious or floral idiosyncrasies fighting for space with the particular practical functions the owners most desired. Though obviously uncoordinated, this row of elaborate backyards seemed like an especially colorful and playfully chaotic English garden, a unified space designed to be an urban oasis for individual respite and easy unforced sociability. This is where these people lived, not in their living rooms.

This would have been in the 1980s, and when I went back more recently to take some pictures, the scene had disappeared. The houses were still there, but their wooden frames had been covered with plastic siding. The front porches were clean, though none had porch furniture, and the backyards were mixed—a few well-tended but far less glorious gardens alongside others with junked cars, rusting appliances, and other cast-off equipment. In the twenty-first century traffic was more occasional than bustling, and coal was no longer delivered to a steel mill at the bottom of Ohio Street.

Still, though I hadn't thought at the time to take pictures or talk with the residents, the original image stuck with me as characteristic of how sensibly creative a making-do working-class culture can be. Whoever put front porches on these houses had thoughtlessly reproduced a conventional pattern that could never have fit into its actual environment. Even without coal trucks, it would have been unpleasant to sit on those porches as traffic whizzed by, making enough noise to interrupt either conversation or peaceful contemplation; plus, the houses were set so close to the highway that sitting on the front porch would have felt dangerous, as at any moment a reckless car or a runaway truck might careen onto your porch and into your living room. It made sense to cede control of the front of your house—give it over to the street, with its dirt, noise, and potential danger—and concentrate your living in the back, where your kitchen looked over a backyard that was, or at least felt, isolated from the wider world over which you could have so little control.

This is more than making-do ingenuity. It is, I now think, a core life strategy common in working-class lives, so common it is hardly noticed as it gets repeated and relied upon in nearly every kind of situation. In broad terms, the strategy fits those who do not have careers but just a job they do purely and simply to earn a living. They may like their jobs or hate them, they may like them on Thursdays and hate them on Mondays, there may or may not be opportunities to move up a job ladder and wage scale, and workers may or may not take pride in the work they do. But every workday they cede control of their lives for 8 hours in return for the cash to sustain them for the other 128 hours each week. These hours are the living part they've earned and over which they do have some control, including, if their pay is high enough to sustain themselves with at least a little extra, 8 hours for what you will.

Embodied in the wage relationship, ceding control of one area of life to gain control of another area often becomes a standard strategy used in a variety of ways, including at work—that is, including places where you've already ceded control but where you find ways to take some control back by practicing different forms of crafty deference.

The Uses of Deference

Deference is a widely misunderstood aspect of human relations. It is almost uniformly seen as negative and a weakness in the official culture of the proactive and professional middle class, even though almost everybody has to defer to somebody else a lot of the time. But deference is part of a very common life strategy among suppressed groups, probably most recognizable among women, especially those of my mother's generation, but in other ways among the working class as a whole. A lot of deference is forced on us at work but also in social situations. When you accept that forced deference without guilt as just the way things are, however, you find that there is considerable room for freedom of thought and action within your deference, and there are many ways to retain your dignity and even shape your life around, within, and against that force. When forced deference is embraced, it is (or can be) a strategy, one that is very common in working-class jobs and lives.

But deference is also often a choice, a recognition not simply that someone is more powerful than you but that somebody is more skilled, more knowledgeable, or stronger willed or in a variety of ways "better at" something you desire to do or be part of. That kind of deference is (or can be) a wise recognition of personal insufficiency and a handing off of a bit of responsibility to others so you can handle your own narrower piece of responsibility better than you otherwise would. In that sense, mutual deferences are at the core not only of personal relationships but also of building communities, whether small circles of families and friends or entire societies, especially democratic ones.

I'm not sure when I realized it, but I had observed nearly all my life how hollow formal deference of even an abject kind could become and how strong and clear informal power could be on the ground, where most of life is lived. As a rule of thumb, the more those who receive deference can take it for granted, the less they pay attention to what their deferrers are doing and the more freedom and autonomy the deferring can gain so long as they don't draw too much attention to themselves. My mother never articulated this principle, but she demonstrated it every day when my father left for work, and she illustrated it to me in indirect ways through stories whose point was something else but through which I learned to appreciate how a certain well-attuned cunning was necessary to be a good person.

Formal deference to men was culturally forced on women of all classes in those days, but there were a variety of ways that deference actually played out in marital relationships, from the strictly formal deference given even to "hen-pecked" husbands all the way to abject humiliation and domestic violence. In my observation, however, many deferent working-class women gained considerable informal power over time, power often available by being on the ground with the children, in the neighborhood, or at church. It is a power that comes from the personal loyalties and moral reciprocities so many working-class women build up through working day by day to make everything come out okay situation by situation. I had seen my mother develop this kind of power, greatly enhanced once she returned to work as a teacher, and Judie's mother as well right up to the time she died at age 102. Judie achieved a spunkier version of it at work and in our immediate neighborhoods.

The deference itself is not a life strategy. Rather, what's required is a certain psychological distance a person can establish from her or his deference, distance that can transform simple deference into a tactic that can search out autonomous spaces for one's own action.

There are particularly stark and therefore clear examples from the early and most dangerous days of the twentieth-century African American freedom struggle. Ruth Needleman's portrait of George Kimbley, a black leader in the Steel Workers Organizing Committee in the 1930s and later in the United Steelworkers union, is a particularly telling one. Kimbley had learned from his mother, who had been born into slavery, how to use acts of kindness and concern to break down racial barriers as you cultivated moral reciprocities with others. "Kimbley avoided symbolic protests against racism; he viewed them as fruitless and dangerous. He saw value in not 'stating his mind,' but rather in speaking and acting with great caution, with an eye toward those behaviors that would keep him safe." Using this cautious deference as a shield, however, Kimbley was a dogged and crafty organizer who advanced the union, the black freedom movement, and himself during very difficult and oppressive times. Retired in his nineties, he regaled Needleman with a wide range of cunning tricks—some manipulative, some humorous, and many inspiring—he used to break down and get around white racism.[1] The stories he tells, however embroidered, reveal Kimbley in control within and around his ceding of control to the boss and the white man.

Kimbley would be seen as Tom-ish by later more militant black Steelworker leaders who, in the heyday of the civil rights movement, favored a more direct and confrontational style, but even they moved the deference line forward rather than abandoning it altogether. Like most effective rank-and-file organizers, they knew they needed first to be exemplary workers and then to strategically probe the limits of what they could get out of the company and the union hierarchy.[2] Charles Payne's account of Mississippi black activist Amzie Moore's struggles in the years prior to the 1964 Freedom Summer provide a more militant example in a much more dangerous situation. "Moore's ability to play the Negro, to adopt the innocent, know-nothing demeanor that whites typically wanted to see in Blacks," was part of his power as an antilynching and voting rights activist. Avoiding direct confrontation when he could and "playing the Negro" even when confronting white power, Moore knew how dangerous his organizing within the black community was and therefore always carried a gun, and "at night the area around his house may have been the best-lit spot" in town.[3]

These heroic examples of the uses of deference are extreme cases of working-class ceding control, refusing to fight or even challenge in one area in order to probe for spaces of autonomy and agency in other areas of life. Less deference and less ingenuity are ordinarily required in the daily practice of working-class ceding of control to gain control. My notion is that there is a continuum from simple obedience to the most heroic forms—that is, from simple deference that is not a tactic but instead purely and simply acceptance of subjection—to cunning personal or activist agency within and around formal deference. In working-class life, it is not uncommon for some people to flat out simply obey and defer from childhood; nor is it unusual for crafty deference to lose its craftiness as life grinds people down to simple subjection. Conversely, some reject deference in any form and straightforwardly confront people and forces that are more powerful than they, at least expressively if not materially. But strategies of deference are very common in working-class life and can take a variety of forms both across individual lives and within them.

Sociologist Jessica Calarco found that working-class parents teach their children "strategies of deference," basically to respect their teachers and other adults and not to burden them by requiring too much attention.[4] As I pointed out in chapter 6, this is not simple obedience. The deference I learned as a child, for example, was more about keeping adult authority out of my business than it was genuine respect (although I had some of that too). I liked ladness because of how we could taunt or slyly challenge authority without (usually) being punished for it. This resonated with the stories from the mill that my father was so good at telling and with a general ethos of avoiding professional people, even preachers and doctors, as much as we could. It was like a craving for our own spaces, places where we could be ourselves among ourselves. But I learned over time, mostly from my father's stories as a union "grievance man" I think, that ladish taunting often weakens your position not only because it exposes you to punishment but also because it succumbs to a desire for immediate emotional satisfaction rather than gaining some real control by "keeping yourself to yourself."

Calarco's longitudinal study of mixed-class students from the third grade into middle school is focused on showing the advantages middle-class kids get by practicing the "strategies of influence" their parents teach them. According to Calarco, middle-class kids are taught to question and negotiate with the authority of their teachers, who are there to serve and help them. They learn that children should ask for help and seek special accommodations when they can. Working-class kids, conversely, are taught to defer to teachers, do what they're told, and

not burden teachers with unnecessary questions and instead work out their problems on their own. The middle-class kids become so good at bargaining for special
arrangements that teachers spend the bulk of their time and attention accommo-
dating them while the working-class kids try to figure things out on their own. In
today's world this sets up a chain reaction of working-class disadvantages in pursuing academic success and then, in a labor market tiered by educational attainment, further disadvantages them in obtaining good jobs with decent wages and
conditions.

Calarco is convincing in detailing the injustice involved here and presents some
school-based remedies for reducing those disadvantages, but I want to focus on
the values of the strategies of deference working-class parents are teaching their
children. In interviewing the parents, Calarco concluded:

> All the parents . . . , regardless of class or mobility, wanted to support their
> children's academic success. At the same time, parents worried that too
> much support could undermine their children's development of good
> character (i.e., respect, responsibility, and work ethic). Middle-class and
> working-class parents alike struggled with how to balance those seemingly
> competing priorities. Ultimately, middle-class parents prioritized good
> grades, and working-class parents prioritized good character.[5]

Good grades or good character? Is that really the choice we want forced on parents and their children? If the situation today is as Calarco describes it, and I think
it is, the root of the injustice is not in parental decision making or school practices but rather in a labor market that denies representation, steady work, and
decent wages to more than half the jobs that need done.[6] In the current arrangement, the working-class preference for good character, simple integrity, and being and belonging conspires to keep them in their place, which has probably been
true for more than a century, but the places they inhabit now have been degrading and eroding for decades. Looking at the culture, at least as I and others have
characterized it, do we want to mobilize an effort to change that culture, as is common among well-intended liberals who see education as the one and only answer?[7] Or should we focus our efforts on dramatically improving labor market
conditions and living standards? The answer seems obvious to me. The culture is
well worth preserving and protecting. The current labor market rules are not.

But look at it too from a middle-class perspective. Do we want to teach our kids
to develop such strong negotiating skills that they come to see human relationships as mostly transactional, with less and less concern for character and integrity
except as public relations branding? Is this really what middle-class parents want,
finagling, transactional grade hounds constantly seeking competitive advantage so
they can find a career, not just a job, a career that may value those same finagling,

manipulative transactional skills they're honing in school? I doubt that is what any parent wants, but those are the pressures being put on us by the increasing distance between good jobs and bad jobs based on educational attainment.[8] Parents should not have to prioritize between good grades and good character. We need to attack our growing inequalities with higher wages and better conditions for all the bad jobs that do much of the work we all depend on. In the long run, even most winners can't really win in a winner-take-all society.[9]

Working-class deference can seem like the resignation of the oppressed, and sometimes that's all it is. But deference is a more valuable part of all human relations than it's usually given credit for, and working-class deference is very often part of a broader pattern of values and proclivities that are (or can be) humanly valuable, societally necessary, and individually rewarding.

Formal and Informal Control at Work

Just because wage workers accept a wage in return for allowing themselves to be bossed around for a set number of hours does not mean they have ceded all control at work. The formal ceding is in fact but a first step in regaining some control on an hourly and daily basis. There is a long history among industrial workers of what Frederick Winslow Taylor called "soldiering." But the phenomenon of gaining control at work is broader than the explicit and often well-organized "goldbricking," "quota restriction," "chiseling" and "banking" that have long been common in factories.[10] Soldiering is practiced in offices, retail work, caring and cooking, and all working-class occupations and is not unknown among professionals.

Let me start with an example from my own experience. When a new dean imposed a curricular rule on our group of faculty, we first opposed it for undermining our traditional faculty authority over the curriculum. When it became clear that fighting the new rule was going to take all our time with little chance of success, one of the faculty who worked extensively with public school teachers suggested their strategy of giving in on the principle so we could do what we wanted in the classroom. "They do it all the time in the publics," he said, "because there is no end of dictates from central office that range from impractical to stupid." This was a hard pill to swallow because we saw the principle as fundamental to academic integrity, but we knew the new dean could not possibly enforce the new rule in our classrooms. We also suspected that his motivation was to establish his authority over us rather than really caring about the curricular rule. We turned out to be right, and he soon forgot about the rule. What's more, we were able to employ this strategy consistently as he was "taking charge" of us, giving up responsibilities that we had not been asked to give up. It wasn't long until such a mess was created that he abandoned his take-charge approach and adopted Mr. Nice Guy instead.

Two things about this experience. One, it might not have worked, and consistently giving in on principles can erode informal as well as formal control; indeed, later a more systematic and consistent approach by the university administration did undermine important principles of faculty control and academic integrity. But the other thing is how good it felt to come to that common resolution—how liberating it felt to give up on one front and take the fight to terrain where we knew we had enormous advantages. Part of that good feeling was that we all agreed with each other, the feeling of solidarity. But the more important part was the sense of control we felt we could have not only in this fight but also in whatever future ones were to come. By ceding formal control, we could keep our informal control and potentially enhance it. And for us, this time, it worked like a charm.

The success of this ivory tower struggle relied heavily on our having professional prerogatives and the fact that our workplace, a college classroom, is difficult to observe on a regular basis. But ceding control to gain control is well documented in even the most highly supervised, rigidly controlled workplaces, such as assembly lines. Perhaps the most famous example is Ben Hamper's *Rivethead: Tales from the Assembly Line*, a best-selling book by an autoworker/rock critic who explained in detail how workers on the line did their own and others' jobs in order to control the pace of work and rest.[11] Hamper even claimed to have been able to leave the plant from time to time to go to a rock concert. I've talked with several autoworkers who are highly skeptical that Hamper could actually leave work without being noticed, but they all confirmed that he had accurately portrayed the dynamics of both work sharing and dealing with supervisors who had to allow this formally forbidden practice if they wanted to meet their production quotas; they also shared their own mostly hilarious stories of winning control over part of their work shift by making sure the work got done and done well. There are similar tales from steel mills where elaborate contests were staged and lunches were cooked and enjoyed, often deer meat or other game, while on the clock.[12] Jill Schennum details a wide range of practices at the Bethlehem, Pennsylvania, plant of Bethlehem Steel, where workers not only controlled their own work pace and created leisure on worktime but also gained "a certain citizenship 'right' to the space of the mill, the space of production," something she calls "inhabitance rights."[13] Likewise, longshoreman Reg Theriault explained how workers in West Coast ports shared their work by "each . . . doing the work of two men" for a stint, thereby earning a period of rest and socialization.[14] And Frank Bardacke casually mentions how California farmworkers, of which he was one, could slow down their pace and entertain visitors in the back part of the workday.[15]

Goldbricking, quota restriction, and work sharing in office work are harder to see and have not been studied, so far as I know. But though typically more individualistic, they surely occur. Many of my adult students worked in offices in Chicago's Loop, and into the 1990s they delighted in telling me and their classmates stories about the ingenuity it took to control their work pace and space. Many of them were able to do reading for class and other homework during work hours, and it was not uncommon for someone to explain that they had not finished the assigned reading because it was a busy day at work. This looseness in the workday got noticeably diminished in the downsizing and "right-sizing" of the 1990s, and by the early years of the twenty-first century it was rare for people to report being able to do school assignments at work. I probably encouraged and indulged these discussions to the detriment of covering all the material, but people loved to talk about their versions of chiseling and to compete with each other's stories, which were especially revealing when there was a roughly equal mix of blue-collar and white-collar workers in the classroom.

I observed a few things in these discussions over the years. One was the sense of exhilaration people felt in gaining and maintaining areas of control, in taking back some of the workday they had given away. Second, there is usually pride in doing the work well, sometimes better than management desired, and in any case, doing the job well is a necessary condition for gaining control, for creating some time for what you will within the time for what they will. Finally, no matter how exaggerated their tales may have been, they also seemed especially delighted in how craftily ingenious many of their ploys were; they enjoyed sharing them and learned new angles from each other. To middle-class professional eyes, these little victories can seem sad, even pathetic, and the ploys can seem juvenile and unproductive. But the most important thing I learned was how uniformly you can tap into a certain underworld of work life, a whole realm of activity and human agency that to be effective needs to be kept secret—"to ourselves, within ourselves"—even when you are busting with pride in getting over on the boss. In labor union settings there is much more consciousness of the value and complexity of this underworld, and for my money, labor historians have greatly underestimated how dedicated most unions have been to preserving and protecting this underworld.[16] But the evidence of my classroom suggests a broader universality across all kinds of occupations. And to me this suggests that in the wage bargain, the initial and fundamental ceding of control is the beginning not of a dance or of a game but instead an existential struggle to find and maintain areas of autonomy, zones of freedom at work.[17] Turning it into a game can enhance the enjoyment, but regaining some control over your workday is as important and universal a working-class value as there is.

Every workplace has complex forms of both formal and informal control, and the less conscious management is of the informal controls, the stronger workers' informal power can be. That this rule of thumb is as universal as it is, as wide-spread in so many different workplaces, is amazing to me because there is no ar-ticulated ideology, let alone a textbook, that explains the value of it or how to do it in any particular workplace. Still, it gets passed on in workplace instruction and imitation and in conversations like those in my classes.

Most systematic studies of these phenomenon—such as Michael Burawoy in the 1970s, Hamper in the 1980s, and Jill Schennum in the 1990s—were done in factories, ones with strong unions back in the day, and are now likely dated. The severe forms of electronic monitoring and control from Amazon warehouses to UPS over-the-road drivers may have made the complexity of regaining control out of reach for many workers today, something from the dinosaur days of strong unions and protective workplace laws. But the practices of what my father called "protecting the slack" are so ancient, passed along by example and word of mouth but also somehow instinctive, that I would not jump to that conclusion without closely observing what is going on in these repressive workplaces. Indeed, in a participant-observer study of an Amazon warehouse, Emily Guendelsberger care-fully explains the totalitarian mechanisms of control employed but then encoun-ters a group of experienced workers who explain why she'd been "working *way* too hard." They explained how to steal time off and control the pace of your work-day. One worker bragged that he took forty-eight minutes of time "off task" be-fore he got called on it.[18]

Nevertheless, I think it's safe to say that in the first quarter of the twenty-first century, so much has been lost at work that there may not be much left to cede—at least not much in comparison to the years around the Glorious Thirty. Many millions of workers likely have smaller and smaller areas of informal control, fewer and weaker zones of autonomy. If so, it is a tragedy of major proportions. If, as we'll see below, losses of control cause declines in health, well-being, and longev-ity, then these new electronically surveilled workplaces may be committing some-thing like manslaughter.

Status versus Control

Two very important and widely hailed studies—Michael Marmot, *The Status Syn-drome*, and Richard Wilkinson and Kate Pickett, *The Spirit Level*—have docu-mented the enormous costs in health and well-being the United States, the United Kingdom, and some other countries endure because of our extreme levels of in-come inequality.[19] Both studies unfortunately use the word "status" as if it were synonymous with class position and, more importantly, with "control." As I sug-gested in chapter 6, this confusion reflects a widespread middle-class assumption that there is one and only one social hierarchy and accompanying status system that everyone recognizes and adheres to. This assumption is incorrect, because though there are measurable objective gradients of income, wealth, educational attainment, power and (formal) authority, working classes generally use a different morality-based system to rank themselves and others. As a result, working-class adults also do not experience anything like the levels of "status anxiety" and "social evaluative threat" that are common among middle-class professionals.[20]

This error is significant, because if we understand how relatively unimportant status is in working-class life and, conversely, how important having a sense of control and actual control is in human life generally, then we will focus on different remedies for inequality and its accumulating negative effects on everybody but especially on poor and working classes.

Marmot's pathbreaking research established that a health gradient strongly correlated with a social gradient of "more money, bigger houses, a more prestigious job, more status in the eyes of others, or simply a higher-class way of speaking."[21] In other words, the more money, prestige, status, etc. you have, the healthier you are likely to be. Wilkinson and Pickett then showed that societies with greater levels of inequality of income and wealth, such as the United States and the United Kingdom, experience a long list of physical and mental health problems far above countries with more equality. As you might expect, people with lower incomes experience greater health and well-being problems than people with higher incomes in all countries.

Why Marmot labeled this "the status syndrome" is a mystery, because his analysis clearly shows that varying levels of control and sense of control are the root causes of disparate health outcomes. At several points he lays this out quite clearly:

> People who reported less control over their lives had worse health. Furthermore, the greater the degree of inequality of material deprivation and of income, the worse the health. We found that the link between income inequality and poor health was low control. The study suggested a causal chain: the greater the degree of inequality, the less control people had over their lives; the less control, the worse their health.[22]

But Marmot loses this focus on control and thus the causal connection between income and control because, as is quite common, he sees status—which is the way others rank you—as precisely synonymous with income levels. This gives equal weight to middle-class ways of ranking "prestigious occupations," possessions, and ways of speaking as it does to income and wealth, thereby missing the uniquely powerful effects of money, its sufficiency or insufficiency, in a society organized around free wage labor.[23] Wilkinson and Pickett, in their most recent work, then further obscure the relationship between insufficient income and low control by seeing status anxiety and social evaluative threat as the central problems of extremely unequal societies such as the United States and the United Kingdom.[24]

These are big errors for such sophisticated social scientists to make. Since they are British, it is possible that they tacitly assume a more singular and rigid class system in Britain than exists in the United States, which never had a true aristocracy and has always had a stronger rhetorical and a sometimes genuine belief in classlessness. But another explanation is more likely. As I've demonstrated in earlier chapters, middle-class professionals are prone to assuming that there is but one culture and thus but one status system that tracks "more money, bigger houses, a more prestigious job, more status in the eyes of others, or simply a higher-class way of speaking." As a result, they grossly underestimate the importance of money in attaining both a sense of control and actual control and thus good mental and physical health.

In Marmot's list of status characteristics above, for example, there is no room for "status in the eyes of others" to vary by social class—that is, by whose eyes are doing the looking. Likewise, there is no room for alternative views of what constitutes a "prestigious job," as, for example, when many skilled trades workers rank themselves above engineers and top management.[25] Nor is there room for more than one kind of judgment about "a higher-class way of speaking" especially in the United States, where perfect diction can draw contempt from even elite middle-class professionals. Rather, Marmot assumes a uniform status system based on the amount of money you have or earn. Status and prestige simply follow from income and wealth. This *is* one common way of thinking in the professional middle class, especially in the United States, but as Michele Lamont has demonstrated, it is not the only status schema even within the middle class, parts of which use aesthetic or, like the working class, moral criteria for ranking people.[26]

The larger and more important point is that before money can reflect status, it is simply money, with many other powers that are clearly more important than how middle-class people rank each other. For wage workers, hardly anything is more important than the size of that wage. If it is insufficient, that insufficiency will affect all aspects of their lives, just as it will if their wage includes a healthy chunk of discretionary income. In a capitalist society money is, as Marmot himself says at one point, a means to increasing one's capabilities, to gaining and maintaining control in some part of your life, a means for having some freedom, a capacity for what you will.[27]

The focus of Marmot as well as Wilkinson and Pickett drifts from the more prosaic lack of money and therefore of control among large sections of the working class to the more perplexing phenomenon that though the top US income tiers have higher incomes than the top tiers in more equal countries, they have substantially worse health and well-being outcomes. Besides a wide range of physical ailments, one particularly striking difference is that one of four people in the United States are mentally ill, while only one of ten are in more equal countries such as Germany and Japan.[28] To explain these phenomena among the top income tiers, it makes sense to look at social psychology and national zeitgeists, as Wilkinson and Pickett do. But this does not mean that those explanations will apply to lower economic tiers, especially to an American working class that is experiencing a debilitating decline in working conditions and living standards. Status anxiety and social evaluative threat are unlikely to account for increasing death rates and decreasing longevity in the United States, especially among adults with no more than high school educations.[29] Lack of money and thus of control may not fully account for declining longevity either, but they are undoubtedly necessary and contributing conditions for a whole range of maladies among lower income groups. Anne Case and Angus Deaton argue that inadequate wages are the foundational causes of the dramatic increase in what they call "deaths of despair"—suicides, drug overdoses, and alcohol-related liver diseases.[30]

The connection between money and control, as obvious as it is, is profoundly important. It is especially important for working classes not only because they usually have less of both but also because of their tendency to view their work as just a job that trades away a large part of life to necessity with the hope of having a measure of freedom and autonomy in the other parts. If there is not enough money and control in those other parts, they have lost their proletarian wager and are in danger of sinking into a spiral of decline. Opportunities to gain informal control at work are nearly as important in working-class life, but a decent enough wage from a secure job can go a long way in compensating for even the most difficult, dirty, tedious, and dangerous jobs.

People with careers mix work and life differently, seeking more formal control at work. And for us degrees of control at work do confer status among other professionals, and that status often enhances our power and control. As a result, we are more subject to social evaluative threat and status anxiety in all parts of our lives in ways that are much less likely in working-class life. Enhanced status, almost always related to our careers, often gains us middle-class professionals more power and control, but it works differently in a different status system. Being thought of as a good worker—meaning reliably adequate and dependable, not necessarily talented, in a morally evaluative status system—does usually lighten supervision and thus increase a worker's daily control. But the ranking system is different, and it is nowhere near as important as money, the wages and benefits that establish some security and control outside the workplace.

Marmot's study was pathbreaking because he showed the concrete link between degrees of control and both physical and psychological health. But he's wrong to think that it isn't absolute amounts of money and control that are determinative but rather that poor health and well-being are generated mostly by "feeling lesser." For working-class people, the presence or absence of a truly living wage, steady work, and ample free time each week, each year, and each work life are far more important than being treated with respect by people who think they are better. There are built-in defenses against middle-class disrespect within working-class culture, and the social experience of the Glorious Thirty shows that when real income is increasing and work time is decreasing, an increasing sense of control both strengthens these defenses and makes them less important because respect, including self-respect, tends to follow from more money and control.

It is true that having "status in the eyes of others" increases one's control among the professional classes, but that does not make it nearly as important in working-class life as money and time, discretionary income and free time for what you will. The very act of ceding control concedes that others have higher status in their own and others' eyes, and, more importantly, more power as well. Ceding control involves formal deference that does not frontally challenge that status, power, and authority but instead seeks to carve out autonomous spaces where you can avoid or deflect their control. It allows your betters to go on thinking they're better but resists internalizing that belief yourself. That resistance is not always successful, but there are strong cultural nudges and support to resist internalizing that feeling of being lesser.

The strategy of ceding control to gain control undoubtedly worked better for the working-class generations formed in and around the Glorious Thirty. Barbara Jensen's Auntie Lu is probably representative of those times more than of our own, but the following passage illustrates the simultaneous strength and casualness of the attitude:

> BARB: Would you call yourself middle class or working class?
> LU: Probably working class. I guess I'd rather be there. I mean, you know, middle class, some of them are pretty hoity-toity, I guess.
> BARB: Snotty, kinda?
> LU: Well, I don't think a lot of people mean to be, but I think they, they like to kinda feel they are *above*. A lot of people—I know people who really aren't above but they think they are. And I just like to slide them people by.[31]

Some working-class people cannot "slide them people by" because they accept the middle-class status system and, as a result, live within the shame of their inferior status in that system. More importantly, most working-class people who do not accept that status system have at one time or another nevertheless experienced the shame of "hidden injuries of class" even if only momentarily and uncharacteristically, as my take-no-shit-from-nobody father did in confronting a college dean. But if I'm right that ceding control to gain control is a core strategy within working-class life, then it's important to understand how that culture can look more cautiously conservative than it is. Or rather, it may be that within its cautious conservatism, there is more potential for agency, both individual and collective, than may seem logical. In fact, the historical record suggests that though ceding control is initially preservative and conservative, it can and often has turned toward collective action both when losing control, especially suddenly, and on the evidence of the Glorious Thirty, when experiencing steady gains in control.

More money and more free time from their wage labor are the essential elements of working-class control and thus of enhancing their freedom and autonomy and thereby their health. Overcoming alienation at work in the young Karl Marx's sense, however desirable in itself, is much less feasible and much less important as modern economies have developed. Working conditions can be and have been improved, even dramatically, without in any way addressing what Marx saw as the estrangement of the worker who "is at home when he is not working and when he is working he is not at home."[32] Rather, working-class men and women have embraced their fate as wage workers and in doing so have found patches of freedom, zones of autonomy, usually individually or in families or other small groups, but every once in a while in large and disciplined collective action.

The working class today is as varied as ever, but in the aggregate it has been losing and continues to lose control as real wages stagnate or decline, as work becomes less regular and steady, as work weeks provide either too many hours or too few, and as pensions for younger workers are making retirement impossible again. Giving a shit about status merely distracts from understanding that extreme inequality is about money, not prestige or social evaluative threat, or how we look "in the eyes of others." Things are simpler than that. We know how to increase real wages and free time because we've done it before. As the wealthiest country the world has ever known, we have the wherewithal today to greatly increase working-class money and control while at the same time reducing the high-stakes, stressful status anxiety now so widespread among younger people aspiring to be or remain in the professional middle class.[33] Falling from the middle class might not be so fearful if nonprofessional workers had much more control, more money, and time for what you will.

Working for a Living

A spicy tuna roll is a wrestling maneuver that I thought would be a perfect analogy for ceding control to gain control. The move involves giving up one leg to your opponent with the intention of turning it into a takedown and pin. Once your opponent grabs the leg you have offered, a quick grab of the interior of the opponent's thigh turns his grip on your leg into an aid to putting him on his back. But when I asked my grandson Max, a former high school wrestler, about it, he explained that a spicy tuna roll is an aggressive move, "a pin move that is high risk/high reward." If you miss your grab of the opponent's thigh, you are very likely to end up on your own back.

Ceding control to gain control is nothing like a spicy tuna roll, because the former involves a genuine recognition of your subordination, a real giving up of control that you would sooner not give up. It is a resigned recognition of necessity, not an aggressive move that slyly hopes to reverse the order of things, but rather a sad reconciliation with reality: you have to work for a living. Working-class parents are not usually explicit in teaching the part about gaining control once you've given up control. Instead, they typically counsel obedience and deference so their children will be capable of working hard and obeying the rules no matter how bad the work or unfair the rules. But working-class parents also allow considerable autonomy in other parts of daily life in growing up, thus cultivating the lived relationship between ceding control here to gain it elsewhere.[34] School therefore often becomes practice in building character, practice in "taking it"—doing something you don't want to do so at the end of the day you can be free to do what you do want to do. This is external ceding of control. In going to work, it is a simple trade of their time for my own time, the character of which is highly dependent on the adequacy of the wage. On the other hand, once at work, workplace chiseling, like other strategies of deference, is an interior form of regaining control, taking back some of what you've given away in trading your time for a wage. This too is often learned at school, as Paul Willis explained how the lads' seemingly rebellious high jinks were actually a part of "learning to labor."[35]

Embracing the necessity of wage work in shaping so much of your life, like all strategies of deference, undoubtedly involves working people "participating in their own subordination."[36] But it's hard to see how most people have any alternative, and it's crucial to see that the mere acceptance of that subordination is not the end of life and the beginning of survival. It's still life, still a struggle but on a different terrain, one where the severe disadvantages you face can often be managed with a widely available working-class grit and on-the-ground ingenuity. Given good times and a little personal luck, life can even flourish, at least for a while, like those backyards on Ohio Street safe from the dirt and chaos of the street. And even when not flourishing, there are ways to have moments of enjoyment, fellowships of richly different balances of tension and support, that can keep you going. This is a drama of working-class life—how bad will it be, and will I be able to take it, not for a day or two but day after singular day despite its potential to grind you down over time?

Most middle-class professionals also accept certain levels and kinds of subordination and trade-offs of control, but the process of professionalization (being recognized as "professional") tends to spell out these trade-offs and thereby formalize areas of professional autonomy. Labor unions can do some of that for working-class jobs and also for many professional ones, but most working-class people with "just a job" generally have to win autonomy on the ground day after day and with a little help from their friends.

TAKING IT AND LIVING IN THE MOMENTS

It ain't about how hard you hit. It's about how hard you can get hit and keep moving forward; how much you can take and keep moving forward.

Rocky Balboa in *Rocky I*

Grandma Ruby would never talk about the past. . . . For decades she endured and suffered wrongs without weakening.

LaToya Ruby Frazier, *The Notion of Family*

Just after the 1959 steel strike—the largest strike in US history, with five hundred thousand workers off their jobs for 116 days, including my father and all my uncles—political sociologist Seymour Martin Lipset published his classic text *Political Man*, wherein he repeated claims that working-class people lacked the capacity for delayed gratification. When I first read the book sometime in the 1960s, I took it personal. Lipset was what was called a "liberal" in those days, actually a prounion social democrat part of whose point in the book was to show how valuably important union leaders were given the dangerous authoritarian tendencies of their rank-and-file members. He painted a bleak portrait of workers as "likely to have been exposed to punishment, lack of love, and a general atmosphere of tension and aggression since early childhood—all experiences which tend to produce deep-rooted hostilities expressed by ethnic prejudice, political authoritarianism, and chiliastic transvaluational religion." Working-class people, according to Lipset, were incapable of complex thinking because they had a "limited time perspective," which led to their difficulty with delaying gratification. "From early childhood, he [the worker] has sought immediate gratifications, rather than engaged in activities which might have long-term rewards."[1]

The steel strike was a refutation of Lipset's thesis. The Steelworkers union had no strike fund in those days, and while they had a strikers' assistance program that could help with individual emergencies, the vast majority of those half million workers had to make do based on whatever savings they had, doing odd jobs, and help from any relatives who had jobs outside the industry. After 116 days they were forced back to work by a government injunction, but according to polls by the union, the companies, and the press, the overwhelming majority would have chosen to resume the strike if the Republican Dwight Eisenhower administration had not leaned on the steel companies to settle on terms highly favorable to the steelworkers.[2] Now that's a bit of delayed gratification it's hard to imagine half a million middle-class professionals of all races and ethnicities across the country ever achieving. And it took complex thinking, a keen understanding of the industry and of the union contract, to accomplish this feat. The strike was not about wages or benefits but instead was about work rules that limited management's ability to rule the workplaces they owned and thought they should control absolutely.

So, are Lipset and all the supporting research that social scientists have done before him and since just full of shit? Well, not quite full. There is some truth in their observations, but that truth is lost within a middle-class perspective that doesn't know it's a perspective.

There *are* loveless families in the working class (as in the middle class), and the stresses of miserable work and poverty can drain whatever love there might once have been. But Lipset, like scores of middle-class researchers before and since, mistakes this part for the whole, thereby missing not only the complex variability within working-class life but also the strengths of a culture that routinely deals with the powerful stresses of bad work and material insufficiency.

The working-class way of delaying gratification is different from the middle-class one. Working-class people are actually champions of not just delaying but also renouncing gratification in large parts of their lives, though they're also good at finding and creating rewards for themselves both within that renunciation and around its edges. The cultural pressure within working-class life to steel yourself so you can "take it" is foundational, I think, in both masculine and feminine forms. To my middle-class eyes there is an enormous downside to their taking-it culture, as in the past several decades most have shown themselves all too good at taking the downscaling of their lives, but that is why it might be important to remember how taking it works in better times and better circumstances when people of all sorts have better prospects—indeed, when there are prospects.

It is hard for middle-class professionals—even, maybe especially, social scientists who are trying to be value free—to understand or even see a working-class taking-it culture and how it relates to a different way of being in time. So, some of what I see as an egregious error is pretty normal in the way of things, merely an innocent mistake we humans are prey to. But this mistake, like some others, often serves a darker purpose of simply affirming our ways as superior and therefore justified in dominating others'.

Marshmallows and Delaying Gratification

The capacity to delay gratification is undoubtedly a good thing, but there's more than one way to do it, and it's valuable for more than one kind of purpose. The working-class way that I call "taking it" is similar to Michele Lamont's concept of "the disciplined self" as engaged in a daily "struggle to 'make it through' and keep the world together in the face of economic uncertainty, physical dangers, and the general unpredictability of life."[3] But making it through requires constant vigilance, what the military calls "readiness," and the ability and willingness to endure not just uncertainty but also certain heartache, pain, tedium, and other sufferings that are seen as inevitable parts of life.

Though systematic studies of delayed gratification aspire to be scientific, they do not recognize taking it as a way of delaying gratification, because these studies are substantially conscribed within professional middle-class assumptions and expectations that can see only one way of doing it.

Shortly after Lipset was writing, Stanford psychologist Walter Mischel began his famous marshmallow study that, when completed, purported to show that greater self-control exhibited by preschool children resulted in greater "cognitive and academic competence and ability to cope with frustration and stress in adolescence."[4] The marshmallow test gave four-year-olds a marshmallow and told them they would get another one if they did not eat the first one within fifteen minutes. Those who lasted eleven minutes, for example, would become more competent teenagers and therefore were more likely to be successful adults than those who lasted just five minutes. Mischel's study made no effort to differentiate by social class (his preschoolers were all middle class, drawn largely from Stanford faculty), but his study appeared within a public discourse that Lipset and others had prefigured to believe that a deficient ability to delay gratification was an important cause for working-class people being "unsuccessful." And this idea has carried into the present around the concept of working-class "cultural deprivation."[5] More recent study challenging the predictive value of the marshmallow test does differentiate by social economic status (SES) by using the simple measure of whether the child's mother had a college degree. This study found only a small difference by SES (with "the lower SES" kids having slightly smaller average wait times), a difference likely to be accounted for by other SES-related factors besides delayed gratification ability.[6] Thus, after decades of assuming otherwise, today there is no solid evidence that working-class children are significantly worse at delaying gratification than middle-class children.

It is actually somewhat comical to read social scientists explaining the elaborate procedures they devise to avoid any bias as they decide when and how to tempt kids with marshmallows—especially when one of their key measures for teenage competence is SAT scores, to which Mischel says "our culture" assigns extraordinary value and importance. The "our culture" here is decidedly middle class and professional, where many parents and teens as well as schools are obsessive about test scores, versus working-class parents and teens who often see these tests as fruitless pains in the ass and, in earlier times when Mischel started his study, most working-class children would not have taken either the SAT or ACT. The "adolescent coping questionnaire" Mischel had parents answer is full of value-loaded ideological questions about goal setting and pursuing, planning and self-control. One question does ask "How skilled is your son or daughter at maintaining friendships and getting along with peers?" But the answers to that question are not reported in the results—either because the researchers do not care about successful relationships as much as they do SAT scores or because a deficiency in accumulating marshmallows has no effect on achieving good interpersonal relations later in life.[7]

If you sift through these professionalist biases, however, you can see a certain logic to the assumption that insufficiency in money and in steady work might logically undermine one's desire to set goals and develop plans for meeting those goals. Sociologist Jessi Streib traces this logic in her analysis of mixed-class couples who have different attitudes toward goal setting and planning:

> Those born into blue-collar families often lived with economic insecurity and in families that possessed little authority. Needing to quickly and flexibly respond to unforeseeable events and others' orders, they likely learned that going with the flow and making decisions spontaneously best allowed them to adapt to events outside their control. . . . In contrast, respondents born to white-collar professional parents grew up with fewer unforeseeable events, a more secure family safety net, and in families that possessed more authority. Their stability allowed them to organize and plan, their surplus resources offered them more choices, and their authority allowed them more freedom from others' demands upon their resources.[8]

Streib presents these different "class sensibilities" as deriving directly from the experience of substantial versus little control in the daily lives of families. That makes sense to me, but there is also a culture within the working class that encourages "going with the flow" by first "taking it" and then developing your ability to "quickly and flexibly respond to unforeseeable events" over which you can have little control. Cultivating your own and your children's capacity for taking it is an attitude and a mental (and even spiritual) skill that is a necessary condition for gaining some autonomy and control in those situations where you have ceded control because you either have to or choose to. This requires a deep commitment to delaying gratification—to surrendering to a necessity that involves, or most likely involves, being tired and miserable a large portion of most days. Logically, you can see how a taking-it culture undermines long-term planning and overly ambitious goals. In fact, that is often an important part of the purpose for cultivating a capacity for taking it: a counsel to take one day at a time and within that day to stay focused on the immediate, whether that is a work task, a family duty, or a moment of creative or passive enjoyment. Delaying gratification is both a daily effort and a renunciation of whole areas of gratification—having interesting work, a really good income, and high status in the eyes of bosses and professors. You may still strive for those things, especially interesting work and a good income, but you have to be willing and learn how to live without them.

The "going with the flow" metaphor is appropriate here, but to middle-class professional minds the phrase can conjure images of passivity, conformity, and even learned helplessness, and all those things can follow from a taking-it culture. But it can also be an effective way of living a life and of being in time. Working-class going with the flow envisions life as a river rather than a highway, and that has consequences for how you delay gratification in living a life.

Life as a river takes you wherever it's going independent of your will—lazily into the Gulf of Mexico or disastrously over Niagara Falls. The best you can do is keep the boat in good order, take care of yourself and others with you in the boat, and be constantly alert for the next rapids, all the while depending on those others doing their jobs, as you do yours, and fully enjoying their company during those calm spots that come along from time to time. Nobody can control the boat or stop it from capsizing by themselves, but by counting on each other you can hold it together and find out where the river is taking you. I fancy that pure middle-class professionals, those without any hybridity, see life as a highway where you have well-developed maps, can choose to go wherever you desire, and can stop for the night whenever and wherever you want. Though it is probably better to be on life's highway in the company of others, that is not a necessity, and to be a complete human being you should be capable of going it alone. You can make mistakes or take the wrong road, but basically you are the master of your fate. Of these two visions, surely the river is the more realistic, the more true to real life, but thinking that you're fully determining your own direction on life's highway can be more motivating and productive, even if illusory. These visions fit different circumstances, however, that are shaped by the necessities and possibilities of pursuing a career or just finding a job.

As an old man now, I know life is more like a river, but I do not regret the time and effort I spent making a concerted effort to create a new and better self and to be master of my fate on life's highway. I appreciate the control-seeking, can-do spirit of professionalism. We're the ones who think to build dams and put up warning signs on the Niagara River to get out before the current takes you away. An achievement culture is, as you'd expect, way better at achieving things. But no real world can work without a being-and-belonging culture that narrows its vision to who and what is immediately before you, to doing your job and counting on others to do theirs, a culture that encourages you to simply be your own true self among others you know well. Envisioning life as a river allows and encourages you to develop all kinds of coping skills in dealing with situations a large part of which are out of your control, taking-it skills that build resilience and grit not just as passive endurance but also as savvy ingenuity in avoiding the worst. Life on the river requires delaying a lot of gratification a lot of the time.

I first learned about the middle-class version of delayed gratification when I was praised for doing it by deans and professors *because* I was going to college! The idea was that I was preparing myself for some future reward, whether a career or a deeper appreciation of the human condition, and while I saw that part, it seemed to me ridiculous that I was delaying much gratification. Most of my friends from high school either got jobs when they graduated or went into the armed forces, beginning with boot camp; I get that they had more income than I did and thus they could start adult lives earlier than I did, but what they did at work didn't seem that gratifying to me, especially if the work was dangerous. My first try at college included some working hard at my studies, but mostly it was a lark of adolescence extension with lots of partying and hanging out. In my second try I became a quasi-nerd who fully enjoyed reading, learning, and writing, and I spent many years doing that even though I was usually working too. That didn't seem like delaying gratification either. What mainstream middle-class culture calls "delayed gratification" has almost nothing to do with not being gratified. Rather, it is about encouraging ambitious aspirations, setting goals, and developing and executing plans to achieve those goals—including learning from your mistakes and a pinch of not being afraid to fail. This is definitely a worthwhile culture. But it works best in circumstances that are pretty favorable for achieving goals while providing a good deal of gratification too. It's not so much about resisting eating a marshmallow as it is about having a lot of marshmallows to begin with.[9]

Taking It

Taking it is an important part of working-class character, though not as important as carrying your own weight and being a positive part of the various groups to which you belong. Taking it is a necessary, not sufficient, condition for developing good character. As such, taking it may look like simply a defensive move, simply a will to endure, but it is more than that. It is a foundation on which the rest of life can be organized, lived, and potentially enjoyed.

Though persistence and endurance are ancient, taking it first appears with free wage labor, mostly in the nineteenth century, when artisans and peasants were being transformed into industrial workers. As Joshua Freeman has so poignantly demonstrated, the transition from precapitalist to capitalist societies always involved a bitter process of breaking the previous work habits of preindustrial workers and forcing time discipline and consistency of work effort across the day. Organizing work around wages for hours even in command economies such as the early Soviet Union and the People's Republic of China required a similar breaking of not only old habits but also wills to autonomy. "Soviet supporters of scientific management . . . saw in Russian culture, especially among peasants and former peasants who had entered industry, an inability to work hard at a steady pace, instead alternating spurts of intense labor with periods of little if any work (the same complaint early English and American factory owners had about their workers)."[10] Factory workers everywhere fought back against this process but could not remain factory workers, which usually meant they could not earn a living, unless they submitted to the will of their paymaster. This moment of submission, repeated millions of times up to today as factory work shaped all modern work in one country after another, is a moment of bitter resignation to ceding control over your life to others, shaping yourself to please them enough that they will tolerate you. But once that submission occurs, in country after country workers begin to organize around increasing their wages, reducing their hours, and improving their conditions at work.[11] The struggle for the formation of labor unions and working-class political parties to enforce better wages, hours, and conditions is premised on that bitter submission. Taking it is not just taking it. Ceding control is what allows you to gain and regain control elsewhere and in different ways. But first you have to be able to take whatever conditions those to whom you've ceded control impose on you.

The submission to and habit of taking it at work gets transferred to other aspects of life. Truck driver/scholar Anne Balay describes the process beginning in childhood:

> Working-class culture tends to place a high value on persistence. History has trained poor, minority, and blue-collar groups to "put up with things they don't like" . . . , and they're good at it; persistence in the face of adversity becomes a useful tool, a point of pride, and a source of honor. My mother and grandmother often told me that . . . "Nobody asked you what you wanted" or "Life isn't fair." Though these comments sound

harsh, especially to middle-class ears, they were a crucial part of class training. My family needed me to learn that the world does not care what people like us want or cater to our needs; our best option is to learn that, and learn to live with it. . . . [But] making a virtue of persistence, and taking pride in your ability to endure hard stuff, is fully compatible with advocating an end to, or diminution of, the hard stuff.[12]

Ceding control, if it is to be a beginning and not just an ending, requires a deep lifelong commitment to taking it while at the same time maneuvering and sometimes fighting to make the "it" easier to take.

Working-class persistence is not the same as the middle-class kind, which Angela Duckworth calls "stamina for long-term goals." Duckworth and her colleagues find an "optimistic explanatory style" (taking failures in stride), a "growth mindset," and an "achievement motivation" as essential to individuals achieving persistence or grit. Taking it is almost the opposite of this, as Duckworth explains: "Grit, however, is distinguished from the general tendency to be reliable, self-controlled, orderly, and industrious, with its emphasis on long-term stamina rather than short-term intensity."[13] Working-class grit is that reliable industriousness taking it one day at a time, building a character and reputation as what the British call "grafters" and Americans call "grinders"—both of which refer to hard workers, where "hard" refers to both the difficulty of the work and the reliable competence and dedication the worker brings to that work.[14] Contrary to Duckworth, taking it requires plenty of long-term stamina as well as short-term intensity, but grafting or grinding is not in the service of long-term goals, personal growth, or achievements. It is the price to pay for the rest of your life, and if there is a long-term goal, it is first to avoid having your paid labor take over the rest of your life and then to make your paid labor easier to take by gradually improving conditions at the same time as you maneuver around and within them to regain bits of control.

Taking it is the working-class form of delayed gratification. It does not have the long time horizon of the middle-class kind but instead has daily, weekly, and annual cycles of delay and gratification. Taking it in working-class life comes in two primary forms. Usually it is seen as a necessary condition for the freer, easier, more pleasurable moments of life—and also for the creative purposeful activities in one's church, union, or other social or civic engagement. It's the necessity that is expected to cycle with freedom and autonomy. On the other hand, when living is hard, too hard for too long, taking it can become all there is of life—not a temporary delay prior to gratification but rather a will to continue without gratification. Often this form is a resigned but steady numbness that allows a modest sense of accomplishment simply by carrying on and doing the best you can for those with whom you belong. Across most working-class lives there is traffic back and forth between simply taking it and taking it as a necessary condition for something better. There are also looming in the background of most working-class lives people who can't or don't take it, people resorting to petty crime or faithlessness or succumbing to alcohol or drugs.

A strong taking-it culture often encourages a certain self-righteousness toward others who are seen as not taking it. Jennifer Silva is the latest ethnographer to find this attitude widespread and often intense, especially among people who are themselves struggling to take it while living in difficult circumstances. "Stories of triumphing over pain anchor their identities [and] draw stark moral boundaries between the deserving and undeserving."[15] In a taking-it culture, being in the presence of relatives and neighbors who are not taking it, or seem not to be taking it, can undermine your own morale if you are on the edge of not taking it yourself. Conversely, pointing to those who cannot or are not taking it can be a source of honor and pride by contrasting your own rectitude with theirs. While these attitudes may sit side by side in a person, the fear of being undermined by proximity is more likely among the hard-living working class. Self-righteousness, on the other hand, is more common among those for whom life is more settled and taking-it has become a routine necessary condition for the good things in one's life.

Taking it has obvious downsides. Within a masculinist industrial culture it was often about "enduring filth, brutality, and risk-taking at work, and those who deviated and objected were pilloried and outcast as 'soft.'" As Arthur McIvor has pointed out, "At its extreme, masculine identities at work endangered lives, sapped energy and undermined health."[16] The Japanese version of taking it is *ganbaru*, meaning "working with perseverance," "toughing it out," or, more poetically, "enduring the seemingly unbearable with patience and dignity."[17] It isn't hard to see how this attitude, this cultural pressure, can serve the interests of the boss and of capitalist economic relations generally. Likewise, as Michael Ignatieff has observed about the recovery of victims of the Fukushima tsunami and nuclear disaster, when outsiders marvel at others' grit or resilience, it "can become an exercise in moral cruelty," a turning away with self-satisfaction from your duty to help.[18]

These downsides cannot be denied, but given the job structure present and future with its huge majority of just jobs rather than careers, what is the alternative? Even if you think that socialist revolution is a real possibility for starting the world anew, what are people supposed to do while they're preparing for that? First, they have to take it to stay alive, and doing that with patience and dignity is not a given. You have to struggle with both yourself and others to achieve it with consistency in a way that can open up other possibilities. The Spanish word for "taking it" is *aguantar*, which translates as "to bear" or "to put up with," a quality

Mexican and Mexican American farmworkers saw as essential both for doing the work and for leadership in the fields and in their union.[19] To have agency to change your circumstances, individually or collectively, you first have to be able to put up with the circumstances you need to change.

Mainstream professionalism sees education, especially higher education, as the one and only alternative, and in that view nobody should simply give up and take it rather than stay in school as long as they can. Education is vital in a lot of different ways, not just as job preparation, but it is not an alternative to taking it. If everybody had a college education today, two-thirds of them would still have to take it with just jobs.[20] Besides, a whole lot of people hate school, even if they can take it, and others are just no good at it. There are plenty of jobs those people can do; the jobs just need to pay better. If you can show up and work hard at one of the tens of millions of jobs that needs done, you should be able to earn a decent living while pursuing noncertified versions of lifelong learning.

But, and this is my main point, there *are* alternatives within a taking-it culture, built-in alternatives. Taking it by itself is mere survival, but as a necessary condition it not only helps working-class people get by day by day but also encourages a stronger focus on wages, hours, and conditions. This enhanced focus is evidenced by the histories of most capitalist (and communist) countries in the last two centuries but especially in the United States. Andrew Arnold, for example, in his study of the complex relationships between coal miners, coal companies, railroads, and local small business owners in America's late nineteenth-century Gilded Age shows how the miners developed an "adaptive culture," one that allowed for both crafty planning and spontaneous, even contradictory, adjustments depending on circumstances. Arnold shows taking it as "the ways that lower-level actors came to acknowledge the power of those above them even while they maneuvered to resist it" and "the ways in which people ad-libbed, fudged, and otherwise squirmed their way through . . . , and through that process created cultures and institutions that rarely ran as originally intended."[21]

Given the job structure, the working-class strategy of ceding control to gain control needs steady, consistent taking it in order to work. The working-class sense of giving away a big part of your day, your week, your life in order to enjoy your real life is an important alternative to the professional middle-class pursuit of work you love to do and through which you define yourself. And as I suggested in the previous chapter, not expecting the work itself to be pleasant or fulfilling—but instead expecting to simply have to take it—fuels a search for spaces of autonomy and the related workmate sociability that is practically required and (mostly) enjoyable in both getting through the day and improving your conditions.

The Working Class Has Parts, and Taking It Works Differently in Different Parts

Of all the noisome middle-class professional misinterpretations of working-class life, one of the most common is the presumption that the whole of the working class is like the one part you have seen or been made aware of. Often that one part is the most troubled part, and middle-class attention to it is often for generous problem-solving reasons. But just as often the whole conglomerate of nonprofessional workers that constitutes the working class is characterized by its least attractive elements, whether absent fathers, alcohol and drug addicts, or Trump voters.

You can see this in Lipset's cavalier claim that all working-class families were loveless and that the worker had sought immediate gratification "from early childhood." But unfortunately, it is not just dead white guys, like Lipset. Living ones, like sociologist Andrew Cherlin, somehow don't even guess how ridiculous it is to claim that all mid-twentieth-century working-class men were "uncommunicative" and "taciturn," unable to express emotion and thereby develop an "expressive self."[22] Cherlin must not ever have known anybody like my voluble midcentury steelworker father or to have ever been in a working-class tavern where eloquent anger so often coexists with men "crying in their beers."[23] He certainly has not been exposed to Jessi Streib's account of different class feeling rules.[24] But never mind, just think how unlikely and illogical it is to imagine that a group of tens of millions of men would all be the same personality type. Think of how isolated in your own class you would have to be to imagine such a thing and then get it past juried reviewers and editors.

Cherlin has recently updated his profile of working-class men, but now he finds men with a "disciplined self" at midcentury being transformed into today's socially unintegrated men who have a "haphazard self." With his coauthors including Kathryn Edin, Cherlin's study of 107 youngish men in four mostly eastern big US cities definitely locates an insightful category of working-class men—those with middle-class aspirations to be more autonomous, expressive, and generative than their fathers and grandfathers but without the opportunities to have steady work and therefore steady family relationships. The midcentury industrial worker is now envisioned as "honest, hardworking, and sober" in contrast to the current drifting, uncommitted working-class man facing a precarious and shifting labor market today.[25] I find this an insightful analysis of one segment of current working-class men. But it is applicable to only one segment, and its partiality gets lost in the authors' then-versus-now simplicity. Cherlin et al. make a sweeping historical contrast that grossly simplifies working-class men both then and now because the authors take one part then and contrast it with a different part now.

I can attest that there were many working-class men with haphazard selves back in the day as well as some women, and I can also testify that there are plenty with disciplined selves today, though not as many men as women. The working class had parts then, and it has parts now. If we could measure it, we would undoubtedly find smaller proportions of disciplined selves and larger proportions of haphazard ones today, especially among men. And that change in proportions is tragically important, but it doesn't mean the parts have changed entirely or that the culture is being eroded to such a degree that it is now at best what Raymond Williams understood as a residual culture.

Besides important gender, racial/ethnic, regional, and religious differences that shape a wild variety of specific cultures within the American working class, there are important economic and cultural parts to the working class that cut across these more richly various specific cultures.

Economically, the division between *hard living* and *settled living* can be measured, with the hard-living part gloriously diminishing in the years around the Glorious Thirty and the settled-living part diminishing ever since.[26] But the hard-living part never disappeared during the golden age, and the settled-living part has not disappeared today. It is important to see the hard and the settled in strictly economic terms, as being about the material circumstances people face, not the culture with which they face them. If we do that, then hard living can be measured and evaluated with some precision. "Hard living" is not synonymous with "the poor," especially not as measured by the US Census Bureau, whose poverty rates are widely understood today as egregiously parsimonious.[27] Rather, living is hard when a person's or a family's income is inadequate to cover basic costs where those people live. Attempts to establish "family economic self-sufficiency" standards, "hardship thresholds," and "living-wage levels" by location have shown the wide differences between costs of living in cities and small towns in various parts of the country as well as within individual urban areas. Census Bureau poverty rates do not adjust for these differences, providing only one poverty rate for each household size regardless of where those households are. Though insisting on the primary importance of regional differences, the various attempts to determine levels of adequacy have arrived at general society-wide estimates of hard living that are from two to four times above the official poverty rate.[28] In 2005 the Economic Policy Institute found that nearly one-third of households across the country were hard living in these terms, or about half of the working class, and this would undoubtedly be higher today.[29]

As with most binaries, there is an intermediate area with people near the threshold on both sides and a lot of traffic back and forth over working-class life courses. As Michael Zweig has pointed out, using official poverty standards, today "more than half the working class experiences poverty in a ten-year period."[30]

Hard living itself ranges widely from a single mother of two making $20,000 a year or less (and thus officially poor) to a married couple with one child and two low-wage jobs that give them a family income of $45,000 a year in a city that requires $50,000 to avoid hardship. There is a wide range among the settled living as well—from a married couple with two kids and two jobs making $75,000 in a smallish city to a UPS truck driver married to a stay-at-home mom making more than $100,000 (with overtime) or a city bus driver married to a postal worker, also with a combined six-figure income. Both the hard and the settled also contain important variety within them based on how long they've been living hard or settled. In fact, there is such a wide range of incomes, wealth, life chances, and circumstances within working-class life—with grinding inequities by race and gender—that you might wonder if it makes sense to see them as all one class with the same cultural proclivities. But before we address that, let's look at a classic breakdown of the cultural parts of the working class and at the various ways they interact with the economic parts.

Herbert Gans long ago laid out a four-part taxonomy with two majority parts (*action seeking* and *routine seeking*) and two secondary parts (*middle-class seeking* and *the maladapted*).[31] These terms denote different orientations, predispositions, and expectations within working-class life, with Gans classifying his urban villagers by their wants and desires rather than by their incomes and occupations. "The maladapted" in Gans's day referred mostly to alcoholics and otherwise irresponsible workers and/or fathers (almost always men), but today it would include the wide array of drug addicts and even more absent fathers. These were very much a minority in Gans's day, and despite troubling increases, they are still a minority now. In a taking-it culture, the maladapted are often seen as unwilling or unable to take it—to reliably endure bad jobs, tense romantic or family relations or to reliably fulfill duties, especially the tedious and ritualistic ones. Likewise, Gans saw his "middle-class mobiles"—those seeking to better themselves by mimicking middle-class ways—as a decided minority. You might think that middle-class seekers would come mostly from the settled living, and they probably do, but it is not unusual for the strongest middle-class aspirations to be among the poorest and hardest living.[32] Cherlin et al.'s "haphazard selves" today come from this predisposition, whereby middle-class aspirations clash with labor market realities with frustrating results.

Whatever you think of these subsidiary categories, Gans captured something crucial when he found routine seeking as a core working-class cultural predisposition in conflict with another core predisposition toward action seeking. These different predispositions can be seen both between individuals and within individual lives. Some folks are more routine seeking, others more action seeking, but both predispositions are present in most working-class lives and in pretty predictable patterns. Looking back over the century-plus of human experience with industrial work, it is clear that the working-class aspiration for a routine and predictable life of steady work at decent wages is the more fundamental impulse.[33] But once that aspiration is frustrated, action seeking becomes more likely, especially among men, whether in political or other collective action or in actions of relief and despondency, as with alcohol, drugs, gambling, stealing, or other risky but adventurous behaviors. Paradoxically, however, the opposite pattern is also predictable. Once a routine and predictable life is achieved, it becomes common for people to feel caught in a rut and become uncomfortable with the predictable routines that seem to define and prescribe every moment of their lives. This leads to more action seeking, including workplace and political activism, most often in controlled and episodic ways that relieve the routines without abandoning or (intentionally) putting them at risk. Thus, there is a unity of opposites between routine seeking and action seeking in working-class life.

Likewise, there is a common dialectic between the economic categories of hard living and settled living and the cultural ones seeking routine or action. You might think that settled living and routine seeking go together, complementing each other, and sometimes they do. But the settled living often are the ones most likely to seek a little action, including in union work and related politics. Similarly, the hard living are usually the most intensely committed to pursuing routine—steady, predictable circumstances where they could feel they have some control over their lives, could let down their guard, and not have to be taking it seemingly every minute of every day. The settled living frequently take their routines for granted, while the hard living are often desperate to establish some.

The categorical purity I'm arguing for here—economics only and culture only—is of analytic value but may seem to rule out messy exceptions. Tom Gorman, for example, lived in a settled-living family by my income and steady work criteria, but his father was one of those alcoholics who seldom missed work but brought chaos and humiliation into his family several times a week. This undoubtedly, as Gorman recounts, made living unsteady and hard for the growing children in that family.[34] On the other end are families who are officially poor and thus hard living by my criteria but are in fact living settled lives, based on low-wage but steady work plus food stamps and housing subsidies; often these are single mothers who have some help from their extended families, but just as often they are isolated mothers and daughters supporting one another in complex but noneconomic ways. For me, the analytic purity of this set of terms allows and encourages us to think more clearly about how economics and culture interact with and are layered within each other. They can even clarify messy exceptions so long as we remember that the categories are analytic and do not directly reflect every possible kind of social reality.

I grew up in a routine-seeking family among other routine-seeking relatives, friends, and neighbors, a family who went from hard living to settled living as I was growing up among many similar families. There was a certain magic to that. Knowing that tomorrow would be pretty much the same as today, that the weekend was just ahead, and that next year would be much the same and likely a little better lent a certain calm and quiet joy to life. But there was a nervousness among our parents and most other adults, a fear that this steady progress wouldn't last, and as a result we got a lot of counsel about how hard and mean life could be and thus the importance of taking it, steady persistence, and stick-to-itiveness—what today is often called resilience and grit. As it happened, those of us who did not have to take much that was hard and mean in our lives never got as good at it as those who faced a lot, but even for us taking it was always there as an attitude, an expectation that in retrospect I think was pretty valuable. As working conditions and living standards deteriorate, however, taking it becomes very much a double-edged sword—not simply a useful recognition of necessity but also a potentially disabling fatalism and passivity where a taking-it mode is all you've got, the only thing you're good at, and is thus merely the survival of the oppressed. In increasingly precarious circumstances, being praised for your resilience and grit by your family and friends and praising yourself for your ability to take it can be cultural nudges to simply go on taking it and nothing else. On the other hand, how would you go on at all without that supportive self-pride?

Scholars, especially progressive advocates, have often focused on the hard living and especially the hardest of the hard living in a generous effort to figure out how public policy might improve their lives. Two problems arise out of this focus. First, for some reason such scholars, as middle-class professionals, too often gravitate toward what they see as cultural deficiencies—bad attitudes toward school, for example—rather than insufficient money and life control; they find a "culture of poverty" they think is a cause of poverty without trying to understand which of these "deficiencies" might actually be not only disabling but also valuable in hard circumstances.[35] Second, problem-solving scholars tend to ignore the settled-living working class, either forgetting that this part exists or lumping the settled living in with a broad middle class, seeing only similarities in economic circumstances, not the differences in cultural emphases—emphases the settled living most often share with the hard living rather than with middle-class professionals. Taking it is one of these.

Taking it is generally more unambiguously fruitful in settled lives than in hard ones. The efficacy of taking it, the positive role it can play in working-class lives, increases as money and time for what you will increase. In that continuum there is a point at which taking it becomes no longer a double-edged sword but instead is an anchoring part of life that both restricts you and frees you to go ashore and explore, so to speak, to seek a little action and take some calculated risks. Settled living, with its adequacy of money and time, frees you to use and expand your zones of autonomy even while you continue to take it. Settled living also allows for more relaxation, which can rejuvenate you in a way that makes taking it both easier to do and more worthwhile.

Taking it also works differently with women than with men. Until quite recently scholarship has focused on working-class men and their problems, thereby missing important gender differences not so much in culture as in the strength of that culture. Working-class men, it seems to me, have always been better at articulating a taking-it ideology, usually under the banner of "toughness," but women have always been more consistently strong in actually taking it and more creative in working within it. As working people and their culture have been challenged with harder and harder circumstances to take in the past half century, more men have weakened in their ability to take it, while women seem stronger and certainly clearer in their abilities to take it with ingenuity. The focus on fatherless families and unsteady, irresponsible working-class men, often addicted to one substance or another, typically overlooks how mothers and grandmothers have adjusted to this widespread new circumstance.[36]

Though two recent best-selling memoirs of working-class life, *Heartland* and *Hillbilly Elegy*, feature drug- and alcohol-addled single mothers who were truly terrible parents, they are not in any way representative of working-class women today.[37] It is worth noting that in both memoirs grandmothers are rugged champions of taking it, filling in for their daughters. I don't doubt that a larger percentage of working-class women are both practically and morally feckless today than decades ago. Women, like men, succumb to the unceasing daily grind of unsteady low-wage jobs surrounded by deteriorating circumstances, especially in deindustrialized and other woebegone places.[38] But as Allison Pugh found in her study of various responses to increased workplace and social insecurity, there is an especially strong "care work ethic" and sense of familial duty among women of all classes, but especially women of limited means. This care ethic encourages a limiting but strongly disciplined self.[39] Such a duty to nurture and care is not unknown among men, but as Pugh points out, it is optional for them, whereas the cultural pressures on women to care are both ancient and enormous. Working-class women are more likely to wholeheartedly embrace their duty to care, maybe especially single mothers, so many of whom ingeniously and bravely combine mothering with low-wage and median-wage jobs and, with a little help from their friends and families, are proud of their ability to make do with no dependency on male partners.[40] Likewise, though only a slim majority of working-class women are married, nearly all of them are in the paid workforce and are both economically and culturally better equipped than previous generations to avoid "gendered traps of dependency," including domestic violence.[41] Taking it is a strategy of the oppressed, a bitter but wise recognition of necessity. Given centuries of multiple oppressions, it should not be surprising that working-class women are better at it than men. Socially and culturally, working-class women have more permission to resist their multiple oppressions today, even though there are fewer economic opportunities that would allow them to effectively do so. While I don't know how you would measure this, the ingenuity and resilience of both married and unmarried working-class women in raising their children and keeping various kinds of families together is pretty astounding given the unsteadiness of so many working-class men and the ruthless deterioration of economic conditions in recent decades. It is when you look at both women and men in the working class that you can see the continuing strength of a being-and-belonging culture, which in the long run could be a mere residual of better times but in the short run is still vital to people getting by and making do in grindingly insufficient circumstances.

Still, though in the aggregate working-class men are not taking it as well as working-class women, it is important not to miss the large part of working-class men who are good to decent fathers and as strong as ever in taking it with difficult work, adverse circumstances, and complicated personal relationships within families. If 27 percent of American children are living in families without fathers present, then 73 percent are living with fathers, some of them (three million, or 4 percent) only with fathers.[42] Not all of these are working class, but a majority are, and it is amazing how that majority gets ignored in all the concern about "the collapse of the working-class family."[43]

Similarly, recent concern with increasing drug addiction and death rates among middle-aged white men uniformly ignores the vast majority of these men who are neither addicted nor killing themselves.[44] The Case-Deaton study that so alarmingly and valuably called attention to the rise in opioid addiction and what the authors called "deaths of despair"—drug overdoses, suicide, and chronic liver cirrhosis—saw these as indicators of increasing stress being experienced by a non-college-educated working class.[45] Even with this troubling increase only a small fraction of whites without bachelor's degrees are killing or poisoning themselves, but the Case-Deaton study tells us nothing about how most people in that population are dealing with those stresses. Nonetheless, this image of disintegrating men using drugs and alcohol to remove themselves from their lives of despair has become the iconic representation of working-class men, especially black men but more recently also white men. The horrendous rise of drug addiction and deaths of despair reflect circumstances of increased pressure in deteriorating conditions, not a broad characterization of working-class life, especially not in more prosperous places. Many deindustrialized men have, as Angus Deaton has remarked, "lost the narrative of their lives," but many more have simply lost their jobs and any possibility for decent employment in the places where they belong and can simply be themselves, cultural deficiencies and all. Somehow most of them manage to take it.[46]

In the deindustrialized working-class family I know best, there are four drug addicts in the last two generations, while there was only one alcoholic in my generation (all men). This is new and troubling—heart-wrenching, in fact. But for every man battling drug addiction there are three who are not, and as I write three of the addicts are in various phases of recovery, some bravely fighting to turn their lives around with unsteady, low-wage jobs and girlfriends who are also recovering. Today it is harder to take it in all the miserable circumstances so many young and middle-aged working-class men now face, but a taking-it culture is actually more visible and probably stronger as a masculine culture even though actual taking it is weaker and much less steady. The "I can take it" protestations I hear seem much more common now, as men need to rally themselves to take it in more difficult circumstances. Though there was a lot of that back in the day as well, as conditions steadily improved and settled for thirty years back then, it became less necessary for working-class men to talk themselves into and support others in taking it. The strength of a culture may be better measured by its necessity and the degree of difficulty it faces than by a count of the actual behavior that meets the standard. By that way of scoring, a working-class taking-it culture may be stronger and more important today than it was during the Glorious Thirty. Culture is about what you expect of yourself, what you try to live up to, not your actual behavior. As far as I can see, most working-class men still live up to the taking-it standard, and even though compared with back in the day many more men do not, they generally accept the standard even as they fail to meet it.

On the other hand, the tacit taken for granted taking-it culture among working-class women is clearly stronger in affecting behavior. When taking it is a base, a foundation and not simply a numb resignation to endure, it can become a source of strength, freeing you to figure ways to work around or change bad circumstances. A deep commitment to taking it—especially along with a commitment to care for others, most importantly your own children—mobilizes a being-and-belonging culture to effectively resist the spiral of despair that most working-class men and women feel is ready to engulf them if they let go, give up, or give in instead of making do. The fact that today working-class women are as or more likely than men to actively protest and engage in other forms of collective action may augur a strengthening of the being-and-belonging culture in a new form, one that can limit and disable in unfavorable circumstances but also one that can break out in collective action and quickly gain strength seemingly out of nowhere, as it has done in the past when men played dominant roles.[47] In such moments, the willingness and ability to take it is a working-class strength no matter how it is distributed among genders.

Living in the Moments

I'm not sure which is cause and which is consequence, but an orientation to living in the present rather than for an envisioned future clearly correlates with taking it and making do.

In the interpretation that follows I am probably too influenced by living with and loving a woman who has gone from hard living to settled living to professional middle class but has always lived one day at a time. When we were younger her approach to life often frustrated me, as it often seemed to undermine my dreams and aspirations. While not intending to do that, she had a natural skepticism about my (in those days patriarchal) planning for our future. She deferred to my plans and followed my lead, not just accepting it but also actively implementing "our" plans on the ground in a way I could not have, often with a wisecracking realism that shamed my more ambitious flights of fancy. Now I think it is still fair to say that I helped lift her up while she helped pull me down, but where I once resented that, I came to realize that both were equally valuable. In later years I also came to envy a bit her roomier sense of now, not just her practical everyday competence from which I have benefited so much but also the enjoyment she takes in being with and helping other people one situation at a time. I have lived a purpose-driven life, and I'm proud of both the purposes and the drivenness, but if purposefulness expands your vision into a possible future, it also contracts your experience of the present and your responsiveness to those immediately around you. I did no substantial harm and have no regrets, but I have missed a lot of the richness of daily life, the intensity of both its joys and its pains, that she has not.

Living in the present, in one moment after another, is initially a defensive move in working-class life. In Judie's case, growing up hard living was intensified by a mean-drunk father who periodically terrorized the household and for which she always had to be ready. As several sociologists have pointed out, working-class present-orientedness is related to a lack of resources and stability, the lack of a broader sense of control over the trajectory of your life. Marianne Cooper, author of *Cut Adrift: Families in Insecure Times*, for example, makes this observation:

> When people's circumstances are constantly shifting such that they have little control over what happens in their lives, it becomes hard to map

out the future and execute long-range goals. . . . [T]he combination of income instability and income scarcity makes the exercise of long-term planning not only pointless but painful. To cope with this hard reality, people with few resources often rely on an emotional plan, which is *not* to plan very far into the future.[48]

You can see how immediate circumstances based on insufficient money and control make a short time horizon existentially useful and therefore necessary. But even when the insufficiency disappears, as it did in Judie's life, the culture (what Cooper calls "an emotional plan") remains. And in those more positive circumstances, living in the present can become not just a defense against hard living and its instability but also a practically effective and even joyful way to live a life.

So say a long tradition of poets, philosophers, and religions. The Roman poet Horace, for example, advised:

> Be wise! Drink free, and in so short a space
> Do not protracted hopes of life embrace;
> Whilst we are talking, envious time doth slide;
> This day's thine own; the next may be denied.[49]

This Epicurean version of living in the moments contrasts with Buddhism's more spiritual mindfulness that also disdains "our regrets or longings of the past, or our hopes or fears about the future."[50] From the Beats during the Glorious Thirty to now, Buddhism attracts many middle-class young people who want to reject the ladder-climbing future-orientedness of middle-class professionalism.[51] Likewise, Friedrich Nietzsche's godlessness saw "a more vital, assertive life" as requiring "affirmation of every moment, exactly as it is, without wishing that anything was different, and without harbouring peevish resentment against others or against our fate."[52]

Frankly, I abhor all versions of this momentary philosophy. For me, if you're not going somewhere, you're going nowhere. I reference the philosophy to illustrate that middle-class professionalism is not the only effective way to live a life—that there are alternative possibilities and that the working-class roomier sense of now is one of them. I am, however, attracted to the rejection of status seeking and "peevish resentment" that is part and parcel of these philosophies and that I think is the bane of middle-class life, a constant source of anxiety and depression.[53] William Deresiewicz quotes a Harvard dean of admissions to describe what Deresiewicz calls a "midlife crisis that is typical of high achievers":

> It is common to encounter even the most successful students, who have won all the "prizes," stepping back and wondering if it was all worth it. Professionals in their thirties and forties—physicians, lawyers, academics,

business people and others—sometimes give the impression that they are dazed survivors of some bewildering life-long boot camp. Some say they ended up in their profession because of somebody else's expectations. . . . Often they say they missed their youth entirely, never living in the present, always pursuing some ill-defined goal.[54]

Singular dedication to a culture strengthens you within that culture, but you can't have it both ways. If you're all about becoming and achieving, you're going to miss some being and belonging, and if you're all about being and belonging, you're going to miss a lot of becoming and achieving.

Working-class living in the moments is not based in either Epicureanism or Buddhism, of course, let alone Nietzsche. Like ceding control, deference, and taking it, it is first a realistic adjustment to limited and limiting circumstances. But it doesn't need to remain that way. If wages, hours, and conditions steadily and over time dramatically improve, as they did during the Glorious Thirty, new options become available. One is to jump into the professional middle class. Others are Epicurean or semi-Buddhist. But still others involve gradually expanding your time sense to have more space for both planning a different future and reflecting on the past, including both nostalgia and reminiscence. I'm inclined to think that this expansion from the present, what Thomas Pynchon called "temporal bandwidth," is an enrichment of working-class life but not quite in the hierarchical way Pynchon envisioned: "'Temporal bandwidth' is the width of your present, your *now*. . . . The more you dwell in the past and future, the thicker your bandwidth, the more solid your persona. But the narrower your sense of Now, the more tenuous you are."[55] This kind of "the more the better" quantitative certainty may work for poets and scholars, but I know and live among many people with narrow temporal bandwidths who have very solid personas and are not as tenuous as I am. As much as I value a forward-looking sense of history, if anything it's the big thinkers who are (sometimes productively and/or delightfully) more tenuous. There are ways to broaden your sense of future and past without losing too much of that roomier sense of now that Barbara Jensen admires in working-class life. I'm not suggesting some kind of golden mean for temporal bandwidths but rather that there's more than one way to be good and solid. Let a variety of temporal bandwidths bloom!

Mixing Classes

Ceding control and taking it are most often viewed with contempt within the world of middle-class professionals. Even middle-class resilience and grit is about being goal-oriented, not about "enduring the seemingly unbearable with patience and dignity." Some portion of working-class young people will always be open to and even obsessively motivated by our urging to be proactive, to fight back, broaden your horizons, take control of your life, and be somebody. But there is not enough room in our job structure for everybody to be our version of somebody, and the idea that being somebody is the goal of life is both ontologically superficial and socially corrosive.

Still, our proactive sense and the counsel to fight back are positives we middle-class professionals can bring to our free wage labor sisters and brothers. We cannot do that effectively, however, if we are so headstrong in our own culture and its superiority that we can't see the value of theirs: how it works in their lives, the strength and sometimes nobility it takes to live within that culture, and its inner workings and potential strengths in moving forward, in making do and sometimes better than making do.[56]

I was part of a group of Chicago academics from mixed-class backgrounds who, when unions started hiring young organizers in the city in the 2000s, came up with the idea of having career days for activist college students who might want to become professional organizers.[57] For several years, we asked three community organizers and three labor organizers to talk about what their work and lives were like to a gathering of such students. I'm not sure how many students we turned on to organizing as a career, but getting the community and labor organizers together was electric. I don't remember whether we asked them to talk about their class backgrounds, but almost all of them did, and while some were from working-class families, most were not. They "admitted" to growing up in the suburbs as if suburbs were not part of real life, and many of them said that though their initial (and continuing) motivation to become organizers was based in a commitment to social justice, now they loved the kind of people they got to work with, referring to the folks they were trying to help organize. Many said "I didn't know there were people like that," and when pressed, they gave a variety of reasons they admired working-class people. "Straightforward" and "no bullshit" were common, and when one young woman said "honest, I mean really honest, not just in words," there was a lot of affirmative head-shaking. The young organizers and students from working-class backgrounds usually beamed at this recognition, but when one of them said about the middle-class-origin organizers "Well, I didn't know there were people like you until I went to college," that got their affirmative head-shaking too.

These were extraordinary moments of class-cultural recognition and mutual respect, but they can occur naturally when people from different classes mix it up a bit.

WORKING-CLASS REALISM

Don't get above your raising
Stay down to earth with me

Earl Scruggs and Lester Flatt

When I began as a part-time night school instructor in 1975, Roosevelt University's "campus" was in the historic Auditorium Building in Chicago's then-deteriorating South Loop. An Adler-Sullivan architectural masterpiece from 1889, at that time the building was a strange combination of historic grand hotel grandeur in the lobby and the tenth-floor library coexisting with dusty blackboards in scrubby classrooms, where I was advised to bring my own chalk. My first class was on the Wabash side of the building, where the noise from the El required both me and the students to pause midsentence when trains passed by our windows. This was frustrating at first, but nobody complained; instead, we all quickly mastered pausing skills, and by the middle of the semester it was so second nature that we were scarcely aware we were doing it. My only other teaching experience then had been at Northwestern University, and the contrast could not have been more striking with the students there, who with much less to complain about did a lot more of it. It seemed they often thought critical thinking simply involved insightfully bitching about almost everything, from their parents to the Vietnam War to poor lighting in a room. In that first course at Roosevelt one of my most perceptive students ever, Jennifer Artis, picked out a tangential passage from an essay in which Anthony Burgess compared life in postwar Italy and the United States that said something like "A bad day in America is when one thing goes wrong. A good day in Italy is when one thing goes right." Artis argued that while this might be true for some Americans, "we're more like the Italians, I think—pushing through, hanging in, carrying on." Artis was black, and she went out of her way to make clear that her "we" covered everybody in that overcrowded, un-air-conditioned room, whites as well as blacks. Her comment initiated a rich conversation that I remember a lot of to this day. Some thought it—taking it, making do, getting by—was a Chicago thing, some more of a black thing, and others a midwestern attitude, while Artis insisted it was about social class. But everybody agreed that we were more like Italians, with lower expectations that actually made us less unhappy. And then we wondered about whether this was a bad characteristic, accepting too many things as they are, not pushing to improve them. A white woman who was a nurse gave personal testimony: "I push to change things, to make them better, every day, but at the end of the day, you got to make do, to simply get by to tomorrow, when you can start over again. For me, they're not opposites, one supports the other. To me the complainers are not the ones who make things better." A black social worker who seldom spoke in class countered: "I agree with that, but maybe we're just trying to make ourselves feel better." Somebody else said, "And what's wrong with that?" To which the social worker answered, "Because we're all here to improve ourselves, and it sure would help if we had a better room." Everybody laughed, and the conversation ended with that contradiction.

Though undoubtedly stylized in my memory, I remember this class discussion because it was early in my encounters with adult students of different ages and races and because I used that Burgess quote to initiate similar discussions for the next decade or so. Subsequent conversations always turned out differently, with some students admitting they were more like Burgess's Americans and others arguing that taking it and getting by were wholly negative habits. But for most people over the years these discussions ended with both a proud acceptance of their ability and willingness to take it and make do alongside a recognition of the potential disadvantages of such an attitude.

Most of my students back then were settled-living working class with decent jobs and fairly stable lives, people who would often have been seen as middle class, and many thought of themselves that way even though they had working-class jobs. Also, their being in college as working adults meant they were open to some middle-class aspirations. Many thought a college degree could transform their lives by leading to a better higher-paying job. Thus, you could say that in the conversation I recount above, the taking-it attitude was working class, and the will to improve things was more of a middle-class attitude. To some extent that is surely apt, but such a clear distinction misses the strong sense of possibility that resides within working-class realism. The effort to be real and to enforce lower expectations in yourself and others is an attempt to locate real possibilities amid the chimera of middle-class propaganda that you can be whatever you want to be. It is not just a fatalistic passivity or a will to simply adjust yourself to circumstances rather than acting to change those circumstances. It is a cultural injunction to not lose the bird in your hand by pursuing the bird in the bush, a counsel to be patient and alert for those moments when the bird in the bush might wander over near your free hand.

Though no student ever stated it as clearly as Jennifer Artis, she saw Burgess's "American" attitude as disabling—always disabling but especially in difficult circumstances. If you can't take it, you won't be able to change your circumstances or adjust yourself to them. Meanwhile, you'll make yourself and often those around you miserable by expecting everything to work out and go your way, which it won't. Sky-high expectations actually undermine your ability to be effective in living your life, in being a good person, pulling your own weight, and meeting your obligations to the groups to which you belong. Hanging in there, making do, and getting by require intelligence and ingenuity, a thorough understanding of the limits and obstacles within your life, and above all a consistent focus on the real possibilities, often narrow and fleeting, available to you.[1]

Working-Class Realism and Its History

Working-class realism is a culture, not a reality. No claim is being made that working-class people, individually or collectively, have a more true and accurate grasp of reality. Rather, the culture encourages people to be realistic and scorns them when they are thought not to be. To middle-class eyes this is a lowering of expectations, a crushing of aspiration, which itself is a cause of lower levels of accomplishment. My middle-class eyes mostly agree, but my residual working-class ones understand that accomplishment, striving to achieve something outstanding, is not valued in working-class life the way it is in the middle class. Other things are, and those other things—character, integrity, and belonging—are valuable too, arguably more humanly valuable, long-lasting, and sustainable and more widely available if you keep it simple. John Lennon captures the culture from the negative point of view of the rebel: "They hate you if you're clever and they despise a fool."[2] The fool is a person who is not being realistic, and the clever are all those who have both aspiration and the talent to justify that aspiration. This is the dark side of the culture—not a caring warning against foolhardy illusions of grandeur but instead a mean-spirited resentment of those you think see themselves as better than you. The culture can be hard on people who are artistic, like Lennon, or are otherwise different, as numerous gays have recounted.[3] And it can be incredibly ignorant, as when one brother tries to persuade his younger brother to no longer be gay. But in a belonging culture ostracism is almost always an attempt to pull you back in to the culture, to persuade you to be people like us, not some other kind of people. And often, even with some resentment, people think they're doing it for your own good based on a fear that your difference will lead you to a bad end.

Teachers like me tend to resist this culture because we think it discourages people from stretching themselves to become what they could be if they just believed they could. But abhorring the culture and preaching the pursuit of excellence, dreaming big, reaching for the stars, and claiming you can become anything you want to be is unlikely to work except for a handful of talented individuals to whom we pay special attention. Rather, there are resources within working-class realism that can stretch aspiration a bit for everybody without getting out of control. I found it often hard to convince working adults that they could do the next thing, but that's what works—convincing them that there are realistic possibilities they're missing, not general possibility for everyone but instead possibilities specific to them and their situations. The goal is not to convince them to transform themselves (which usually means becoming more like me) but rather to convince them of some specific possibility—you can do *this*, not you can do whatever you put your mind to. This may be different for young people, traditional-aged students with whom I have little experience, but I fear it is not—that unfounded grand expectations can distort and misdirect lives by being too American, in Jennifer Artis's terms.

The low expectations of working-class realism are not superficial, not just bad advice that can be dispensed with by replacing it with good advice and a little inspiration. Rather, it goes deep and is likely rooted in a centuries-long peasant culture of survival. Immigration historian John Bodnar found not only that the culture of European peasants survived being immersed in an urban-industrial proletariat but also that their place within industrial capitalism reinforced that culture. Strategies for survival changed, but "what remained the same was the framework in which this was done—a framework where survival was the preoccupation. This framework was as much an element of working-class status as of peasant traditionalism." For Bodnar, "urban industrial society . . . positively nurtured behavioral patterns such as limited horizons, familial cooperation, fatalism, and anti-materialism which were as functional for proletarians as for peasants."[4] He called special attention to familial cooperation to claim that American workers' famously narrow focus on bread-and-butter economic issues were not "goals in themselves . . . [but] part of a larger cultural system which focused energies on the maintenance of the family unit."[5] And this was just as true of the blacks and other native-born toilers he later studied in the mines and mills of Pennsylvania.[6]

Bodnar was writing about the late nineteenth and early twentieth centuries when standards of living and working conditions were worse, much worse than they are now even after nearly half a century of deterioration and decline. A lot of things have changed pretty dramatically since then, but what he characterized as peasant behavioral patterns are still recognizable even if modified—limited horizons, familial cooperation, fatalism, and antimaterialism.

The well-publicized and scorned "consumerism" of the Glorious Thirty surely undermined antimaterialism, but habits and traditions of religiosity and frugality are still common in the working class even when not needed for survival, which they still often are. So is suspicion of showy expenditure, status measured by belongings, and pleasure-seeking hedonism that is not subordinated to larger social or religious goals. Familial cooperation is certainly not as prominent as it used to be, undermined both by increased social isolation in the hard-living working class and by the influence of middle-class individualism's child-centered family arrangements where the family is expected to serve the individual rather than the other way around.[7] But on a comparative basis, and including both nuclear and extended families and not just the proportion of single-parent families, my guess is that family commitments are still more intense and loyal in the working class.[8] Limited horizons and fatalism are undoubtedly less limited and severe today than back then, but in comparison with middle-class professionalism, horizons are still more constricted and fatalism still has a steady if weakened presence, whereas official middle-class culture disdains any role for fate (or luck) with its exaggerated sense of individual freedom and determination.

The dramatic increases in time and money in working-class life across the twentieth century greatly expanded horizons as, for a while, new possibilities emerged. Likewise, familial cooperation, fatalism, and antimaterialism all weakened. But the "culture of constraint" that Annette Laureau found in late twentieth-century working-class families surely has a through line of continuity from the medieval peasant of all continents to today.[9]

Though my father drove most things in our family, my mother was the philosopher of working-class realism. He virtually forced-marched my sister and me to have ambition, to aspire to better ourselves, but was himself suspicious of ambition, and my mother was the one who sought to reconcile that contradiction for us. Two instances stick out in my memory.

In the seventh grade, that important transitional year when I had to choose between nerdness and ladness, I got my Balboa haircut and learned how to tuck a black T-shirt into my jeans. I thought I looked pretty good and should be more attractive to girls than I seemed to be. I asked Mom, "Am I handsome?" After hesitating a moment she answered, "No, Jackie, you're just sort of plain. You're not bad-looking, but you're not really handsome." This seemed uncharacteristically cruel in that moment, but I also recognized how valuable it was to know that for sure. It helped me situate myself in my world, gently nudging me toward the lads, and helped me avoid the worst practical mistake a person could make:

aspiring to the impossible. Avoiding unrealistic aspirations is not simply about avoiding the inevitable heartbreak of failing to achieve them but more importantly is about staying on track to discovering who and what you actually are and what is actually possible for you in the real world. Sorting that out and achieving the achievable are difficult. You can't afford to get distracted by aiming too high or in the wrong direction.

The other remembrance occurred earlier and is fuzzier, but I remember the quiet intensity of my mother's instruction very well. I was complaining about the Pittsburgh Pirates' very mediocre catcher in the early 1950s, Joe Garagiola, and she told me a story about how he had stuck up for and protected Pirate superstar Ralph Kiner, whom she knew I idolized as a nine-year-old. I don't remember what Garagiola did, but the point was that daily character was as important as how you performed on the field and that not everybody could be a star. A winning team needed players who just did their job without distinction and were reliably loyal to their teammates. There was also something about the humble craft of catching, being there for every pitch at the center of the game but unnoticed unless you made an error.

My mother was literally counseling me not to seek distinction but that if I cultivated daily character and was reliably loyal to my teammates, I might become a good player, a mediocrity like Joe Garagiola, and that should be enough for me. Being on the team and contributing was what I should aspire to, not stardom.

Why I remember this conversation about baseball with my mother more than sixty years later is a mystery to me. For nearly a decade after that I did aspire to become a big league player, not ever a star but just to make it to the bigs. My dad counseled hard work and to always hustle, advice I also took, but he had a better sense of how good you had to be to make it to the majors, and he didn't mind telling me I was probably not going to be that good. My father's approach was to divert my ambition in a more realistic direction, such as going to college and staying out of the mill. My mother, on the other hand, was offering a different set of goals about being good, not great, and common, not outstanding. That little bit about "the humble craft of catching" was about the value and importance of being common, of living well without the need for recognition, and, in fact, how wise it could be to avoid the spotlight and simply do a good job and be a good teammate. As she knew well, commonness and mediocrity, no matter how plentiful they might be, were hard to come by; they took effort, focus, and dedication, and you needed to be going in the right direction to achieve them.

Working-class realism is not just about low expectations, but about different expectations. A being-and-belonging culture tends to fear that aspiration and ambition will not just miss their mark but can also move you away from the things that really matter. An achievement-oriented life can get too complicated on the self-esteem side and not complicated enough on the tangled-relationships side. Working-class realism starts off as a defensive measure in severely limited circumstances, but even as some limits retreat and new possibilities emerge, as they did for me and my family, the attitude remains to affirm the values of keeping it simple to maintain your integrity.

Working-class realism is not without aspiration, but there are two sides to achieving mediocrity, to being and staying common. One is to be true to your real self and to those with whom you belong. It's not getting a big head, not overestimating yourself and what you can be and do, but also not being overcome with ambition that takes you away from where you belong, ambition that can change you inside and turn you into a phony. But the other side is to control your aspiration, to focus your intelligence and ingenuity on negotiating limiting circumstances and always have downscaled aspirations ready when you do take a big chance. Most working classes are from somewhere else, especially the US working class. Immigrants took a big chance in coming here, but so did blacks fleeing the South to find jobs and freedom in the North and rural and small-town folks of every race migrating to cities for work that was often stifling, hard, dangerous, and degrading. English historian Alison Light captured working-class aspiration perfectly when she imagined the country-to-city migration as setting out "to find the place where the streets are paved with gold, or at least paved, or at least where there are jobs paving them."[10] Big aspirations are permissible but only so long as you retain a sly wariness of "expecting too much" and a bemused commitment to remaining "down to earth."

Upward Mobility and the Working Class

A willingness to defer, cede control, and take it are aspects of working-class realism that are often seen by empathetic professionals as encouraging low expectations and thereby undermining, indeed disabling, working-class young people from achieving upward mobility. The whole education reform movement championed by both George W. Bush and Barack Obama saw education as the only path to upward mobility, the key to education as overcoming "the bigotry of low expectations," and high-stakes testing as both the instrument and the measure of improvement. This approach stacked illusion atop illusion, but the foundational one is that moving up income quintiles is the only kind of upward mobility or the only one that matters.[11]

Upward mobility comes in two forms: relative and absolute. *Relative upward mobility* is about children born in one income quintile moving up to a higher quintile as adults. For example, if you are born in the lowest quintile, your chances of earning enough money as an adult to be in the top quintile has been about one in ten, versus about one in three for those born into the top quintile.[12] According to Raj Chetty and his colleagues, the degree of relative upward mobility has not changed much since the mid-twentieth century.[13] The chances of reaching the top income quintile as an adult improve as a person is born to parents in each higher quintile, and there was then and is now considerable upward and downward mobility between income quintiles. Perfect equality of opportunity would mean that at any point in time, 20 percent of all adults in the top income quintile would have been born into each of the five quintiles. As it is, the origins of top earners are 30 percent from the top quintile, 25 percent from the next quintile, 20 percent from the middle quintile, 15 percent from the next, and 10 percent from the bottom.[14] Though there is enough movement here to undermine the notion that the United States is a "hereditary meritocracy," despite the frenzied efforts of so many professional middle-class parents, it shows that opportunity is not nearly equal and is in fact severely limited for the bottom 40 percent.[15]

A few years ago I explained data similar to these to a class of traditional-aged college students, and one from a settled-living working-class background noticed something that disturbed her: "So, this means if I move up, as I want to do, then somebody else has to move down. That's not what I wanted. Can't everybody or most people move up without taking other people's spots?" The answer for relative mobility, of course, is no; every move up requires a move down in a hierarchy of incomes. But there is another kind of upward mobility, one that is not about advancing your position in a hierarchy.

Absolute upward mobility is when someone moves up not in relation to others but simply from where they were before or where children at midlife do not move up income quintiles but nonetheless earn more than their parents did in midlife. This is where you can move up, improve your own and your children's income and conditions, "without taking other people's spots." Whereas relative upward mobility has been basically stable for more than half a century, absolute upward mobility has seen a slow-moving but dramatic decline. Raj Chetty and his colleagues put it succinctly in one comparative statistic: People born in 1940 had a 90 percent chance of having a substantially better real income in midlife than their parents had. People born in 1980, on the other hand, had only a 50 percent chance.[16]

This is a huge difference. It means that for someone like me, born in 1943, you had to screw up numerous times to miss out on the higher real wages that were growing across the economy based on sharing the benefits of productivity growth. Those born in 1980, on the other hand, had to make all the right moves to have a fifty-fifty chance of improving their economic situation, and those born now will have an even smaller margin of error and will most likely have a lower income than their parents did.

It is characteristic that the professional middle-class attempt to reform public education would see upward mobility only in a hierarchy, focusing on a chimeric equality of opportunity while ignoring the growing inequality of condition, of income and of wealth. Equalizing the quality of education, which the reformers never came close to doing, could be helpful in equalizing life chances and conditions but not if at the same time actual incomes and conditions are becoming more unequal. Equality of opportunity requires a rough equality of condition across the board, not just in one subsidiary area such as education.

Absolute is the kind of upward mobility that is most important to the working class. Working-class realism works so much better, both in itself and by expanding horizons and engaging new possibilities, when there is nearly universal absolute upward mobility. You don't have to take anyone's spot to do better across a lifetime and for your children. To restore the kind of absolute upward mobility we had during the Glorious Thirty is going to require moving some money around—that is, redistribution of income and wealth. The restorative nostalgia for the Glorious Thirty's strong unions, productivity sharing, and a steeply progressive tax code are what is essential for moving money at scale from the top few percent to everybody else. Such radical changes are realistic, not utopian, because we've successfully done it before.

I know how to raise expectations. I grew up at a time when our reality outran our low expectations for more than a decade, and eventually we raised our expectations to meet the new realities and then went beyond that. Improve the reality, and expectations will expand.

Chetty et al.'s study of absolute and relative upward mobility was done against the background of our extraordinary increase in the inequality of income and wealth. Several of Chetty's group were responsible for documenting this increase against an onslaught of pseudoscientific happy talk.[17] They were surprised to find that relative upward mobility has been fairly stable, but they warned that because of the dramatic increase in inequality, the "rungs on the ladder [of income distribution] have grown further apart."[18] Though the greatest inequality is between the top 1 percent or the top one-tenth of 1 percent and the rest of us, secondary inequalities are growing as well. We are left with a situation whereby the professional middle class is still thriving or comfortably stagnant, while life in the working class is deteriorating. This division is the source of much working-class resentment, more prominent and dangerous among white men than in the rest of the working class, but present throughout—and directed mostly at the political and communications elite, but not without touching us standard-issue middle-class professionals as well. But it also means that the stress of living with a fear of falling grows among middle-class professionals, if not for ourselves then for our children. This class inequality among free wage labor is not sustainable. It leaves all of us testy—them less willing to overlook standard middle-class classism and microaggressive injuries of class, and us more anxious in general and increasingly isolating ourselves from lives that are going downhill and might take us with them.[19] This is not sustainable, and today middle-class professionals could use some working-class realism to negotiate a situation that is all the more difficult to confront because we're so good at keeping it out of our purview.

Working-Class Realism and Collective Action

The picture of working-class culture I have presented in these last three chapters does not support the idea that the working class is by its nature a revolutionary class or even one prone to large-scale protest and collective action. Ceding control, taking it, and the managed expectations of working-class realism, I have argued, all have both moments of passivity and moments of autonomous agency, often in ways that complement each other. But the moments of autonomous agency are usually either individual tactics and strategies or are based on organically developed local solidarities among families, friends, neighbors, and workmates. If I am right to characterize working-class culture in these ways, then it is hard to see how they could ever have acted to change the world, as they clearly have from time to time. With their limited horizons and existential bird-in-the-hand conservatism, it is hard to imagine, for example, how half a million steelworkers from all parts of our vast country could have repeatedly struck and backed down some of the largest corporations in the world from 1946 through 1959.[20]

I do not have the complete answer to this puzzle, but I hope (and expect) that labor and community organizers will recognize the culture as I have presented it and the difficulties of organizing within that culture. On the one hand, it is less individualistic and is full of complicated local solidarities that are capable of being mobilized given the right circumstances. But on the other hand, working-class culture is highly risk-averse and pragmatic, is suspicious of romantic visions and utopian schemes, and generally lacks confidence in its own collective efficacy. There are rebels within the culture, as there are in all cultures, but they are not necessarily the best leaders or leaders at all—often they are breaking away rather than building upon the possibilities within the culture. Professional organizers usually come from the outside; even if from working-class backgrounds, they often are not part of the community or workplace they are attempting to organize. They bring organizing skills and potentially a culture of organizing that demonstrates the power of collective action, whether in service activities or in union or community activism. My hope is that thinking more clearly, more systematically, about the two primary class cultures in our society can illuminate part of this puzzle.

In the 1980s I was part of a variety of efforts to fight plant closings in the Chicago area and through a national network. At the Midwest Center for Labor Research, we engaged in various kinds of fight-back organizing activities, but mostly we provided research that showed alternative profitable uses and ownership structures for specific factories that were closing or in danger of closing. Our job was to convince local and state officials that there were viable alternatives to letting a particular plant close, but to do that we first had to convince the workers in that plant that there was a realistic chance of saving the plant and their jobs if they mobilized to resist the closing. Though this persuasion job was mostly the responsibility of local union and community leaders who hired us as outside experts, we had a vital piece of it. Among ourselves I argued that in our presentations we should point out to workers that mobilizing to fight the plant closing would likely result in a better severance package—last paychecks, pension and health insurance continuance, and assistance with job search and training—even if they didn't save the plant and their jobs.[21] This was repeatedly shouted down as undermining the fight. Merely mentioning it would undermine the will to fight back against the closing and would focus people on accepting the closing and getting a better severance package. My view sometimes resonated with local leaders, but I was eventually forbidden through democratic discourse from raising it with them.

I don't know who was right or wrong, as there were very few genuine fight-backs and fewer still effective ones, and looking back, given the national political situation, it is hard to imagine any approach that would have achieved a substantially different result. But I now think our differences reflected class outlooks in a complicated but revealing way. I was the middle-class academic, and those who argued for a tightly focused, all-or-nothing, save-the-plant approach were workers, mostly steelworkers, who had been laid off during the recession of the early 1980s. By some accounts they were not "real workers" because they came from professional middle-class families, had college educations, and had entered the mills as revolutionary students with the express purpose of sparking broadscale revolt. Most had been in their jobs for about a decade and had moved up both the job ladder in the plants and within their unions. I'm not sure how long you have to be in a working-class occupation before you become a "real worker," but though most still had revolutionary convictions, they were as savvy a bunch of organizers as I have ever known. In the various plant closing campaigns that I was involved in or witnessed, they were the ones who made something out of nothing, who found avenues for action that others had not seen.[22] They had the high expectations, runaway aspirations, and self-confidence they could achieve them that were likely rooted in their middle-class families of origin. I, on the other hand, had that working-class wariness of hoping for too much and an instinct for always having a Plan B—that even if the streets weren't paved, there might at least be jobs paving them. I wish I had argued more strongly for my view of how to make our case for fighting back, as I think it might have resonated better with workers in most of the situations we faced. But there would have been no fightback at all without these not quite real workers, without their sturdy middle-class sense of entitlement and their savvy influencing skills. They were aware that they were bringing middle-class professionalism, its skills and attitudes, to the struggle, but their achievement-oriented zeal could have adjusted better to the constraints and possibilities within working-class realism.

Though I didn't know it then, the principle behind my view is that a simple "what do you have to lose" approach often has an answer that is not "nothing." But when combined with a persuasive "here's a supplementary benefit you could win" argument, it has both greater realism and the attraction of a fallback position that can make an improbable risk seem more calculated and less foolish. Working-class realism's sense of possibility is constrained, but not nonexistent. Collectively, those in the working class can dream big when they see others in movement, but they need to have fallback positions and secondary survival goals and to be in circumstances where they can see new possibilities emerging. On the other hand, it was amazing to me then and still is that in plant closing situations, so few workers or community members were motivated to resist even though they knew their lives were about to be turned upside down.

The history of the US labor movement is replete with long periods of quiescence followed by dramatic upsurges. These seemingly emerge out of nowhere but are built on years of smaller-scale organizing, some successful and some not but over time greatly expanding workers' sense of collective efficacy.[23] The goal of gradually expanding people's experience of the power (and gratification) of collective action is a staple among community organizers in working-class neighborhoods—for example, the iconic tactic of beginning by simply getting a stop sign placed at a dangerous intersection. Working-class culture is more solidaristic than middle-class professionalism, but working-class solidarity tends to be very local and its horizons for expanding pretty limited. It is the work of labor and community organizers to not just organize people's preexisting proclivities but also nurture an expanding sense of what is possible. These organizers, historically and now, often come from middle-class backgrounds where they meet with an activist tenth within the working class—a minority temperamentally given to action and motivated to move up a learning curve of effectiveness. When working-class organizing works, it is almost always founded on a productive meshing of middle-class and working-class cultures, of middle-class aspiration, vision, and knowledge with working-class on-the-ground ingenuity and ability to take it. What is not productive is top-down orders from headquarters, as I witnessed so many times among AFL-CIO staff coming to a local struggle from Washington, D.C. These staff invariably had a wider vision and knowledge than we had locally, but by and large they were a conservative influence, telling us what we could not do rather than showing us what advantages and possibilities we might have and how they might provide some help for such an effort. This latter sometimes did happen, and when it did it was powerfully effective, but the real potential of the cross-class meshing of cultures is revealed on the ground: middle-class organizers adopting some working-class ways, often enthusiastically, and working-class organizers eager to learn and to be influenced but without allowing their feet to leave the ground.[24]

Still, though based on long-term organizing efforts, working-class upsurges of organized collective action do not occur unless there are favorable circumstances. Specific situations are so complexly different that it would be folly to try to develop a list of what circumstances are generally favorable. But I think the last forty years evidence that deteriorating conditions in themselves, especially if they happen slowly, do not spur collective action without some real change in circumstances that reveals new possibilities. The desperate conditions of the Great Depression are often seen as the primary circumstance that motivated the most effective working-class upsurge in US history in the 1930s. But the increasingly desperate circumstances of the first four years of the Depression did not spur widespread revolt, even though it did spur some very creative organizing among the unemployed.[25] It was not until Franklin Roosevelt's first one hundred days in 1933 and its wild initiation of try-anything programs with immediately visible effects that people could believe in the possibility of massive change. Unemployment went from about 25 percent down to 15 percent, and as it did both hope and anger emerged in a series of dramatic strikes in the summer of 1934. From that point on a new labor movement developed that eventually won a Second New Deal and an unprecedented period of union and working-class power during the Glorious Thirty.

Looked at closely, the upsurge of the 1930s supports Alexis de Tocqueville's analysis of the French Revolution:

> Experience teaches us that the most hazardous moment for a bad government is normally when it is beginning to reform . . . [,] setting out to relieve [its] subjects' suffering after a long period of oppression. The evils, patiently endured as inevitable, seem unbearable as soon as the idea of escaping them is conceived. Then the removal of an abuse seems to

cast a sharper light on those still left and makes people more painfully aware of them; the burden has become lighter, it is true, but the sensitivity more acute.[26]

Expectations increase in response to improving circumstances, not the other way around. And given our political, social, and cultural power as middle-class professionals, we are in a position to improve some circumstances. We should do that both because it is the right thing to do and because in the long run it will enhance our own class interests as it expands our own and others' sense of possibility.

Organizing and Circumstances

I'd like to say to organizers and others who are trying to aid in bringing working-class people into civic, workplace, or political action that they need to work within working-class culture, not against it. And that is one thing I would say. But my instinct on this is countered by too many instances of working-class individuals, and not just young ones, who are trying to reject some aspects of their culture and are often attracted to middle-class professionalism and its proactive ways. These are often though by no means always leaders who will work with organizers and organizations to advance collective goals. In these contexts, professionals can help change both expectations and circumstances—but only if their professionalism liberates itself from the pursuit of individual accomplishment and status or at least strongly leans against those aspects of its culture. When professionalism consistently draws on the common-good idealism embedded (if sometimes buried) within most professions and when professionals can restrain their headstrong commitment to the singular superiority of their culture, they can bring not just knowledge and skills to working-class struggle but also a broader vision and proactive attitude. That attitude needs to be tempered by working-class realism and to work within its constraints, as most on-the-ground organizers in my experience know. But I'm guessing they also have to imbibe some of that working-class culture not only because it makes them better organizers but also because it will likely make them better, more trustworthy human beings. Of all the different kinds of people who live on and around the edges between our two great proletarian cultures, organizers do it best. Some part of that may be what is sometimes called "going native," but the more important part is about being who you are, whatever that happens to be.

In the great CIO upsurges in the 1930s—in steel, auto, rubber, and radios—most of the action was driven by workers themselves or, crucially, by people who had started their lives as workers but then became professional unionists, leaders, and organizers. But it's hard to imagine those upsurges without broader circumstances being changed by the first New Deal spurred by a man of the landed gentry and furthered by a progressive middle-class lawyer named Robert F. Wagner and a middle-class organizer and intellectual named Frances Perkins. The National Industrial Recovery Act and the National Labor Relations Act, known as the Wagner Act, changed the landscape for working-class organizing, and a handful of unions took advantage of those changes to reorganize themselves and then others. The way workers rushed to join unions and learn unionism after the sit-down strikes in rubber and auto plants and after General Motors and U.S. Steel signed barebones union contracts in 1937 exhibit the way a stolid, seemingly inert mass of people can relatively quickly turn into an organized and highly effective mob. Circumstances had changed, and the sit-down and other strikers demonstrated that those changes had opened up new possibilities, changing expectations and then actions.[27] Similar dynamics can be seen in the twentieth-century civil rights movement initiated by middle-class and settled-living working-class leaders, painstakingly built by local organizing and nationally illustrative struggles, until in a relatively few years new possibilities had brought wide ranges of working-class blacks into action.[28]

All our middle-class prejudices against working-class culture have some basis in reality, but as long as our only move in solidarity with them is to help educate a handful of them to become more like us, we will limit both their and our possibilities. Rather, deep within our professionalism is a desire and a range of abilities to change circumstances for the common good. We standard-issue middle-class professionals need to realize that given the opportunity, the capitalist class will degrade our working conditions and living standards too, something you can already see happening in many professions. In most ways our interests align with those of the working class as I have broadly defined it. Our own politics and collective action need to focus on improving their circumstances with an eye to increasing their sense of possibility and initiating a new upsurge of organized collective action. It's a good bet that such an eventuality will end up benefiting us as much as them, as it did in the Glorious Thirty.

TWO GOOD CLASS CULTURES

In broad terms, my argument is that working-class culture is not a problem, but an asset—an asset for the people who live within it and for a modern capitalist society like ours.

Reading the last three chapters, you might be tempted to think that what I'm describing is similar to what others have called a "culture of poverty," one that cedes, defers, takes it, and approaches life with a narrow realism that undermines people's capacity for agency. Even though formally denounced as an idea, the "culture of poverty" thesis frames a lot of middle-class professional thinking about "the unfortunate." Middle-class conservatives tend to use this thesis to blame the victim, thinking that if poor people would just change their culture, the poverty could be overcome. Progressives, on the other hand, start off with the opposite notion—eliminate the poverty and the culture will dissipate—but then somehow default to thinking that education is the key to providing opportunity and thus alleviating hardship. Both views see the culture as negative and something to be overcome.

Neither of these, I hope you have noticed, is my view. For starters, I don't see the working class as uniformly "unfortunate." Part of the working class is subject to hard times and difficult living, and a part of that part is affected by living hard for too long, even through generations. But other parts of the working class are getting by, and still others are mildly prospering. All these parts broadly share a culture, and though economic circumstances shape how the culture works, their way of life is basically the same. Low expectations, taking it, and emphasizing being and belonging are a large part of what enables people to get by and get through living hard. But in better economic circumstances, these same and other aspects of the culture become a foundation for expanding one's prospects and possibilities without necessarily abandoning your way of seeing and being in the world.

Working-class culture does not need to be undermined, overcome, or reformed. What is needed is a change in the economic circumstances of the class—specifically, much more time and money for what you will. The culture, like the people within it, will flourish in better, more settled and reliable circumstances. Some, and not just young ones, would *choose* to slide into professional middle-class ways, but they would not be forced to because that was the one and only path to decent standards of living and working. Discretionary time and money, especially an ample amount of them, expand human freedom. More freedom, of course, does not mean that everybody will use that freedom in good and productive ways, but on the evidence of history so far, most will. As Benjamin Friedman has documented, "a rising standard of living, over time . . . usually leads to the positive development of . . . a society's moral character."[1]

As an educator, I value education. I have experienced and I have seen how enormously positive, often life-transforming, it can be. But education cannot and should not play any role in improving the economic circumstances of the working class. Too many progressive discussions of our outrageous levels of income and wealth inequality end up seeing educating people for better jobs as the primary equalizer. Education cannot do that, because there are not nearly enough jobs that require much education beyond on-the-job training. More education can help some individuals, but only significant changes in labor market rules can improve working-class standards and conditions. The jobs that we have need to pay better, way better—period. In addition, where education is simply or primarily not about learning but instead is about individuals advancing their economic prospects, our culture inevitably dominates theirs. That domination is not a good thing in itself but it also tends to be educationally counterproductive because it sets up a negative dialectic between the class cultures.[2] Besides, defining ourselves as and requiring others to become part of the exam-passing classes is not exactly leading with the best aspects of our middle-class professionalism.

Can we substantially increase both wages and leisure time not only for the working class but also for all workers, including most of us standard-issue middle-class professionals? We can. We have enough wealth to dramatically increase living standards across the board, starting from the bottom up, if only we would systematically address our savagely inequitable distribution of income and wealth. The experience of the Glorious Thirty provides a template: share the gains from productivity growth and severely tax the very top income groups to pay for a greatly enhanced social wage. How to strengthen labor unions so they can once again enforce productivity sharing is difficult to determine, but democratic government can establish better rules for fostering workplace representation, just as it can regulate minimum wages and time off. Though they have not used the term "social wage," more and more Democrats are advocating forms of it—from government-funded early childhood education and subsidized day care, subsidized rents, and public building of affordable housing to baby bonds and guaranteed annual incomes, not to mention universal health care. Taxing the high-income wealthy to build an awesome social wage in the United States is a no-brainer economically by now, though of course the politics is a very different matter. Nonetheless, the magnitude of our wealth and the degree of its maldistribution are such that even a very thorough redistribution of income and wealth would leave the wealthy pretty damn wealthy and thus hopefully not too pissed off.[3]

Those kind of policy issues may be above my pay grade, but the point is that working-class culture is not the problem. Thinking that it is the problem *is* the problem.

If I am right that our two primary class cultures push and nudge us in opposite directions and that both directions are pretty good ways to go, then we need each other as both productive antagonists and complements. We need to be engaged with one another as adversaries who respect each other enough to also be coalition partners. We can be too aspirational and achievement-oriented and they not enough. They can be too rigidly character-oriented, but our purpose-driven lives can erode our characters. We lack their ingenuity when our plans go awry, but they are too exclusively reactive. They tend to be too parochial and concrete, but we can be too rootless and abstract. We are ruining ourselves with status anxiety and social evaluative threat. They undermine their capacity to change broad socioeconomic circumstances with their awesome ability to take it and their peasant-derived realism. A doing-and-becoming culture needs a being-and-belonging one to not only do most of the work that needs to be done but also to offset our relentless drive to improve our individual selves. But a being-and-belonging culture needs our sense of capacity and broader horizons to help them transform their taking-it culture from a tactic to a strategy for fighting back and changing their circumstances.

The English historian Alison Light wisely concludes her reflection on common people: "As we grow older we see not how unique our lives have been, but how representative we were and are; that we are part of the figure in the carpet woven by events, by chance and accident, and by the play of forces more powerful than us."[4] Cultures, including class cultures, are "forces more powerful than us," but as with other such forces, the more we know and understand them, the more we can both shape those forces and adjust to them. It is helpful to remind ourselves, as working-class culture does, that we are not very powerful, that we are carried along by where the river of life is going regardless of what we do. On the other hand, the full-scale individual responsibility that middle-class culture encourages is without doubt a productive and valuable illusion, an illusion that working-class culture would do well to cultivate a bit. The sense of individual powerlessness, fostered in working-class culture, can be a wise recognition of our limits if and probably only if it leads to a mutual dependence on and reciprocity with others. A similar interdependence, or solidarity, in mutually sharing our cultures of class is what can make us stronger.

I am not arguing for a happy medium, a cultural synthesis that would be the one right way for everybody all the time. That's neither possible nor desirable, and pursuing it might be something like totalitarian. But a more equal interchange between the cultures could allow some of us to mix and match while others maintain the real strengths of less hybrid, more pure versions of the cultures. We need, for example, those obsessively aspirational people of talent who often achieve great things for all of us, not just for themselves. And we also need those who work hard to just be okay, who pull their own weight and both enjoy and are bound by the tangled webs of their preexisting relationships. Neither group, nor all the mediocrities in between, should get all the honor or, most importantly, all the income and time for what you will. There is now plenty of all that to go around.

Cultural differences of all sorts make talking and acting with each other difficult. When you add up all our differences in class, race, ethnicity, gender, sexuality, religious beliefs, age, region, life stage, and even personality type, it can seem a wonder that we ever understand each other enough to get things done together. But we often do, and when we do it is because each of us has enough experience of the rest of us that we cannot blindly insist on the superiority of our own way of doing things. We cannot move forward, separately or together, if they think we are not "real" people or "real Americans," while we think they are just backward and need to try harder to be more like us.

My critique of middle-class professionalism is not focused on how its competitive status anxiety can turn so ugly, both socially and psychologically. Though that is the part I find most debilitating and distasteful, it also seems to motivate people of talent to do good as well as well. The problem is middle-class culture's parochial self-assurance that there is only one right way, and we're it. On the other hand, that culture's earnest streak in doing good and becoming better is what I'm appealing to. Not everybody, but a substantial chunk of us actively cultivate a social conscience and feel empowered to think about how we can become a better, more just and sustainable society. It's not only that social conscience I'm appealing to, however. Our class interest is also involved. Many standard-issue professionals, for example, would benefit economically from a greatly expanded social wage. But more than that, as I have tried to indicate, we middle-class professionals have a lot to gain culturally, maybe even spiritually, from more exposure to a prosperous working class. Where both their culture and ours are stronger in themselves and more secure, we are more likely to be open to each other, as I think we were once upon a time. I'm thinking we might at least be able to renew that interrupted century of the common and make America glorious again.

Notes

INTRODUCTION

1. *Merriam-Webster*, "mediocre," https://www.merriamwebster.com/dictionary/medio cre#synonyms.

2. Benjamin Franklin, "Information to Those Who Would Remove to America: 1782, Excerpts," America in Class, https://americainclass.org/sources/makingrevolution/indepen dence/text8/franklininfoamerica.pdf; Alexis de Tocqueville, *Democracy in America*, trans. Arthur Goldhammer (New York: Library of America, 2004, originally published in French, 1835–1840), 3.

3. Thomas Piketty, *Capital in the Twenty-First Century*, trans. Arthur Goldhammer (Cambridge, MA: Harvard University Press, 2014), 161.

4. Peter McPhee, *Liberty or Death: The French Revolution* (New Haven, CT: Yale University Press, 2016), 278–79.

5. Raymond Williams, *The Long Revolution* (New York: Harper Torchbooks, 1961).

6. Geoff Eley, "Corporatism and the Social Democratic Moment: The Postwar Settlement, 1945–1973," in *The Oxford Handbook of Postwar European History*, ed. Dan Stone (Oxford: Oxford University Press, 2012), 37–59; Nicholas Crafts and Gianni Toniolo, "'*Les trente glorieuses*': From the Marshall Plan to the Oil Crisis," in *The Oxford Handbook of Postwar European History*, 356–411; Adam Roberts and Timothy Garton Ash, eds., *Civil Resistance & Power Politics: The Experience of Non-violent Action from Gandhi to the Present* (Oxford: Oxford University Press, 2009).

7. Paul Willis, *Learning to Labor: How Working-Class Kids Get Working-Class Jobs* (New York: Columbia University Press, 1977), 54.

8. Willis, *Learning to Labor*, 1–3.

9. For accounts of female "lads" in (roughly) my generation, see Barbara Jensen, *Reading Classes: On Culture and Classism in America* (Ithaca, NY: Cornell University Press, 2012), chap. 5; Marge Piercy, *Sleeping with Cats: A Memoir* (New York: HarperCollins, 2002), chap. 3. Jensen, who grew up in a working-class Minneapolis suburb, recounts how "the cool kids . . . were powerfully bound together—in part *against* school," 117. Piercy grew up in a working-class Detroit neighborhood where she belonged to a gang that "forgave" her for "doing well in school" because she could pick locks and was gifted at shoplifting, 40. A more contemporary study of Latinx and Anglo girl "lads" in California is Julie Bettie, *Women without Class: Girls, Race, and Identity* (Oakland: University of California Press, 2003). Bettie explores a wide variety of antischool tactics that working-class girls employ, commenting that "girls may resist school without violently confronting it, and their strategies, often less sensational than those of boys, are easily overlooked" (47). What is fundamental for both genders of ladness is, as Bettie puts it, the rejection of "official school activities and, by association middle-class cultural norms."

10. Robert Bellah, Richard Madsen, William Sullivan, Ann Swidler, and Steven Tipton, *Habits of the Heart: Individualism and Commitment in American Life*, updated ed. (Berkeley: University of California Press, 1996), 20–21. See especially: "In the language they [Americans] use, their lives sound more isolated and arbitrary than . . . they actually are."

11. For a brief but insightful discussion of various current conceptions of "culture," see Mario Luis Small, David J. Harding, and Michele Lamont, "Reconsidering Culture and Poverty," *Annals of the American Academy of Political and Social Science* 629 (May 2010): 6–27, esp. 13–19. Within that taxonomy, my view would be closest to the notion of culture as "frames"—certain "shared taken-for-granted understandings" that "highlight certain aspects of social life and hide or block others" (14, 19, and 23). But I am more insistent that culture is first outside and beyond the individual, with each of us interacting with our culture, some viewing it as guide and comfort while others view it as unwanted pressure and constraint but mostly just taking it for granted without another thought.

12. For an excellent brief historical overview of free wage labor up to the present day, see Jurgen Kocka, *Capitalism: A Short History* (Princeton, NJ: Princeton University Press, 2015), 124–45. However, even Kocka fails to recognize the significance of managerial and professional occupations that are wage-dependent as an important part of free wage labor in today's advanced capitalist countries.

13. Michael Zweig, *The Working Class Majority: America's Best Kept Secret*, 2nd ed. (Ithaca, NY: Cornell University Press, 2012), 90. For a fuller discussion of this issue, see Jack Metzgar, "Are 'the Poor' Part of the Working Class or in a Class by Themselves?," *Labor Studies Journal* 35, no. 3 (2010): 398–416.

14. Bureau of Labor Statistics, "Median Usual Weekly Earnings of Wage and Salary Workers by Occupation and Sex, Quarterly Averages, Not Seasonally Adjusted," Table 4, regularly updated at https://www.bls.gov/news.release/wkyeng.nr0.htm, Bureau of Labor Statistics, "Employment Situation Summary Table A: Household Data, Seasonally Adjusted," regularly updated at bls.gov/news.release/empsit.a.htm.

15. According to the BLS, the median salary for "food service managers" was about $45,000 in 2019, meaning half of such managers made less than that. Bureau of Labor Statistics, "Median Weekly Earnings of Full-Time Wage and Salary Workers by Detailed Occupation and Sex," regularly updated at bls.gov/news.release/wkyeng.t104.htm. See also Stewart O'Nan, *Last Night at the Lobster* (New York: Penguin Books, 2007), whose central character is a manager of a Red Lobster that is closing.

16. Bureau of Labor Statistics, "Median Usual Weekly Earnings of Wage and Salary Workers," Table 4.

17. Though I could not calculate a racial/ethnic breakdown from BLS statistics, which double-counts Hispanics, Colby King used the 2017 American Community Survey to determine that nonwhites were about 42 percent of the working class, using three different occupation-based definitions including mine. Colby King, "Counting the Working Class for Working-Class Studies: Comparing Three Occupation-Based Definitions," *Journal of Working-Class Studies* 4, no. 1 (June 2019): Table 4, https://workingclassstudiesjournal.files .wordpress.com/2019/06/jwcs-vol-4-issue-1-june-2019-king.pdf. Likewise, by the commonly used education binary—working-class equals adults without bachelor's degrees—people of color are 40 percent of working-class adults, as calculated from US Census Bureau, "Educational Attainment in the United States: 2018," February 21, 2019, https:// www.census.gov/data/tables/2018/demo/education-attainment/cps-detailed-tables.html.

18. Though the 2016 presidential election showed an eight-point advantage for Donald Trump among the working class versus the educated middle class (all colors), that margin was completely the result of a huge shift in the white part of the working class. In 2008 and 2012, the education-defined middle and working classes (all colors) voted virtually the same. See the presidential exit polls for 2008, 2012, and 2016.

19. The most important of these are Michele Lamont, *The Dignity of Working Men: Morality and the Boundaries of Race, Class, and Immigration* (New York: Russell Sage Foundation, 2000), which found some relatively minor differences by race among black and white working-class men who, however, shared the same broad "cultural repertoire,"

and Annette Lareau, *Unequal Childhoods: Class, Race, and Family Life*, 2nd ed. (Berkeley: University of California Press, 2011), which found that shared patterns in child-rearing approaches by class were much more significant than by race or levels of poverty. Likewise, Bettie, *Women without Class*, found that Latina and white working-class girls shared similar antischool cultures, even though the unavailability of class terms in their experience caused them to interpret that experience strictly through an ethnic lens. Jessica Calarco, *Negotiating Opportunities: How the Middle Class Secures Advantages in School* (New York: Oxford University Press, 2018), likewise tends to confirm the strength of class cultures among Latinx and Asian elementary school students and their parents.

20. I have asked this open-ended question a lot—very unsystematically, or randomly but not in a good way—sometimes with groups of students in my classes, sometimes one-on-one with people I know or those who engage in conversation in public settings. Amazingly, few give answers outside the rich/poor/middle-class framework. For a full discussion see Jack Metzgar, "Politics and the American Class Vernacular," in *New Working-Class Studies*, ed. John Russo and Sherry Lee Linkon, 189–208 (Ithaca: Cornell University Press, 2005).

21. General Social Survey of the National Opinion Research Center at the University of Chicago, 1972–2018, https://gssdataexplorer.norc.org/variables/568/vshow. For a discussion of these survey results, see Michael Hout, "How Class Works: Objective and Subjective Aspects of Class since the 1970s," in *Social Class: How Does It Work?*, ed. Annette Lareau and Dalton Conley (New York: Russell Sage Foundation, 2008), 28–32.

22. Larry M. Bartels, *Unequal Democracy: The Political Economy of the New Gilded Age* (New York: Russell Sage Foundation, 2008), 137.

23. All issues of *Labor Research Review*, from 1982 through 1996, have been archived at Cornell University's School of Industrial and Labor Relations, https://digitalcommons.ilr .cornell.edu/lrr/.

24. Raj Chetty, David Grusky, Maximilian Hell, Nathaniel Hendren, Robert Manduca, and Jimmy Narang, "The Fading American Dream: Trends in Absolute Income Mobility since 1940," *Science* 356, no. 6336 (2017): 398–406.

25. Daniel Markovits, *The Meritocracy Trap: How America's Foundational Myth Feeds Inequality, Dismantles the Middle Class, and Devours the Elite* (New York: Penguin, 2019), captures the basic dynamics of this class relationship: "Elite children strain themselves in meritocratic schools and elite adults accept the relentless rigors of the meritocratic workplace because the returns to gloomy jobs are so low, the returns to glossy jobs are so high, and so few jobs are glossy" (34).

PART I: NOSTALGIA FOR THE THIRTY-YEAR CENTURY OF THE COMMON

1. A potential exception to this dismissive usage might seem to be Yuval Levin's chapter "Blinded by Nostalgia," in *The Fractured Republic: Renewing America's Social Contract in the Age of Individualism* (New York: Basic Books, 2016). But though that chapter very insightfully charts the reliance on nostalgia by both the Left and the Right, it does not actually show or even address how this nostalgia "blinds" rather than guides both progressive and conservative thinking. Though much conservative nostalgia is now superficially for the Ronald Reagan era, not the Glorious Thirty, as Levin insightfully points out, "Key to what Reagan achieved, in the eyes of conservatives, was that he recaptured something of the magic of the midcentury decades. So in a sense the Right is awaiting a second renaissance while the Left awaits a first one, but both have in mind the postwar decades as the original model to be recovered—the model of America in its prime" (22).

2. The quote is from the call for papers for the German Historical Institute London's October 2015 conference "Nostalgia: Historicizing the Longing for the Past." This conference points to a scholarly literature that does not simply dismiss nostalgia but also investigates it

from many different angles. I have not drawn on this literature much because it is not reflective of general public and intellectual discourse in the United States, but I have been kept apprised of it through many hours of conversation with my friend Tim Strangleman, whose thinking on the potential value of nostalgia has very much informed my own. See Strangleman, "The Nostalgia of Organization and the Organization of Nostalgia: Past and Present in the Contemporary Railway Industry," *Sociology* 33, no. 43(1999): 725–46. See also "Nostalgia for Nationalisation?," in Strangleman, *Work Identity at the End of the Line? Privatisation and Culture Change in the UK Rail Industry,* 164–77 (New York: Palgrave Macmillan, 2004).

3. N. Geoffrey Bright, "'The Lady Is Not Returning!': Educational Precarity and a Social Haunting in the UK Coalfields," *Ethnography and Education* 11, no. 2 (2016): 142–57.

4. I am using the term "restorative nostalgia" in a very different sense than Svetlana Bohm's *The Future of Nostalgia* (New York: Basic Books, 2001), 41–48. For Bohm, the term refers to right-wing nationalism's use of monuments to evoke a mythical origin narrative of a nation; though her essays are primarily on Europe and Russia, the closest American analogue would be the way southern segregationists used Confederate monuments and symbols to create and enforce Jim Crow laws. For me, nostalgia is an emotion or an emotional state that can be brought into thought in many different ways, some of them distasteful and dangerous, as Bohm explores, and this is one of the reasons nostalgia should not be simply dismissed. But my sense is that restorative nostalgia just as often leads to golden age thinking, which first identifies an exemplary period and then engages in an intellectual process to determine what made it exemplary.

5. This personal anecdote is an extreme example of a larger trend. During the 1980s the premium for a college education versus a high school education across the US economy went from 36 percent to 60 percent. Reynolds Farley, *The New American Reality: Who We Are, How We Got Here, Where We Are Going* (New York: Russell Sage Foundation, 1996), 97–99. In 2017 the premium was 165 percent. See Bureau of Labor Statistics, "Unemployment Rates and Earnings by Educational Attainment, 2017," September 4, 2019, https://www.bls.gov/emp/chart-unemployment-earnings-education.htm.

6. See Jack Metzgar, *Striking Steel: Solidarity Remembered* (Philadelphia: Temple University Press, 2000), 126–27.

7. Benjamin M. Friedman, *The Moral Consequences of Economic Growth* (New York: Vintage Books, 2005), esp. chap. 4.

8. Golden age thinking far predates the European Renaissance, of course. Mary Beard explains that "a typical style of Roman reform" justified "radical action as a return to past practice," citing Tiberius Gracchus's attempt in 133 BCE to "restore land to the poor" by enforcing an "old legal limit" to owning 120 hectares of land. Mary Beard, *SPQR: A History of Ancient Rome* (New York: Liveright Publishing, 2015), 222–23. Golden age thinking such as this has sometimes been productively creative, as when seventeenth-century English politicians transformed a thirteenth-century "treaty among feudal antagonists" into a Magna Carta that made Parliament dominant over the king and then American Revolutionists claimed it as the basis for a series of rights for "free-born subjects of England." See "The Uses of History: How Did a Failed Treaty between Medieval Combatants Come to Be Seen as the Foundation of Liberty in the Anglo-Saxon world," *The Economist,* December 20, 2014.

9. Jacob Hacker and Paul Pierson, *American Amnesia: How the War on Government Led Us to Forget What Made America Prosper* (New York: Simon & Schuster, 2016); Jacob Hacker, *The Great Risk Shift: The Assault on American Jobs, Families, Health Care, and Retirement, and How We Can Fight Back* (Oxford: Oxford University Press, 2006); Jacob Hacker and Paul Pierson, *Winner-Take-All Politics: How Washington Made the Rich Richer—And Turned Its Back on the Middle Class* (New York: Simon & Schuster, 2010).

10. Hacker and Pierson, *American Amnesia,* 119; Tony Judt, *Ill Fares the Land* (New York: Penguin, 2010), 229.

11. Sam Pizzigati, *The Rich Don't Always Win: The Forgotten Triumph over Plutocracy That Created the American Middle Class, 1900–1970* (New York: Seven Stories, 2012).

12. David Weil, *The Fissured Workplace: Why Work Became So Bad for So Many and What Can Be Done to Improve It* (Cambridge, MA: Harvard University Press, 2014).

13. Steven Pearlstein, "When Shareholder Capitalism Came to Town," The American Prospect, April 19, 2014, https://prospect.org/economy/shareholder-capitalism-came-town /, and more recently, in *Moral Capitalism: Why Fairness Won't Make Us Poor* (New York: St. Martin's Griffin, 2020).

14. Robert Kuttner, *Can Democracy Survive Global Capitalism?* (New York: Norton, 2018), 26, 37.

1. WHAT WAS GLORIOUS ABOUT THE GLORIOUS THIRTY?

1. Jean Fourastie, *Les Trentes Glorieuses, ou la revolution invisible de 1946 a 1975* (Paris: Fayard Press, 1979).

2. James T. Patterson, *Grand Expectations: The United States, 1945–1974* (New York: Oxford University Press, 1996).

3. Burton J. Bledstein, *The Culture of Professionalism: The Middle Class and the Development of Higher Education in America* (New York: Norton, 1976), 14; US Census Bureau, *The Statistical History of the United States: From Colonial Times to the Present* (New York: Basic Books, 1976), Series F 10–16, 225.

4. "U.S. GDP Growth Rate 1961–2020," Macrotrends, https://www.macrotrends.net /countries/USA/united-states/gdp-growth-rate.

5. For unemployment, see US Census Bureau, *The Statistical History of the United States*, Series D 85–86, 135, which shows the seven years from 1923 through 1929 at or below 5 percent followed, of course, by a decade of double-digit unemployment. Inflation as measured by the Consumer Price Index is a somewhat more complicated story, since the beginning and end of the Glorious Thirty saw substantial spikes in inflation, whereas the 1920s and 1930s was an overall period of deflation. See *Statistical History*, Series E 136–166, 210–11.

6. *Statistical History*, Series D 722–727, 164. In 1940 dollars, the average annual wage in 1940 was $1,299. The 2020 average annual wage is calculated from "Usual Weekly Earnings of Wage and Salary Workers, First Quarter 2020," Bureau of Labor Statistics, October 16, 2020, https://www.bls.gov/news.release/pdf/wkyeng.pdf.

7. For manufacturing and other sectors, see Susan B. Carter, Scott Sigmund Gartner, Michael R. Haines, Alan L. Olmstead, Richard Sutch, and Gavin Wright, eds., *Historical Statistics of the United States*, Vol. 2, *Work and Welfare* (Cambridge: Cambridge University Press, 2006), 275–77. This source reports wages in current dollars, and I adjusted them to 2020 constant dollars using the Bureau of Labor Statistics inflation calculator.

8. Frank Levy, *The New Dollars and Dreams: American Incomes and Economic Change* (New York: Russell Sage Foundation, 1998), 27.

9. At the end of the Glorious Thirty, however, the poverty rate for African Americans was double that of whites for prime-age adults and even worse for black seniors (36 percent) and children (42 percent). At that point it got worse for both blacks and whites for the next twenty years. "Historical Poverty Tables: People and Families—1959 to 2018," US Census Bureau, https://www.census.gov/data/tables/time-series/demo/income-poverty/historical -poverty-people.html.

10. By one highly sophisticated analysis, poverty in the United States would have disappeared by 1985. See Economic Policy Institute, "Poverty Rate, Actual and Simulated, 1959–2013," in *The State of Working America*, http://www.stateofworkingamerica.org /chart/swa-poverty-figure-7m-poverty-rate-actual/.

11. Jacob S. Hacker and Paul Pierson, *American Amnesia: How the War on Government Led Us to Forget What Made America Prosper* (New York: Simon & Schuster 2016), 337.

Most relevant for the decades prior to 1945 is Robert J. Gordon, *The Rise and Fall of American Growth: The U.S. Standard of Living since the Civil War* (Princeton, NJ: Princeton University Press, 2016). Gordon argues that 1870–1970 was the best period for the most people, despite economic depressions and wars, and emphasizes especially the introduction and dispersion of indoor plumbing, household electricity, and telecommunications as bringing our daily lives "from dark and isolated to bright and networked" (94).

12. Louis Hyman, *Debtor Nation: The History of America in Red Ink* (Princeton, NJ: Princeton University Press, 2011), 123.

13. Hyman, *Debtor Nation*, chap. 5.

14. Witold Rybczynski, *Waiting for the Weekend* (New York: Viking, 1991), 144.

15. Robert Whaples, "Hours of Work in U.S. History," Economic History Association, https://eh.net/encyclopedia/hours-of-work-in-u-s-history/.

16. Gordon, *The Rise and Fall of American Growth*, 12.

17. "Life Expectancy for Social Security," Social Security, https://www.ssa.gov/history /lifeexpect.html.

18. Gordon, *The Rise and Fall of American Growth*, 516. The percentages of workers with employer-based pensions is now and always has been higher among those employed by large firms, but large-firm coverage shows the same pattern of postwar rise and post-1970s decline, reaching a high of 85 percent in 1981 but falling to about 50 percent by the turn of the century. See William J. Wiatrowski, "The Last Private Industry Pension Plans: A Visual Essay," *Monthly Labor Review*, December 2012, http://www.bls.gov/opub/mlr /2012/12/art1full.pdf.

19. Carter et al., *Historical Statistics of the United States*, Vol. 2, 550–51.

20. Gordon, *The Rise and Fall of American Growth*, 207.

21. These complaints are usually posed as questions that are legitimately concerned with the possibility that I, as a straight white man, might be purposely or accidentally whitewashing history. I have learned to respect this concern when it is expressed by nonscholars or even by scholars from social science traditions that are aggressively ignorant of history. I am less tolerant of historians who should know better. Jonathan Levy, for example, has declared that "the postwar decades were a good time to be a worker, but only if you were white, male, and straight. . . . . what has come to an end is a golden age for white men with nothing more than a high school education" ("Stuck in a Gilded Age," *Dissent*, Summer 2016), 157. Evidently, Levy thinks white women and people of color with nothing but high school educations and less—a group that constitutes nearly half of the adult population—are making more progress today than they were from 1945 to 1975. They're not. See US Census Bureau, "Educational Attainment in the United States: 2019," https://www.census.gov/data/tables /2019/demo/educational-attainment/cps-detailed-tables.html; Bureau of Labor Statistics, "Earnings and Unemployment Rates by Educational Attainment, 2019," https://www.bls .gov/emp/tables/unemployment-earnings-education.htm.

22. Christine Stansell, *The Feminist Promise: 1792 to the Present* (New York: Modern Library, 2010), chaps. 7 and 8.

23. Alexis de Tocqueville, *The Ancien Regime and the French Revolution*, trans. and ed. Gerald Bevan (London: Penguin Books, 2008, first published in 1856), 174–75.

24. Carter et al., *Historical Statistics of the United States*, Vol. 2, Table Ba4954-4964, "Work Stoppages, Workers Involved, Average Duration, and Person-Days Idle: 1881–1998," 354–55. For the postwar strike wave, see Jack Metzgar, "The 1945–1946 Strike Wave," in *The Encyclopedia of Strikes in American History*, 216–25 (Armonk, NY: M. E. Sharpe, 2009). For the broader context of the 1967–1971 strike wave, see Jefferson Cowie, *Stayin' Alive: The 1970s and the Last Days of the Working Class* (New York: New Press, 2010), esp. chap. 1.

25. Jack Metzgar, *Striking Steel: Solidarity Remembered* (Philadelphia: Temple University Press, 2000), 141–48.

26. See, however, Barry Bluestone and Bennett Harrison, *Growing Prosperity: The Battle for Growth with Equity in the 21st^t Century* (Boston: Houghton Mifflin, 2000). In chapter 2, "A History of American Growth," they conclude that "on its own, however, postwar growth would likely have petered out in a decade [i.e., by 1955] or so if it were not for three critically important factors," of which "organized labor and collective bargaining" was the most important. The other two are "the role of the federal government in stimulating aggregate demand" and "the unexpectedly strong expansion in labor supply as women entered the labor force in record numbers" (35–36).

27. Lillian Faderman, *The Gay Revolution: The Story of the Struggle* (New York: Simon & Schuster, 2015). Pages 11, 98–102, and 279–287 recount the fight from 1952 to 1974 to get "homosexuality" removed from the *Diagnostic and Statistical Manual of Mental Disorders* as a sickness that needed curing. The Mattachine Society, which most historians see as the origin of the gay liberation movement, was formed in 1950, and many gay activists saw the American Psychiatric Association's 1952 declaration as a reaction to the beginnings of that movement. See Eric Marcus's oral history *Making Gay History: The Half-Century Fight for Lesbian and Gay Equal Rights* (New York: HarperCollins Perennial, 2002). For the containment strategy against women, see Elaine Tyler May, *Homeward Bound: American Families in the Cold War* (New York: Basic Books, 1988).

28. Patterson, *Grand Expectations*, 642.

29. The direct quotes are from Patterson, *Grand Expectations*, 205 and 342, though the penultimate passage is on 374: "By the late 1950s millions of Americans were enjoying the bounties of affluence and the consumer culture, the likes of which they had scarcely imagined before. In the process they were developing larger expectations about life and beginning to challenge things that seemed set in stone only a few years earlier. Older cultural norms, however, still remained strong until the 1960s, when expectations ascended to new heights and helped facilitate social unrest on a new and different scale."

30. Tocqueville, *The Ancien Regime and the French Revolution*, 174–75.

31. Erik S. Gellman, *Death Blow to Jim Crow: The National Negro Congress and the Rise of Militant Civil Rights* (Chapel Hill: University of North Carolina Press, 2012). For a basic explanation of the origin and trajectory of the campaign, see "Double V Campaign," Wikipedia, https://en.wikipedia.org/wiki/Double_V_campaign.

32. Levy, *The New Dollars and Dreams*, 27, 34, and 50.

33. Economic Policy Institute, "Median Family Income, by Race and Ethnicity, 1947–2010," *The State of Working America*, http://www.stateofworkingamerica.org/chart/swa-income-table-2-5-median-family-income/.

34. Economic Policy Institute, "Black Median Family Income, as a Share of White Median Family Income, 1947–2013," *The State of Working America*, http://stateofworkingamerica.org/charts/ratio-of-black-and-hispanic-to-white-median-family-income-1947-2010/.

35. Andrew J. Cherlin, *Labor's Love Lost: The Rise and Fall of the Working-Class Family* (New York: Russell Sage Foundation, 2014), 94.

36. Cherlin, *Labor's Love Lost*, 9.

37. Randall Kennedy, "Black America's Promised Land: Why I Am Still a Racial Optimist," *The American Prospect*, no. 5 (Fall 2014), https://prospect.org/civil-rights/black-america-s-promised-land-still-racial-optimist/.

38. Anne Case and Angus Deaton, *Deaths of Despair and the Future of Capitalism* (Princeton, NJ: Princeton University Press, 2020), 189.

39. Thomas Piketty, *Capital and Ideology* (Cambridge, MA: Harvard University Press, 2020), 353.

40. Patrick Bayer and Kerwin Kofi Charles, "Divergent Paths: Structural Change, Economic Rank, and the Evolution of Black-White Earnings Differences, 1940–2014," Working

Paper No. 2279, National Bureau of Economic Research, September 2017, https://www.nber
.org/system/files/working_papers/w22797/w22797.pdf.

41. "Poverty Rate by Race/Ethnicity," Kaiser Family Foundation, 2018, at https://www.kff
.org/other/state-indicator/poverty-rate-by-raceethnicity/?currentTimeframe=0&sortModel
=%7B%22colId%22:%22Location%22,%22sort%22:%22asc%22%7D.

42. See Marianne Cooper, *Cut Adrift: Families in Insecure Times* (Berkeley: University
of California Press, 2014); Victor Tan Chen, *Cut Loose: Jobless and Hopeless in an Unfair
Economy* (Oakland: University of California Press, 2015); Allison J. Pugh, *The Tumbleweed Society: Working and Caring in an Age of Insecurity* (Oxford: Oxford University
Press, 2015); Arne L. Kalleberg, *Good Jobs, Bad Jobs: The Rise of Polarized and Precarious
Employment Systems in the United States, 1970s to 2000s* (New York: Russell Sage Foundation, 2011); David Weil, *The Fissured Workplace: Why Work Became So Bad for So Many
and What Can Be Done to Improve It* (Cambridge, MA: Harvard University Press, 2014).

43. Benjamin M. Friedman, *The Moral Consequences of Economic Growth* (New York:
Vintage Books, 2005), 4.

44. Samuel P. Huntington, *Political Order in Changing Societies* (New Haven, CT: Yale
University Press, 1968), 50–51.

45. Friedman, *The Moral Consequences of Economic Growth*, 14. See, in general, Huntington, *Political Order in Changing Societies*, 47 and 32–59. Writing in 1968, Huntington
was more focused on what were called third world countries at the time, and his book is in
part a warning to the American foreign policy establishment not to be in such a hurry to
encourage literacy, democracy, economic development, and prosperity in those countries;
he compiles an impressive list of well-known instances where improved conditions of various sorts led to more "social unrest"—more activism and agency among people—rather
than less, as still is conventionally expected.

46. John Kenneth Galbraith, *The Affluent Society* (Boston: Houghton Mifflin, 1998),
was originally published in 1959, when real median household income was about three-
fourths of what it would become by 1975, by which time it had reached nearly the level it
is now. In 2019 dollars, median household income was $31,000 in 1947 (when this series
begins), $42,000 in 1959, and $57,000 in 1975. See Carter et al., *Historical Statistics of the
United States*, Vol. 2, Table Be1-18, "Distribution of Money Income among Households,
1947–1998," 652.

47. In 1956, for example, fewer than one in four whites thought blacks and whites
should be treated equally in hiring. See Nancy MacLean, *Freedom Is Not Enough: The
Opening of the American Workplace* (Cambridge, MA: Harvard University Press, 2006),
54. Likewise, Tamara Draut cites the opposition of the *New York Times* and the *New Republic* to the "sex equality" provision of the 1964 Civil Rights Act to show how the "very
idea that women should be able to have the same jobs as men was seen as both ridiculous
and contrary to nature." Tamara Draut, *Sleeping Giant: How the New Working Class Will
Transform America* (New York: Doubleday, 2016), 123–24.

48. On productivity, see "Labor Productivity and Costs: Productivity Change in the
Nonfarm Business Sector, 1947–2015," Bureau of Labor Statistics, http://www.bls.gov/lpc
/prodybar.htm. On innovation, see "The 85 Most Disruptive Ideas in Our History," *Bloom-
berg Businessweek*, 2014, special issue celebrating the magazine's eighty-fifth anniversary,
http://www.bloomberg.com/businessweek/85ideas/. Nearly half of the ideas named came
during the Glorious Thirty, including exactly five of the top ten and ten of the top twenty.
Also noteworthy is that "between the late 1950s and early 1970s, the legal underpinnings of
the right to vote were transformed more dramatically than they had been at any earlier
point in the nation's history." Alexander Keyssar, *The Right to Vote: The Contested History of
Democracy in the United States* (New York: Basic Books, 2000), 256. Chapter 8, "Breaking

Barriers," lays out the case for this claim, reading like an ode to the Glorious Thirty in a realm I have not covered in this chapter.

49. Based strictly on income quintiles, there was not a significant increase in the chances of a person born in the lowest quintile reaching the highest (they were slim before and still are), but this does not take into account the enormous shift in the occupational structure during the Glorious Thirty and the working conditions and life circumstances that went with that change. Political theorist Adam Swift calls "the 'Golden Age' of social mobility" an "expansion of 'room at the top,'" explaining that "the postwar increase in the proportion of better jobs . . . constitutes an upgrading of the class structure." Adam Swift, "What's Fair about That?," *London Review of Books* 42, no. 2 (January 23, 2020), https://www.lrb.co.uk /the-paper/v42/n02/adam-swift/what-s-fair-about-that. Still, the continuity in "rank-based measures of intergenerational mobility" (often called "relative mobility") merely emphasizes the greater importance of across-the-board increases in real wages and family incomes (often called "absolute mobility" and metaphorically "a rising tide that lifts all boats"). For evidence of the continuity in "rank-based measures" of income across the second half of the twentieth century, see Raj Chetty, Nathaniel Hendren, Patrick Kline, Emmanuel Saez, and Nicholas Turner, "Is the United States Still a Land of Opportunity? Recent Trends in Intergenerational Mobility," *American Economic Review* 104, no. 5 (2014): 141–47.

2. THE RISE OF PROFESSIONAL MIDDLE-CLASS LABOR

1. Susan B. Carter, Scott Sigmund Gartner, Michael R. Haines, Alan L. Olmstead, Richard Sutch, and Gavin Wright, eds., *Historical Statistics of the United States*, Vol. 2, *Work and Welfare* (Cambridge: Cambridge University Press, 2006), Table Ba1033–1046, "Major Occupational Groups—All Persons: 1860–1990," 133. From the table's occupational categories, I defined "blue collar" as including "craft workers," "operatives," and "laborers," who grew from 18.5 million workers in 1940 to more than 30 million in both 1980 and 1990 but declined as a percentage of the total workforce from just under 40 percent to about 25 percent by 1990.

2. Camille Ryan and Julie Siebens, *Educational Attainment in the United States: 2009*, US Census Bureau, 2012, http://www.census.gov/prod/2012pubs/p20-566.pdf. Despite fierce racial discrimination during the entirety of the period, blacks increased their college graduation rates from nearly zero in 1940 to 10 percent by 1975. National Center for Education Statistics, *120 Years of American Education: A Statistical Portrait* (Washington, DC: US Department of Education, 1993), https://nces.ed.gov/pubs93/93442.pdf.

3. Carter et al., *Historical Statistics of the United States*, Vol. 2, Table Ba1033–1046, "Major Occupational Groups—All Persons: 1860–1990."

4. John Kenneth Galbraith, in *The Affluent Society* (Boston: Houghton Mifflin Company, 1998, originally published in 1958), first identified a "new class" of workers who expected to enjoy their work, and his examples were all professionals and managers (chap. 23, "Labor, Leisure and the New Class"). He would later develop this notion into what he called "the technostructure" in *The New Industrial State* (Boston: Houghton Mifflin, 1971). Barbara and John Ehrenreich's justly famous article "The Professional Managerial Class" was reprinted in 1979 and matched with a book's worth of critique, debate, and commentary in Pat Walker, ed., *Between Labor and Capital* (Boston: South End Press, 1979).

5. See Christopher Jencks and David Riesman, *The Academic Revolution* (Garden City, NY: Doubleday, 1968); Martin Trow, *Twentieth-Century Higher Education: Elite to Mass to Universal* (Baltimore: John Hopkins University Press, 2010).

6. The literature on middle-class professionalism is outrageously slim given its importance in our society today and for at least the last one hundred years. Burton J. Bledstein's *The Culture of Professionalism: The Middle Class and the Development of Higher Education*

in America (New York: Norton, 1976) is focused strictly on the nineteenth century but is valuable in establishing the university as *the* agent for developing "the culture of professionalism," which he presents as a contradictory jumbo of high-minded social idealism and a relentless pursuit of status and affluence. Paul Starr's masterful *The Social Transformation of American Medicine: The Rise of a Sovereign Profession and the Making of a Vast Industry* (New York: Basic Books, 1982) is revelatory about the rise of doctors mostly in the twentieth century and mostly absent any "high-minded social idealism;" but as important as the health care industry is, physicians have played a minor, nearly nonexistent role in shaping the broader professional middle-class culture of the Glorious Thirty and after. Rakesh Khurana's *From Higher Aims to Hired Hands: The Social Transformation of American Business Schools and the Unfulfilled Promise of Management as a Profession* (Princeton, NJ: Princeton University Press, 2007) was especially helpful to me; see note 7 in this chapter. Jeff Schmidt's *Disciplined Minds: A Critical Look at Salaried Professionals and the Soul-Battering System That Shapes Their Lives* (Lanham, MD: Rowman & Littlefield, 2000) is not without insight but is so single-minded in its moralistic ax grinding that I couldn't finish reading it.

7. See Khurana, *From Higher Aims to Hired Hands.* Khurana, a Harvard Business School professor, presents the Glorious Thirty (for him 1941–1970) as merely a way station in the long-term erosion of what he calls management's "professionalization project," but his treatment of the period after 1970 is nonetheless cast within a certain angry nostalgia for the era of managerial capitalism.

8. John Kenneth Galbraith, *The New Industrial State* (Princeton, NJ: Princeton University Press, 2007), esp. chaps. 6–8.

9. Carter et al., *Historical Statistics of the United States*, Vol. 2, Table Bc713–718, "Professional and Instructional Staff at Institutions of Higher Education, by Sex and Public-Private Control: 1869–1993," 462.

10. Carter et al., *Historical Statistics of the United States*, Vol. 2, Table Ba1159-1395, "Detailed Occupations—All Persons: 1859–1990," 142–49.

11. Carter et al., *Historical Statistics of the United States*, Vol. 2, Table Bc97–106, "Public Elementary and Secondary Day School Teachers and Instructional Staff—Average Annual Salary and Number, by Sex: 1869–1996," 412–13.

12. For the massification of higher education, see Trow, *Twentieth-Century Higher Education*, esp. chap. 16.

13. Sarah Bakewell, *At the Existentialist Café: Freedom, Being, and Apricot Cocktails* (New York: Other Press, 2016), 283–85. Bakewell is one of several younger historians, born in the mid-1960s, who have joyfully documented the dynamism of the 1950s as prelude and prologue to the 1960s. Referring to "the great liberation movements of the 1950s and 1960s," Bakewell claims that "existentialist ideas flowed into the widening stream of 1950s anti-conformism, and then into the full-blown idealism of the late 1960s" (29, 31). Painting on a wider canvas, Alan Petigny's *The Permissive Society: America, 1941–1965* (New York: Cambridge University Press, 2009), covers everything from blue jeans and Abstract Expressionism to child-rearing manuals and the "ascendancy of science," along with sexual norms and values, psychology, and religion to argue that "Americans during the 1950s were moving in a more open and democratic direction and away from a conservative, hierarchal vision. . . . [S]nobbery became a character trait increasingly held in low regard . . . [and] the valorization of democracy deepened suspicions toward those who fancied themselves, or simply appeared to think of themselves, as superior to the general population" (192–93). Another more narrowly political attempt to redefine the decade is Jennifer A. Delton, *Rethinking the 1950s: How Anticommunism and the Cold War Made America Liberal* (New York: Cambridge University Press, 2013).

14. You may think I exaggerate the spread of "intellectual ferment" in the 1950s, but I look back and wonder. What was I—an Appalachian mill town teenager aspiring to be a sportswriter in Connecticut when I wasn't looking up some girl's skirt and about as intellectually unfermenting as I could be—doing reading *Dharma Bums* on my own, writing a research paper on Fauvists and Cubists as a senior, and listening to Charlie Parker and Thelonious Monk under the tutelage of one of my steelworker coaches for Franklin Local 2634's baseball team? How did such a thing happen in 1960, all before the world turned upside down? The moral panic and authenticity dramas must have been really widespread by then for these pieces of it to get all the way to someone like me.

15. Carter et al., *Historical Statistics of the United States*, Vol. 2, Table Ba1159-1395, "Detailed Occupations—All Persons: 1859–1990," 142–49.

16. Avner Offer, *The Challenge of Affluence: Self-Control and Well-Being in the United States and Britain since 1950* (Oxford: Oxford University Press, 2006). Offer opens the book with what he calls his core argument: "Affluence breeds impatience, and impatience undermines well-being." His argument is not as narrowly focused on impatience as this line suggests, but looking back from the twenty-first century, he fails to see the anxious exhilaration and exploratory nature of those initial decades of living with discretionary income and time, especially among the wildly expanding professions in the United States.

17. Though it initially affected scholarship more than middle-class professionalism as a whole, there were darker notes of class domination and prejudice being sung at the time. The idea that working-class people had authoritarian personalities was developed in the 1950s as a middle-class fear fantasy and has spread more widely in the middle-class imagination up to the present. See Michael Lind, *The New Class War: Saving Democracy from the Managerial Elite* (n.p.: Portfolio/Penguin, 2020), 103–12. I address this subject more fully in chapter 8.

18. Though higher education is a small and likely more elite part of the emerging professional middle class of this time, by 1975 about one of four college faculty were from working-class backgrounds, about the same percentages as studies in 1995 and 2013 found. Lynn Arner, "Survival Strategies for Working-Class Women as Junior Faculty Members," in *Working in Class: Recognizing How Social Class Shapes Academic Work*, ed. Allison L. Hurst and Sandi Kawecka Nenga (Lanham, MD: Rowman & Littlefield, 2016), 50.

19. Jason Isbell, Drive-By Truckers, "Outfit," *Decoration Day*, released June 17, 2003, by New West Records.

3. WORKING-CLASS AGENCY IN PLACE

1. David Kynaston, *Modernity Britain: Opening the Box, 1957–1959* (London: Bloomsbury Publishing, 2013), 26–27. The epigraph for this chapter is also from Kynaston, 56–57.

2. Richard Hoggart, *The Uses of Literacy: Aspects of Working-Class Life with Special Reference to Publications and Entertainments*, reprint ed. (New York: Oxford University Press, 1970).

3. Stephen Meyer, *Manhood on the Line: Working-Class Masculinities in the American Heartland* (Urbana: University of Illinois Press, 2016), 4.

4. Meyer, *Manhood on the Line*, 5.

5. Meyer, *Manhood on the Line*, 3–6.

6. These distinctions will be explained and explored in more detail in forthcoming chapters. The routine-seeking/action-seeking distinction is from Herbert Gans, *The Urban Villagers: Group and Class in the Life of Italian Americans* (New York: Free Press, 1962), 28–32. The settled-living/hard-living binary is from Lillian Breslow Rubin, *Worlds of Pain: Life in the Working-Class Family* (New York: Basic Books, 1976), 30–34.

7. See Stephanie Coontz, *The Way We Never Were: American Families and the Nostalgia Trap* (New York: Basic Books, 1992), esp. chap. 2.

8. Sarah Attfield, who grew up in the working class in London, argues that "respectability" is exclusively a middle-class or upper-class (even "bourgeois") concept imported into the working class from outside. Though that happens too, Attfield's analysis misses how common it is for working-class people to have a very different idea of what it takes to earn the respect of oneself and others, especially in autonomous or semiautonomous working-class worlds. See Attfield, "Rejecting Respectability: On Being Unapologetically Working Class," *Journal of Working-Class Studies* 1, no. 1 (December 2016): 45–57, https://workingclassstudiesjournal .files.wordpress.com/2016/06/jwcs-vol-1-issue-1-december-2016-attfield.pdf.

9. Wlliam Julius Wilson, *The Declining Significance of Race: Blacks and Changing American Institutions*, 2nd ed. (Chicago: Chicago University Press, 1980), 128, shows large increases in the proportions of black men in manufacturing from 1940 to 1970—from 5 percent to 15 percent of craft jobs and from 13 percent to 29 percent of "operatives." For black women workers, see Andrew J. Cherlin, *Labor's Love Lost: The Rise and Fall of the Working-Class Family* (New York: Russell Sage Foundation, 2014), 94. In Chicago, African American men and women became majorities in the post office and the transit authority by 1968. Erik Gellman, "In the Driver's Seat: Chicago's Bus Drivers and Labor Insurgency in the Era of Black Power," *LABOR Studies in Working-Class History* 11, no. 3 (Fall 2014):49–76/

10. Gans, *The Urban Villagers*, 29.

11. Arthur McIvor, *Working Lives: Work in Britain since 1945* (New York: Palgrave Macmillan, 2013), 274.

12. Jeff Torlina, *Working Class: Challenging Myths about Blue-Collar Labor* (Boulder, CO: Lynne Rienner Publishers, 2011). See also Torlina's "Power at the Point of Production: Explaining Complexity in Social Stratification," unpublished manuscript, 2016.

13. Sociologist Michele Lamont carefully elaborated this working-class "critique of the moral character of upper middle-class people" in her study of blue-collar men in the United States and France, *The Dignity of Working Men: Morality and the Boundaries of Race, Class, and Immigration* (Cambridge, MA: Harvard University Press, 2000); see, for example, 146–48.

14. In their classic history of higher education in the United States, Christopher Jencks and David Riesman initially assumed that the rapid growth in college enrollments in the postwar years was "largely a consequence of increased lower-middle and working-class access to and interest in college," but their research determined that most of the academic explosion in enrollments was actually "among upper-middle class children." Working-class high school graduates like me did enter colleges in greater numbers than before, but as I observed, there was a decided lack of interest across the class even as access improved. Christopher Jencks and David Riesman, *The Academic Revolution* (Garden City, NY: Doubleday, 1968), 95. Such negative attitudes toward college educations continue today. Despite the apparent unanimity on the importance of higher education, only about half of Americans think universities are having a positive effect on the country. Kim Parker, "The Growing Partisan Divide in Views of Higher Education," Pew Research Center, August 19, 2019, https://www.pewsocialtrends.org/essay/the-growing-partisan-divide-in-views-of -higher-education/.

15. See Kathy Newman, "How the Fifties Worked: Mass Culture and the Decade the Unions Made," book in progress, 2020; John Bodnar, *Blue-Collar Hollywood: Liberalism, Democracy, and Working People in American Film* (Baltimore: John Hopkins University Press, 2003); Judith E. Smith, *Visions of Belonging: Family Stories, Popular Culture, and Postwar Democracy, 1940–1960* (New York: Columbia University Press, 2004).

16. The Debs quote is cited in Martin Trow, *Twentieth-Century Higher Education: Elite to Mass to Universal* (Baltimore: John Hopkins University Press, 2010), 212.

4. "AT LEAST WE OUGHT TO BE ABLE TO"

1. Marc Levinson, *An Extraordinary Time: The End of the Postwar Boom and the Return of the Ordinary Economy* (New York: Basic Books, 2016). Though Levinson argues that this "extraordinary time" can never be repeated, he fully agrees that it was glorious:

> The very fact that life was so good—that jobs were easy to find; that food was plentiful and decent housing commonplace; that a newly woven safety net protected against unemployment, illness, and old age—encouraged individuals to take risks, from marching in the streets to joining the antimaterialist counterculture. Rising living standards and greater economic security made it possible for many people in many countries to join in the cultural ferment and social upheaval of the 1960s and early 1970s, and arguably engendered the confidence that brought vocal challenges to injustices—gender discrimination, environmental degradation, repression of homosexuals—that had long existed with little public outrage. (4–5)

2. Jefferson Cowie, *The Great Exception: The New Deal & the Limits of American Politics* (Princeton, NJ: Princeton University Press, 2016).

3. Emmanuel Saez, "Income and Wealth Inequality: Evidence and Policy Implications," Neubauer Collegium Lecture, University of Chicago, October 2014, https://eml.berkeley.edu/~saez/lecture_saez_chicago14.pdf.

4. This is a back-of-the-envelope calculation: net national income ($17.5 trillion in 2018, from the World Bank) × a 16 percent loss of share for the bottom 90 percent = $2.8 trillion. That $2.8 trillion loss is then divided by the number of workers who constitute 90 percent of the employed labor force (142 million at-work full- and part-time workers in 2019, from the Bureau of Labor Statistics), resulting in a per capita gain of $19,700. World Bank, "Adjusted Net National Income (Current US$)," http://data.worldbank.org/indicator/NY.ADJ.NNTY.CD; Bureau of Labor Statistics, "Labor Force Statistics from the Current Population Survey CPS CPS Program Links," https://www.bls.gov/cps/cpsaat11.htm. A more thorough study by the RAND Corporation in 2020 found that my rough approximation is rather conservative. See Carter C. Price and Kathryn A. Edwards, "Trends in Income From 1975 to 2018," September 2020, https://www.rand.org/pubs/working_papers/WRA516-1.html.

5. See Samuel Bowles, David M. Gordon, and Thomas E. Weisskopf, *Beyond the Waste Land: A Democratic Alternative to Economic Decline* (Garden City, NY: Anchor/Doubleday, 1983), 54–59 on capital shortage, 95–97 on profit squeeze.

6. Another back-of-the-envelope calculation: Using data from figure 4.1 (from the Economic Policy Institute), real hourly compensation grew about 15 percent from 1973 to 2018, while productivity increased by about 70 percent during the same period. I have been tracking Bureau of Labor Statistics reports of "real weekly wages for production and nonsupervisory workers" for decades, so I used those numbers and figured the difference in 2020 dollars between a 70 percent increase from 1973 ($26,608) and a 15 percent increase from that year ($5,701), which amounts to an average loss of $20,907 per worker. Calculated from "Average Weekly Earnings of Production and Nonsupervisory Employees, Financial Activities," Federal Reserve Bank of St. Louis Economic Research, https://fred.stlouisfed.org/series/CES5500000030. Since production and nonsupervisory workers in the private sector number about one hundred million (see "Table B-6. Employment of Production and Nonsupervisory Employees on Private Nonfarm Payrolls by Industry Sector, Seasonally Adjusted," Bureau of Labor Statistics, https://www.bls.gov/news.release/empsit.t22.htm), the total aggregate loss is $20,907 × 100 million = $2 trillion. Steven Greenhouse, in *The Big Squeeze: Tough Times for the American Worker* (New York: Knopf, 2008), 5, calculated that the annual loss in 2007 was $22,000 for "the average full-time worker" or more

than $2 trillion, but he does not explain how he arrived at that figure. While greater precision is to be desired, these rough estimates are enough to confirm that sharing productivity gains again would be as transformative now as it was during the Glorious Thirty.

7. Richard Phillips, "The Facts Missing from the Debate Over Tax Fairness," Tax Justice Blog, March 3, 2015, http://www.taxjusticeblog.org/archive/2015/03/the_facts_missing_from_the_deb.php#.WMwUGPkrLcs.

8. Sam Pizzagati, *The Rich Don't Always Win: The Forgotten Triumph over Plutocracy That Created the American Middle Class, 1900–1970* (New York: Seven Stories, 2012), 247, 263.

9. Thomas Piketty, *Capital in the Twenty-First Century*, trans, Arthur Goldhammer (Cambridge, MA: Harvard University Press, 2014), 505–8.

10. Pizzagati, *The Rich Don't Always Win*, chap. 11.

11. Much of the discussion among international economists has been about determining what would be an "optimal top tax rate" for any advanced economy. Piketty (*Capital in the Twenty-First Century*, 512–13) hypothesized that it would be at least 80 percent on incomes above $500,000 or $1 million), and then a more thorough study determined that it would be 83 percent! See Thomas Piketty, Emmanuel Saez, and Stefanie Stantcheva, "Optimal Taxation of Top Labor Incomes: A Tale of Three Elasticities," *American Economic Journal: Economic Policy* 6, no. 1 (February 2014): 230–71. A more comprehensive analysis by Saez and Gabriel Zucman estimates that a total package of tax reforms focused strictly on the top 1 percent could produce $750 billion a year for government investments in health, education, green infrastructure, and other forms of income redistribution. Emmanuel Saez and Gabriel Zucman, *The Triumph of Injustice: How the Rich Dodge Taxes and How to Make Them Pay* (New York: Norton, 2019), 143.

12. Joshua Freeman, *American Empire: The Rise of a Global Power, the Democratic Revolution at Home, 1945–2000* (New York: Viking, 2012). Freeman frames the second half of the twentieth century as a conflict between empire and "the democratic revolution," with Henry Luce's "American century" contesting for resources and attention, hearts and minds, against Henry Wallace's "century of the common man." In Freeman's telling, after 1975 empire wins decisively, as the democratic revolution recedes.

13. Tony Judt, *Ill Fares the Land* (New York: Penguin, 2010), 229.

14. Pizzagati, *The Rich Don't Always Win*, 264 and 277.

15. Pizzagati, *The Rich Don't Always Win*, 267 and 270.

PART II: FREE WAGE LABOR AND THE CULTURES OF CLASS

1. "Manifesto of the Communist Party," in *Karl Marx and Frederick Engels, Selected Works*, Vol. 1ne (Moscow: Progress Publishers, 1969), 116.

2. See E. J. Hobsbawm, *The Age of Revolution, 1789–1848* (New York: Mentor, 1962), chaps. 9 and 11.

3. See "Wage Labor and Capital," in *Karl Marx and Frederick Engels, Selected Works*, 1:150–54. See also Lawrence B. Glickman, *A Living Wage: American Workers and the Making of Consumer Society*, (Ithaca, NY: Cornell University Press, 1997), esp. chap. 1.

4. Edward Wolff cited in Neal Gabler, "The Secret Shame of Middle-Class Americans," *The Atlantic*, May 2016, https://www.theatlantic.com/magazine/archive/2016/05/my-secret-shame/476415/.

5. THERE IS A GENUINE WORKING-CLASS CULTURE

1. Jack Metzgar, *Striking Steel: Solidarity Remembered* (Philadelphia: Temple University Press, 2000), 203.

2. Robert Bellah, Richard Madsen, William M. Sullivan, Ann Swidler, and Steven M. Tipton, *Habits of the Heart: Individualism and Commitment in American Life*, updated ed. (Berkeley: University of California Press, 1996), xliii.

3. Barbara Jensen, "Becoming versus Belonging: Psychology, Speech, and Social Class," paper presented at the 1997 Youngstown Working-Class Studies Conference, Class Matters, http://www.classmatters.org/2004_04/becoming_vs_belonging.php. Jensen's more fully developed interpretation of class cultures is in her book *Reading Classes: On Culture and Classism in America* (Ithaca, NY: Cornell University Press, 2012).

4. Jake Ryan and Charles Sackrey, *Strangers in Paradise: Academics from the Working Class* (Boston: South End, 1984); C. L. Barney Dews and Carolyn Leste Law, eds., *This Fine Place So Far from Home: Voices of Academics from the Working Class* (Philadelphia: Temple University Press, 1995); Michelle M. Tokarczyk and Elizabeth A. Fay, eds., *Working-Class Women in the Academy: Laborers in the Knowledge Factory* (Amherst: University of Massachusetts Press, 1993). Two books by nonacademics are especially important for tracing the depth and extent of class culture clash: Barbara Jensen, a counseling psychologist, *Reading Classes,* and Alfred Lubrano, a journalist, *Limbo: Blue-Collar Roots, White-Collar Dreams* (Hoboken, NJ: Wiley, 2004). Of the numerous class-crossover memoirs, among the best are bell hooks, *Where We Stand: Class Matters* (New York: Routledge, 2000); Richard Rodriguez, *Hunger of Memory: The Education of Richard Rodriguez* (New York: Bantam Books, 1983); Cheri Register, *Packinghouse Daughter: A Memoir* (St. Paul: Minnesota Historical Society Press, 2000); Renny Christopher, *A Carpenter's Daughter: A Working-Class Woman in Higher Education* (Rotterdam: Sense Publishers, 2009); Milan Kovacovic, *Ma's Dictionary: Straddling the Social Class Divide* (Duluth, MN: Greysolon, 2011).

5. See Allison L. Hurst and Sandi Kawecka Nenga, eds., *Working in Class: Recognizing How Social Class Shapes Our Academic Work* (Lanham, MD: Rowman & Littlefield, 2016).

6. Raymond Williams, "Base and Superstructure in Marxist Cultural Theory," in *Problems in Materialism and Culture* (London: Verso, 1973/1980). Williams defines a residual culture as "experiences, meanings and values which cannot be expressed in terms of the dominant culture" but "are nevertheless lived and practiced on the basis of residue—cultural as well as social—of some previous social formation."

7. Lou Martin, *Smokestacks in the Hills: Rural-Industrial Workers in West Virginia* (Urbana: University of Illinois Press, 2015), esp. chap. 5; Andrew B. Arnold, *Fueling the Gilded Age: Railroads, Miners, and Disorder in Pennsylvania Coal Country* (New York: New York University Press, 2014), 224; Jensen, *Reading Classes,* 60.

8. Peter N. Stearns, *American Cool: Constructing a Twentieth-Century Emotional Style* (New York: New York University Press, 1994), 4. See also E. Anthony Rotundo, *American Manhood: Transformations in Masculinity from the Revolution to the Modern Era* (New York: Basic Books, 1993), ix and 294–97.

9. Claude S. Fischer, *Made in America: A Social History of American Culture and Character* (Chicago: University of Chicago Press, 2010), 12.

10. Benjamin DeMott, *The Imperial Middle: Why Americans Can't Think Straight about Class* (New Haven, CT: Yale University Press, 1990). Though I am focused on American social science, American journalism generally follows similarly blind assumptions about the singularity and ubiquity of professional middle-class culture, what DeMott labels "the omni syndrome" (73–93). A particularly prominent example is feature reporters' unending fascination with tracking generational attitude changes by going to elite college campuses. Only about two-thirds of millennials who graduate high school, for example, go on to a four-year college, and the vast majority of those are not at the top fifty schools, let alone the Princetons and Yales favored by New York–based reporters. See "College Enrollment and Work Activity of Recent High School and College Graduates," Bureau of Labor Statistics, April 28, 2020, https://www.bls.gov/news.release/hsgec.nr0.htm.

11. Fischer, *Made in America,* 12.

12. Colin Woodard, *American Nations: A History of the Eleven Rival Regional Cultures of North America* (New York: Viking, 2011).

13. Bellah et al., *Habits of the Heart*, 119.

14. Bellah et al., *Habits of the Heart*, 119–20.

15. Two more recent studies follow *Habits of the Heart*'s lead pretty directly. Rakesh Khurana's *From Higher Aims to Hired Hands: The Social Transformation of American Business Schools and the Unfulfilled Promise of Management as a Profession* (Princeton, NJ: Princeton University Press, 2007) confirms *Habits of the Heart*'s declension narrative from management as a professional calling to a merely utilitarian career. And Jennifer Silva's *Coming Up Short: Working-Class Adulthood in an Age of Uncertainty* (Oxford: Oxford University Press, 2013) finds working-class young people adopting a hand-me-down version of the middle-class mainstream's therapeutic culture, mostly without the help of psychological professionals. Claude Fischer, on the other hand, is more positive than *Habits of the Heart* about "American" individualism, which he says affirms the importance of community while insisting on "the freedom to choose one's community": "What is most notable about America is not radical individualism, the principle of going it alone, but voluntarism, the principle that individuals choose with whom they go" (Fischer, *Made in America*, 98).

16. Joan C. Williams, *White Working Class: Overcoming Class Cluelessness in America* (Boston: Harvard Business Review Press, 2017), 1.

17. Harris Interactive does a large national workplace survey, which it considers proprietary information, but Career Vision's headline summary of Harris reports that 45 percent of American workers are satisfied with their jobs. "Job Satisfaction Statistics," Clear Vision, https://careervision.org/job-satisfaction-statistics/

18. For a full set of links to Bureau of Labor Statistics occupational projections for various years, see Jack Metzgar, "Our Overeducated Workforce: Who Benefits?," Working-Class Perspectives, September 29, 2014, https://workingclassstudies.wordpress.com/2014/09/29/our-overeducated-workforce-who-benefits/..

19. Paul Willis, *Learning to Labor: How Working-Class Kids Get Working-Class Jobs* (New York: Columbia University Press, 1977); Julie Bettie, *Women without Class: Girls, Race, and Identity* (Oakland: University of California Press, 2014). I should also mention Jay MacLeod's *Ain't No Making It: Aspirations and Attainment in a Low-Income Neighborhood*, 3rd ed. (Philadelphia: Westview, 2009), which contrasts two groups of teenage boys, one of which rejects the middle-class aspirations of the school and one of which embraces them. MacLeod followed up his initial detailed and insightful ethnography from the 1980s with two subsequent revisits with these same groups, and he concludes that these young men were so objectively disadvantaged that their different aspirations made no difference in the long run.

20. For average UPS wages and salaries, see "Average Salary for United Parcel Service (UPS), Inc. Employees," PayScale, http://www.payscale.com/research/US/Employer=United_Parcel_Service_(UPS)%2C_Inc./Salary.

21. Michele Lamont, *The Dignity of Working Men: Morality and the Boundaries of Race, Class, and Immigration* (New York: Russell Sage Foundation, 2000), for example, found "having integrity" in "keeping the world in moral order" at the core of "the distinctions that [settled-living working-class male] whites and blacks draw toward other classes." Most of the men Lamont interviewed shared a "detailed critique of the moral character of upper middle-class people, mostly by pointing to their lack of personal integrity, lack of respect for others, and the poor quality of their interpersonal relationships." Using alternative definitions of success, these men "locate themselves above, or side by side with, 'people above'" (146–47). Other researchers have found similar working-class assessments of "fakes" and "phonies" among the upper and middle classes. Among the high school girls Julie Bettie interviewed in California's Central Valley, for example, both white and Latina working-class girls made "claims of authenticity" for themselves in contradistinction to "prep" girls from educated middle-class families (*Women without Class*, 194–96). There is likely more than a little class prejudice in these views, especially in how sweeping they can often be, but there is also sub-

stantial social science evidence that there is a solid core of truth in these working-class accusations. For comparative studies suggesting that middle-class behavior exhibits more independence and individual selfishness while working-class behavior relies more on interdependence and community, see Nicole M. Stephens, Stephanie A. Fryberg, and Hazel Rose Markus, "It's Your Choice: How the Middle-Class Model of Independence Disadvantages Working-Class Americans," in *Facing Social Class: How Societal Rank Influences Interaction*, ed. Susan T. Fiske and Hazel Rose Markus, 87–106 (New York: Russell Sage Foundation, 2012); Paul K. Piff, Daniel M. Stancato, Andres G. Martinez, Michael W. Kraus, and Dacher Keltner, "Class, Chaos, and the Construction of Community," *Journal of Personality and Social Psychology* 103, no. 6 (2012): 949–62; Nicole M. Stephens, Jessica S. Cameron, and Sarah S. M. Townsend, "Lower Social Class Does Not (Always) Mean Greater Interdependence: Women in Poverty Have Fewer Social Resources Than Working-Class Women," *Journal of Cross-Cultural Psychology* 45, no. 7 (2014): 1061–73.

22. Bettie, *Women without Class*, 125–127; Andrew Cherlin, *Labor's Love Lost: The Rise and Fall of the Working-Class Family in America* (New York: Russell Sage Foundation, 2014), 111–13.

23. Paul K. Piff, Daniel M. Stancato, Stephane Cote, Rodolfo Mendoza-Denton, and Dacher Keltner, "Higher Social Class Predicts Increased Unethical Behavior," *Proceedings of the National Academy of the Sciences* 109, no. 11 (March 13, 2012): 4086–91. This study found "a psychological dimension to higher social class that gives rise to unethical action": "Relative to lower-class individuals, individuals from upper-class backgrounds behaved more unethically in both naturalistic and laboratory settings." Lead author Paul Piff presented a brief on this research in a 2013 Ted Talk titled "Does Money Make You Mean?," TED, October 2013, https://www.ted.com/talks/paul_piff_does_money_make_you_mean#t-1729.

24. Metzgar, "Our Overeducated Workforce: Who Benefits?"; Jack Metzgar, "Graduating College Is Highly Overrated," Working-Class Perspectives, March 17, 2014, https://workingclassstudies.wordpress.com/2014/03/17/graduating-college-is-highly-overrated/.

25. David Kusnet, *Love the Work, Hate the Job: Why America's Best Workers Are Unhappier Than Ever* (Hoboken, NJ: Wiley, 2008).

26. The phrase "fear of falling" and the phenomena it denotes comes, of course, from Barbara Ehrenreich's influential book *Fear of Falling: The Inner Life of the Middle Class* (New York: Harper Perennial, 1990).

27. See Robert Putnam, *Our Kids: The American Dream in Crisis* (New York: Simon & Schuster, 2015); Richard Reeves, *Dream Hoarders: How the American Upper Middle Class Is Leaving Everyone Else in the Dust, Why That Is a Problem, and What We Can Do about It* (Washington, DC: Brooking Institution Press, 2017); Cherlin, *Labor's Love Lost.*

28. See "Occupations with the Most Job Growth, 2018–2028," Bureau of Labor Statistics, https://www.bls.gov/emp/tables/occupations-most-job-growth.htm.

29. Alfred Lubrano, *Limbo: Blue-Collar Roots, White-Collar Dreams* (Hoboken, NJ: Wiley, 2004).

30. See David Greene, "Reflections on the Production of a Working Class Academic," *Public Voices* 5, no. 3 (2002): 91–96, https://efbd7714-b1f3-4f1a-86a0-22d8babb400d.filesusr.com/ugd/d3a2e5_cafffa298c0c4d43a5f45cad9cfc6fe9.pdf; David Greene, "The Matrix of Identity Revisited," paper presented at the Sixth Biennial Conference of the Center for Working-Class Studies, Youngstown State University, May 15, 2003.

31. A great example of this is Didier Eribon's *Returning to Reims* (South Pasadena: Semiotext(e), 2013), translated by George Chauncey from the French 2009 edition. In late midlife after becoming a well-established Parisian intellectual, Eribon returned to visit his working-class mother and Reims neighborhood, having been away for a very long time. Similarly, Raymond Williams's autobiographical character Matthew in *Border Country* (Wales: Parthian, 2006, first published in 1960), had a much less troubled childhood than

Eribon but was equally alienated in returning to his Welsh village in midlife after a very long absence. I cannot imagine being away from my family of origin for a full year at that stage of life, let alone for decades.

32. Annette Lareau, *Unequal Childhoods: Class, Race, and Family Life* (Berkeley: University of California Press, 2003).

33. Lareau, *Unequal Childhoods*, 13.

34. French sociologist Pierre Bourdieu used the term "*doxa*" for those parts of a culture that are "so ingrained that they seldom come to conscious recognition" or "what agents immediately know but do not know that they know." See Sean McCloud, "Class as a Force of Habit," in Hurst and Nenga, *Working in Class*, 16.

35. Betsy Leondar-Wright, *Missing Class: Strengthening Social Movement Groups by Seeing Class Cultures* (Ithaca, NY: Cornell University Press, 2014). The graph referred to is on page 62. Another kind of current class straddling is involved in the educated middle-class young people who return to or move to Rust Belt cities and towns to find what they see as a more authentic way of life as well as cheaper housing. As Sherry Linkon comments, "the hybrid class identity in Rust Belt chic also offers an alternative class location for writers and readers for whom the old suburban, professional version of middle-class life is largely out of reach. For people living in a contingent economy, where the middle class is—together with the working class, of course—on the losing end of the expanding inequality gap, reclaiming the values of belonging and grit may not only offer a way to reconcile the contrast between the promise of the American Dream and the reality of the contemporary economy; it may also serve as a first . . . move toward solidarity and resistance." Sherry Lee Linkon, *The Half-Life of Deindustrialization: Working-Class Writing about Economic Restructuring* (Ann Arbor: University of Michigan Press, 2018), 161.

36. Jessi Streib, *The Power of the Past: Understanding Cross-Class Marriages* (Oxford: Oxford University Press, 2015), 202–3.

37. See Bill Bishop, *The Big Sort: Why the Clustering of Like-Minded America Is Tearing Us Apart* (Boston: Houghton Mifflin, 2008). This class isolation should not be exaggerated, however. People from working-class backgrounds are still entering the professions in some numbers, because despite their considerable advantages, the children of professional middle-class parents experience considerable downward mobility. See Jessi Streib, *Privilege Lost: Downward Mobility in a Gilded Age* (New York: Oxford University Press, 2020), 3. Among professors, for example, there has been only a small decline in the percentage of faculty from working-class backgrounds, from a little more than one-quarter in 1975 to a little less than one-quarter in 2013. Lynn Arner, "Survival Strategies for Working-Class Women as Junior Faculty Members," in Hurst and Nenga, *Working in Class*, 50–51.

38. Bellah, et al., *Habits of the Heart*, 69.

39. Bellah, et al., *Habits of the Heart*, 69.

40. Paul Osterman, *The Truth about Middle Managers: Who They Are, How They Work, Why They Matter* (Boston: Harvard Business Press, 2008), 121–22; see chap. 5 for the analysis.

41. Tim Strangleman and Tracey Warren, *Work and Society: Sociological Approaches, Themes and Methods* (London: Routledge, 2008), 96–97.

6. CATEGORICAL DIFFERENCES IN CLASS CULTURES

1. Jessi Streib, *The Power of the Past: Understanding Cross-Class Marriages* (Oxford: Oxford University Press, 2015), 168. The concept of feeling rules was pioneered by Arlie Hochschild in *The Managed Heart: Commercialization of Human Feeling* (Berkeley: University of California Press, 1979), where it was used to describe employer-prescribed practices for customer service workers for whom "emotional labor" is part of their jobs. Other sociologists have applied it more broadly to basic cultural practices or "scripts,"

such as Allison J. Pugh, *The Tumbleweed Society: Working and Caring in an Age of Insecurity* (Oxford: Oxford University Press, 2015), 36–38.

2. Streib, *The Power of the Past*, 170–71, 179, 186, and 193.

3. The original version was used in Barbara Jensen and Jack Metzgar, "Working Class and Middle Class as Competing Cultures," presentation at the Fifth Biennial Conference of the Center for Working-Class Studies, Youngstown State University, May 2001. That version is reproduced in Jack Metzgar, "Politics and the American Class Vernacular," in *New Working-Class Studies*, ed. John Russo and Sherry Lee Linkon (Ithaca, NY: Cornell University Press, 2005), 207.

4. The key role of "toughness" in working-class culture is more fully developed in chapter 8, "Taking It and Living in the Moments."

5. Allison Light, *Common People: The History of an English Family* (London: Fig Tree Penguin Books, 2014), 118.

6. See Victor Tan Chen, *Cut Loose: Jobless and Hopeless in an Unfair Economy* (Oakland: University of California Press, 2015); Marianne Cooper, *Cut Adrift: Families in Insecure Times* (Berkeley: University of California Press, 2014); Jennifer M. Silva, *Coming Up Short: Working-Class Adulthood in an Age of Uncertainty* (Oxford: Oxford University Press, 2013); Pugh, *The Tumbleweed Society: Working and Caring in an Age of Insecurity* (Oxford: Oxford University Press, 2015).

7. William Deresiewicz, *Excellent Sheep: The Miseducation of the American Elite & the Way to a Meaningful Life* (New York: Free Press, 2014), 46.

8. Andrew J. Cherlin, *Labor's Love Lost: The Rise and Fall of the Working-Class Family in America* (New York: Russell Sage Foundation, 2014), 46.

9. Jessica Calarco, *Negotiating Opportunities: How the Middle Class Secures Advantages in School* (New York: Oxford University Press, 2018).

10. Krista M. Soria, "Working-Class, Teaching Class, and *Working* Class in the Academy," in *Working in Class: Recognizing How Social Class Shapes Our Academic Work*, ed. Allison L. Hurst and Sandi Kawecka Nenga (Lanham, MD: Rowman & Littlefield, 2016), 132.

11. See Paul Willis, *Learning to Labor: How Working-Class Kids Get Working-Class Jobs* (New York: Columbia University Press, 1977).

12. Paul K. Piff, Daniel M. Stancato, Stephane Cote, Rodolfo Mendoza-Denton, and Dacher Keltner, "Higher Social Class Predicts Increased Unethical Behavior," *Proceedings of the National Academy of the Sciences* 109, no. 11 (March 13, 2012): 4088, 4086, and 4089.

13. See Pamela Fox, *Natural Acts: Gender, Race, and Rusticity in Country Music* (Ann Arbor: University of Michigan Press, 2009).

14. Michele Lamont, *The Dignity of Working Men: Morality and the Boundaries of Race, Class, and Immigration* (New York: Russell Sage Foundation, 2000), 146–47; Julie Bettie, *Women without Class: Girls, Race, and Identity* (Oakland: University of California Press, 2014), 194–96.

15. Barbara Jensen, "Becoming versus Belonging: Psychology, Speech, and Social Class," paper presented at the 1997 Working-Class Studies Conference at Youngstown State University, Class Matters, http://www.classmatters.org/2004_04/becoming_vs_belonging.php. Jensen's more fully developed interpretation of class cultures is in her book *Reading Classes: On Culture and Classism in America* (Ithaca, NY: Cornell University Press, 2012).

16. If Mary Beard is to be believed, the contrast was visible in first-century BCE Rome when proletarian laundry workers experienced "a sense of belonging that Cicero would never have dreamt of." Mary Beard, *SPQR: A History of Ancient Rome* (New York: Liveright Publishing, 2015), 454–55.

17. William Foote White, *Street Corner Society: The Social Structure of an Italian Slum* (Chicago: University of Chicago Press, 1955), 107.

18. Jay MacLeod, *Ain't No Makin' It: Aspirations & Attainment in a Low-Income Neighborhood*, 3rd ed. (Boulder, CO: Westview, 2009).

19. J. D. Vance, *Hillbilly Elegy: A Memoir of a Family and Culture in Crisis* (New York: HarperCollins, 2016); Sarah Smarsh, *Heartland: A Memoir of Working Hard and Being Broke in the Richest Country on Earth* (New York: Scribner, 2018).

20. Likewise, using the language of community with very similar findings, see Paul Piff, Andres Martinez, Daniel Stancato, Michael Kraus, and Dacher Keltner, "Class, Chaos, and the Construction of Community," *Journal of Personality and Social Psychology* 103, no. 6 (2012): 949–62.

21. "Sarah Townsend," University of Southern California Marshall School of Business, https://www.marshall.usc.edu/personnel/sarah-townsend-0.

22. Nicole Stephens and Sarah Townsend, "Research: How You Feel about Individualism Is Influenced by Your Social Class," *Harvard Business Review*, May 22, 2017, https://hbr.org/2017/05/research-how-you-feel-about-individualism-is-influenced-by-your-social-class. See also Nicole Stephens, Sarah Townsend, and Jessica Cameron, "Lower Social Class Does Not (Always) Mean Greater Interdependence: Women in Poverty Have Fewer Social Resources Than Working-Class Women," *Journal of Cross-Cultural Psychology* 45, no. 7 (2014): 1061–73.

23. Nicole M. Stephens, Hazel Rose Markus, and Sarah S. M. Townsend, "Choice as an Act of Meaning: The Case of Social Class," *Journal of Personality and Social Psychology* 93, no. 5 (2007): 814–30.

24. Lynsey Hanley, *Respectable: Crossing the Class Divide* (London: Penguin Books, 2016), 105.

25. *Striking Steel: Solidarity Remembered* (Philadelphia: Temple University Press 2000) is focused on the 1959 steel strike. I also wrote the essay "The 1945–1946 Strike Wave," in *The Encyclopedia of Strikes in American History*, ed. Aaron Brenner, Benjamin Day, and Immanuel Ness, 216–25 (Armonk, NY: M. E. Sharpe, 2009).

26. Jensen, *Reading Classes*, 214.

27. Light, *Common People*, 242.

28. Jensen, *Reading Classes*, 215.

29. Svend Brinkmann, *Stand Firm: Resisting the Self-Improvement Craze*, trans. Tam McTurk (Cambridge, UK: Polity, 2017), 123.

30. Charles Murray, *Coming Apart: The State of White America, 1960–2010* (New York: Crown Forum, 2012); Robert Putnam, *Our Kids: The American Dream in Crisis* (New York: Simon & Schuster, 2015); Cherlin, *Labor's Love Lost*.

31. These gender differences are explored in chapter 8, "Taking It and Living in the Moments." See also Lois Weis, *Class Reunion: The Remaking of the American White Working Class* (New York: Routledge, 2004); Kathryn Edin and Maria Kefalas, *Promises I Can Keep: Why Poor Women Put Motherhood before Marriage* (Berkeley: University of California Press, 2007).

32. Putnam, *Our Kids*, 72 and 69.

33. Cooper, *Cut Adrift*, chap. 3. Though I am critical of Cooper's interpretive framework, the portrait of Laura Delgado she provides is rich in nuanced detail, with an abundance of quotes in Delgado's own voice. The very richness of detail Cooper provides allows readers to develop other interpretations of Delgado's behavior and perspective. The direct quotes in this paragraph are from 88, 78, and 84.

34. David Roediger, *The Wages of Whiteness: Race and the Making of the American Working Class* (London: Verso, 1991).

35. Julie Bettie, *Women without Class*, 125–27; Cherlin, *Labor's Love Lost*, 111–13.

36. Richard Wilkinson and Kate Pickett, *The Spirit Level: Why Greater Equality Makes Societies Stronger* (New York: Bloomsbury, 2009); Richard Wilkinson and Kate Pickett,

The Inner Level: How More Equal Societies Reduce Stress, Restore Sanity and Improve Everyone's Well-Being (New York: Penguin, 2019), 36.

37. Benjamin DeMott, *The Imperial Middle: Why Americans Can't Think Straight about Class* (New Haven, CT: Yale University Press, 1990).

38. Wilkinson and Pickett, *The Inner Level*, 20.

39. Cf. "American workers are amazingly clear on the shape of the American class system and their place within it. . . . What matters is power, not status." Reeve Vanneman and Lynn Weber Cannon, *The American Perception of Class* (Philadelphia: Temple University Press, 1987), 283.

40. Light, *Common People*, 243, 47, and 242.

41. Jeff Torlina, *Working Class: Challenging Myths about Blue-Collar Labor* (Boulder, CO: Lynne Rienner Publishers, 2011).

42. Elizabeth R. Gottlieb, *We Are One: Stories of Work, Life and Love* (n.p.: Hard Ball, 2015), 79.

43. "The Making and Remaking of a Labor Historian: Interview with James R. Barrett," *Labor: Studies in Working-Class History* 13, no. (2 (May 2016): 63–79.

44. Quoted in Thomas B. Edsall, "Hillary Clinton's Juggling Act," *New York Times*, November 3, 2016. Jonathan Haidt is a social psychologist at New York University and the author of *The Righteous Mind: Why Good People Are Divided by Politics and Religion* (New York: Pantheon, 2012).

45. James R. Barrett, "Blue-Collar Cosmopolitans: Toward a History of Working-Class Sophistication in Industrial America," *History from the Bottom Up & the Inside Out: Ethnicity, Race, and Identity in Working-Class History* (Durham, NC: Duke University Press, 2017), chap. 4.

46. Michael Ignatieff, *The Ordinary Virtues: Moral Order in a Divided World* (Cambridge, MA: Harvard University Press, 2017), 71–72. In the passage quoted, Ignatieff is writing about multiethnic, multiracial twenty-first-century Los Angeles, but he found similar ordinary virtue in studies of New York City, Rio de Janeiro, Bosnia, Myanmar, Japan, and South Africa, all places with actual and potential violence between "in-turned tribes" of different ethnicities and religions.

47. Richard Pipes, "The Cleverness of Joseph Stalin," *New York Review of Books*, November 20, 2014.

48. Ignatieff, *Ordinary Virtues*, 135.

49. Ignatieff, *Ordinary Virtues*, 114.

50. In addition to Ignatieff, there are sympathetic and insightful treatments of political parochialism and cosmopolitanism in David Goodhart, *The Road to Somewhere: The Populist Revolt and the Future of Politics* (London: Hurst, 2017); Jonathan Haidt, "The Ethics of Globalism, Nationalism, and Patriotism," *Minding Nature* 9, no. 3 (Fall 2016): 18–24. Among the more common and simplistic cosmo-good/parochial-bad treatments is Marc Hetherington and Jonathan Weiler, *Prius or Pickup? How the Answers to Four Simple Questions Explain America's Great Divide* (Boston: Houghton Mifflin Harcourt, 2018).

51. See, for example, Jensen, *Reading Classes*, chap. 4. See also Annette Lareau, *Unequal Childhoods: Class, Race, and Family Life* (Berkeley: University of California Press, 2011); Jessica Calarco, *Negotiating Opportunities: How the Middle Class Secures Advantages in School* (New York: Oxford University Press, 2018).

52. Goodhart's Somewheres would be at least the 57 percent of Americans who have lived their entire lives in their home state or the average American who lives within eighteen miles of her or his mother. Michael Lind, *The New Class War: Saving Democracy from the Managerial Elite* (n.p.: Portfolio/Penguin, 2020), 25.

53. Goodhart, *Road to Somewhere*, 2–5.

54. Eric Idle, *Always Look on the Bright Side: A Sortabiography* (New York: Crown, 2018), as cited in interview with Idle on *Amanpour & Co.*, October 10, 2018, https://www.pbs.org/video/eric-idle-monty-python-tpxwsv/.

55. Jean Boucher, "Class Hybridity: The Coming of Age of a Sociological Blind Spot," paper presented at the Joint Conference of the Labor and Working-Class History Association and the Working-Class Studies Association, Georgetown University, May 30, 2015.

PART III: STRATEGIES AND ASPECTS OF WORKING-CLASS CULTURE

1. Quoted in Betsy Leondar-Wright, *Missing Class: Strengthening Social Movement Groups by Seeing Class Cultures* (Ithaca, NY: Cornell University Press, 2014), 117.

2. Tim Strangleman, "Gendering the Closure of Industrial Workplaces: Towards a Comparative European Perspective," unpublished manuscript, 7.

3. Thomas Gorman, for example, sees the "ranking out" he suffered in the City Line neighborhood of Brooklyn as an "injury of class" that undermined his self-confidence for most of his life, but he also recounts how in midadolescence, when he started to hang out on a neighboring block, he experienced ranking that was "good-natured teasing" rather than a mean-spirited "putting others down." Thomas Gorman, *Growing Up Working Class: Hidden Injuries and the Development of Angry White Men and Women* (n.p.: Palgrave Macmillan, 2017), 147–51. Robin D. G. Kelley, on the other hand, sees "the dozens" as creative verbal sparring that is simply meant "to get a laugh," and his critique of the class dynamics of white social scientists overinterpreting the dozens as evidence of a pathological masculine defense mechanism in a matriarchal urban black culture is both devastating and hilarious. Kelley also makes a compelling case that the dozens is cross-gendered, with women practicing somewhat different forms of it no less humorously. Robin D. G. Kelley, *Yo' Mama's Dis-FUNKtional!: Fighting the Culture Wars in Urban America* (Boston: Beacon, 1997), 1–4 and 32–36. Betsy Leondar-Wright provides a brilliant overview of this phenomenon in "Class Speech Differences I: Humor and Laughter," *Missing Class*, 115–20.

7. CEDING CONTROL TO GAIN CONTROL

1. Ruth Needleman, *Black Freedom Fighters in Steel: The Struggle for Democratic Unionism* (Ithaca, NY: Cornell University Press, 2003), 15. The profile of George Kimbley is chap. 1.

2. Needleman, *Black Freedom Fighters*, 36–132, profiles William Young, John Howard, Curtis Strong, and Jonathan Comer.

3. Charles M. Payne, *I've Got the Light of Freedom: The Organizing Tradition and the Mississippi Freedom Struggle* (Berkeley: University of California Press, 1995), 44. The profile of Amzie Moore is on 29–47.

4. Jessica McCrory Calarco, *Negotiating Opportunities: How the Middle Class Secures Advantages in School* (New York: Oxford University Press, 2018).

5. Calarco, *Negotiating Opportunities*, 190.

6. Our widely tiered labor market has been thoroughly documented as it has emerged over the last forty years. Among the best sources are Steven Greenhouse, *The Big Squeeze: Tough Times for the American Worker* (New York: Knopf, 2008); Arne Kalleberg, *Good Jobs, Bad Jobs: The Rise of Polarized and Precarious Employment Systems in the United States, 1970s to 2000s* (New York: Russell Sage Foundation, 2011); David Weil, *The Fissured Workplace: Why Work Became So Bad for So Many and What Can Be Done to Improve It* (Cambridge, MA: Harvard University Press, 2014); Tamara Draut, *Sleeping Giant: How the New Working Class Will Transform America* (New York: Doubleday, 2016); Emily Guendelsberger, *On the Clock: What Low-Wage Work Did to Me and How It Drives America Insane* (New York: Little, Brown, 2019).

7. Many sources could be cited, but among the most influential are Robert Putnam, *Our Kids: The American Dream in Crisis* (New York: Simon & Schuster, 2015); Richard V. Reeves,

Dream Hoarders: How the American Upper Middle Class Is Leaving Everyone Else in the Dust, Why That Is a Problem, and What to Do about It (Washington, DC: Brookings Institution Press, 2017). Reeves actually advocates "home visiting to improve parenting" (128) and thereby "equalizing human capital development." (124) Just to be clear, Jessica Calarco is not in this group; she values working-class culture, and her school-based ameliorations involve reducing the opportunities for middle-class students to negotiate special deals.

8. See "Unemployment Rates and Earnings by Educational Attainment, 2019," Bureau of Labor Statistics, https://www.bls.gov/emp/chart-unemployment-earnings-education.htm.

9. Parts of my discussion of Calarco here are taken from my review of *Negotiating Opportunities*. Jack Metzgar, "Middle-Class Influence vs. Working-Class Character," *Working-Class Perspectives*, September 10, 2018, https://workingclassstudies.wordpress.com/2018/09/10/middle-class-influence-vs-working-class-character/.

10. Michael Burawoy, *Manufacturing Consent: Changes in the Labor Process under Monopoly Capitalism* (Chicago: University of Chicago Press, 1979), 57–58.

11. Ben Hamper, *Rivethead: Tales from the Assembly Line* (New York: Warner Books, 1986).

12. See Robert Bruno, "Fried Onions and Steel," in *Steelworker Alley: How Class Works in Youngstown*, 62–79 (Ithaca, NY: Cornell University Press, 1999); Stacy James and Jimmy Santiago Baca, eds., *The Heat: Steelworker Lives & Legends* (Mena, AK: Cedar Hill Publications, 2001), a collection of stories written by northwest Indiana steelworkers; Jill Schennum, "The Labor Process at the Works" and "The Moral Economy of the Works," in "Bethlehem Steelworkers: Reshaping the Industrial Working Class," a manuscript I reviewed for Vanderbilt University Press.

13. Schennum, "Bethlehem Steelworkers." For a more recent study of factory workers, see Marek Korczynski, *Songs of the Factory: Pop Music, Culture, & Resistance* (Ithaca, NY: Cornell University Press, 2014), 64–65.

14. Reg Theriault, *How to Tell When You're Tired: A Brief Examination of Work* (New York: Norton, 1995), 96.

15. Frank Bardacke, *Trampling Out the Vintage: Cesar Chavez and the Two Souls of the United Farm Workers* (London: Verso, 2011), 3.

16. The value of labor-union protections of local control in the workplace was a major theme in Jack Metzgar, *Striking Steel: Solidarity Remembered* (Philadelphia: Temple University Press, 2000). The 1959 Steel Strike, which I focused on, was the largest strike in US history (five hundred thousand workers on strike for 116 days), and it was about a section of the Basic Steel contract that conferred substantial formal and informal power on the shop floor to workers who knew how to use (and "abuse") it. Schennum, "Bethlehem Steelworkers," supports my view in detail in her chapter "The Moral Economy of the Works."

17. This directly contradicts Michael Burawoy's classic study, *Manufacturing Consent*, which presents this struggle as a "game" where workers, with the help of their unions where present, participate in their own subordination. For me, Burawoy's 1970s Marxism is an embarrassing example of professional middle-class ignorance, arrogance, and misunderstanding—all the more embarrassing because it reflects my own view of things in the 1970s.

18. Guendelsberger, *On the Clock*, 15–125. See also Gabriel Winant, "Life under the Algorithm," *New Republic*, December 4, 2019.

19. Michael Marmot, *The Status Syndrome: How Social Standing Affects Our Health and Longevity* (New York: Henry Holt, 2004); Richard Wilkinson and Kate Pickett, *The Spirit Level: Why Greater Equality Makes Societies Stronger* (New York: Bloomsbury, 2009).

20. Cf. Michele Lamont, *The Dignity of Working Men: Morality and the Boundaries of Race, Class, and Immigration* (New York: Russell Sage Foundation, 2000).

21. Marmot, *The Status Syndrome*, 1.

22. Marmot, *The Status Syndrome*, 207. "Autonomy—how much control you have over your life—and the opportunities you have for full social engagement and participation are crucial for health, well-being, and longevity. It is inequality in these that plays a big part in producing the social gradient in health" (2).

23. Marmot, *The Status Syndrome*, 11. Marmot's error occurs early in the book when he says that extreme inequality's negative impact on health "is not just a matter of money" but instead of "where one stands in the hierarchy."

24. Richard Wilkinson and Kate Pickett, *The Inner Level: How More Equal Societies Reduce Stress, Restore Sanity and Improve Everyone's Well-Being* (New York: Penguin, 2019).

25. Lamont, *The Dignity of Working Men*; Jeff Torlina, *Working Class: Challenging Myths about Blue-Collar Labor* (Boulder, CO: Lynne Rienner Publishers, 2011).

26. Michele Lamont, *Money, Morals, & Manners: The Culture of the French and American Upper-Middle Class* (Chicago: University of Chicago Press, 1992). In fact, Elizabeth Currid-Halkett, *The Sum of Small Things: A Theory of the Aspirational Class* (Princeton, NJ: Princeton University Press, 2017), sees professional middle-class status as based solely on aesthetic and moral criteria and not at all on socioeconomic position, which she says middle-class professionals take for granted.

27. Marmot, *The Status Syndrome*, 71.

28. Wilkinson and Pickett, *The Spirit Level*, 67.

29. Sherry L. Murphy, Jiaquan Xu, Kenneth D. Kochanek, and Elizabeth Arias, "Mortality in the United States, 2017," National Center for Health Statistics Data Brief No. 328, Centers for Disease and Control Prevention, November 2018, https://www.cdc.gov/nchs/data/databriefs/db328-h.pdf; Anne Case and Angus Deaton, "Rising Morbidity and Mortality in Midlife among White Non-Hispanic Americans in the 21st Century," *Proceedings of the National Academy of Sciences* 112, no. 49 (December 8, 2015), https://www.pnas.org/content/pnas/112/49/15078.full.pdf

30. "Run out over half a century, [the upward redistribution of income] has slowly eaten away at the foundations of working-class life, high wages and good jobs, and has been central in causing deaths of despair. . . . If we are to stop deaths of despair, we must somehow stop or reverse the decline of wages for less educated Americans." Anne Case and Angus Deaton, *Deaths of Despair and the Future of Capitalism* (Princeton, NJ: Princeton University Press, 2020), 127.

31. From Barbara Jensen's oral histories of her family, in this case with Luella (Jensen) Sharpe, used with permission of the interviewer.

32. Karl Marx, "Estranged Labor," in *The Economic & Philosophical Manuscripts of 1844* (New York: International Publishers, 1964), 110.

33. See Rachel Sherman, *Uneasy Street: The Anxieties of Affluence* (Princeton, NJ: Princeton University Press, 2017); Jessi Streib, *Privilege Lost: Who Leaves the Upper Middle Class and How They Fall* (New York: Oxford University Press, 2020); Malcolm Harris, *Kids These Days: Human Capital and the Making of Millennials* (New York: Little Brown, 2017); Walter Kirn, *Lost in the Meritocracy: The Undereducation of an Overachiever* (New York: Doubleday, 2009); Miya Tokumitsu, *Do What You Love and Other Lies about Success and Happiness* (New York: Regan Arts, 2015).

34. Elliot Weininger and Annette Lareau, "Paradoxical Pathways: An Ethnographic Extension of Kohn's Findings on Class and Childrearing," *Journal of Marriage and Family* 71, no. 3 (August 2009): 680–95. Melvin Kohn, *Class and Conformity: A Study in Values* (Homewood, IL: Dorsey, 1969), found that working-class parents "emphasized children's conformity to external authority" (680), but Weininger and Lareau point out the paradox that "working-class and poor parents tended to grant children considerable autonomy in certain domains of daily life, thereby limiting their emphasis on conformity" (680).

35. Paul Willis, *Learning to Labor: How Working Class Kids Get Working Class Jobs* (New York: Columbia University Press, 1977).

36. The phrase comes from Christopher Tomlins, *The State and the Unions: Labor Relations, Law, and the Organized Labor Movement in America, 1880–1960* (Cambridge: Cambridge University Press, 1985), 327, but the most complete articulation of this notion as applied to individual workers is probably Burawoy, *Manufacturing Consent.*

8. TAKING IT AND LIVING IN THE MOMENTS

1. Seymour Martin Lipset, *Political Man: The Social Bases of Politics*, expanded ed. (Baltimore: John Hopkins University Press, 1981), 114. The discussion of delayed gratification begins on 108. The famous chapter I'm referencing, chapter 4, "Working-Class Authoritarianism," was originally drafted in 1955 for a conference of the Congress of Cultural Freedom, later revealed to be a creation of the US Central Intelligence Agency (87).

2. Jack Metzgar, *Striking Steel: Solidarity Remembered* (Philadelphia: Temple University Press, 2000), chap. 2.

3. Michele Lamont, *The Dignity of Working Men: Morality and the Boundaries of Race, Class, and Immigration* (Cambridge, MA: Harvard University Press, 2000), 23.

4. Yuichi Shoda, Walter Mischel, and Philip Peake, "Predicting Adolescent Cognitive and Self-Regulatory Competences from Preschool Delay of Gratification: Identifying Diagnostic Conditions," *Developmental Psychology* 26, no. 6 (1990): 978–86. I do not know why the study is most often identified by only one of its authors, Mischel, but I follow that convention in the text for convenience and readability.

5. See, for example, Karl Thompson, "The Effect of Cultural Deprivation on Education," ReviseSociology, February 15, 2014, https://revisesociology.com/2014/02/15/the-effect-of -cultural-deprivation-on-education/. Or just google "immediate gratification" or "cultural deprivation."

6. Tyler Watts, Greg Duncan, and Haonan Quan, "Revisiting the Marshmellow Test: A Conceptual Replication Investigating Links between Early Delay of Gratification and Later Outcomes," *Psychological Science* 29, no. 7 (July 2018): 1159–77.

7. Shoda, Mischel, and Peake, "Predicting Adolescent Cognitive and Self-Regulatory Competences from Preschool Delay of Gratification," tables 2 and 3.

8. Jessi Streib, *The Power of the Past: Understanding Cross-Class Marriages* (Oxford: Oxford University Press, 2015), 192.

9. Jessica McCrory Calarco, "Why Rich Kids Are So Good at the Marshmellow Test," *The Atlantic*, June 1, 2018.

10. Joshua Freeman, *Behemoth: A History of the Factory and the Making of the Modern World* (New York: Norton, 2018), 177.

11. Lawrence B. Glickman, *A Living Wage: American Workers and the Making of Consumer Society* (Ithaca, NY: Cornell University Press, 1997), traces in detail the political and intellectual debates in the Gilded Age labor movement between advocates of abolishing the wage system altogether and those focusing on fighting for a living wage.

12. Anne Balay, *Semi Queer: Inside the World of Gay, Trans, and Black Truck Drivers* (Chapel Hill: University of North Carolina Press, 2018), 143–44. Chapter 8, "Draggin' Ass: Persistence and Endurance Are Working-Class Values," is a thorough exploration of what I'm calling "taking it."

13. Angela Lee Duckworth and Lauren Eskreis-Winkler, "True Grit," Association for Psychological Science, April 2013, https://www.psychologicalscience.org/observer/true -grit. Duckworth's fully developed interpretation is in *Grit: The Power of Passion and Perseverance* (New York: Scribner, 2016).

14. The "grafters" designation comes from Arthur McIvor, *Working Lives: Work in Britain since 1945* (New York: Palgrave Macmillan, 2013), 271.

15. Jennifer Silva, *We're Still Here: Pain and Politics in the Heart of America* (New York: Oxford University Press, 2019), 3.

16. McIvor, *Working Lives*, 113.

17. Michael Ignatieff, *The Ordinary Virtues: Moral Order in a Divided World* (Cambridge, MA: Harvard University Press, 2017), 152.

18. Ignatieff, *The Ordinary Virtues*, 153.

19. Frank Bardacke, *Trampling Out the Vintage: Cesar Chavez and the Two Souls of the United Farm Workers* (London: Verso, 2011), 31.

20. My own blogs are still a good introduction to understanding the job structure, and they have multiple links to the supporting material. See "Our Overeducated Workforce: Who Benefits?," Working-Class Perspectives, September 29, 2014, https://workingclassstudies .wordpress.com/2014/09/29/our-overeducated-workforce-who-benefits/. Or just google "occupations with the most job growth" to get the latest Bureau of Labor Statistics snapshot of the job structure now and ten years out.

21. Andrew Arnold, *Fueling the Gilded Age: Railroads, Miners, and Disorder in Pennsylvania Coal Country* (New York: New York University Press, 2014), 6–7.

22. Andrew J. Cherlin, *Labor's Love Lost: The Rise and Fall of the Working-Class Family in America* (New York: Russell Sage Foundation, 2014), 158–64.

23. Two excellent studies of working-class tavern life are Julie Lindquist, *A Place to Stand: Politics and Persuasion in a Working-Class Bar* (New York: Oxford University Press, 2002); E. E. LeMasters, *Blue-Collar Aristocrats: Life-Styles at a Working-Class Tavern* (Madison: University of Wisconsin Press, 1975).

24. Streib, *The Power of the Past*, chap. 8. I summarize Streib's account in my introduction to chapter 6.

25. Kathryn Edin, Timothy Nelson, Andrew Cherlin, and Robert Francis, "The Tenuous Attachments of Working-Class Men," *Journal of Economic Perspectives* 33, no. 2 (Spring 2019): 211–28, https://www.aeaweb.org/articles?id=10.1257/jep.33.2.211. Cherlin and his coauthors borrow the concept of a "disciplined self," contrasted with a "caring self," from Michele Lamont, *The Dignity of Working Men*, 23 and 46–47.

26. The distinction between hard living and settled living in working-class life comes from Joseph T. Howell, *Hard Living on Clay Street: Portraits of Blue Collar Families* (Garden City, NY: Anchor, 1973), 6–7; Lillian Breslow Rubin, *Worlds of Pain: Life in the Working-Class Family* (New York: Basic Books, 1976), 30–36. Both Howell and Rubin refer to hard living and settled living as "lifestyles," which suggests too great a degree of freedom to choose among a menu of lifestyles. Conversely, I see them as individual or family economic conditions based on good or bad wages and the steadiness or unsteadiness of work, circumstances that are greatly affected by macroeconomic cycles, business models, the presence or absence of labor unions, and luck more than by individual character or choice. See Jack Metzgar, "Are 'the Poor' Part of the Working Class or in a Class by Themselves?," *Labor Studies Journal* 35, no. 3 (Spring 2010): 398–416, where I argue for drawing a clear distinction between routine seeking and action seeking as opposing cultural proclivities within working-class life and hard living and settled living as strictly economic conditions. In neither case are individuals or families fixed in these designations, and it is common for individuals and families to move into and out of these economic conditions and cultural proclivities across their lifetimes.

27. "Poverty Thresholds by Size of Family and Number of Children," US Census Bureau, updated each year, https://www.census.gov/data/tables/time-series/demo/income -poverty/historical-poverty-thresholds.html.

28. Diana Pearce was a pioneer in these efforts, with the work she did for Wider Opportunities for Women compiled in *Six Strategies for Family Economic Self-Sufficiency*, which unfortunately is no longer available. For her methodology in a 2008 study she did

for Colorado, see *The Self-Sufficiency Standard for Colorado 2008: A Family Needs Budget*, http://selfsufficiencystandard.org/sites/default/files/selfsuff/docs/CO2008.pdf. The Economic Policy Institute has developed the comprehensive "Family Budget Calculator" (https://www.epi.org/resources/budget/) that determines levels of income adequacy, or "hardship thresholds," for different locations across the country. More recently, focused on individual workers rather than households, the Massachusetts Institute of Technology has developed the "Living Wage Calculator" (https://livingwage.mit.edu/), which estimates living wages (an adequacy standard) by location across the country.

29. Sylvia Allegretto, "Basic Family Budgets Better Reveal the Hardships in America," Economic Policy Institute, August 31, 2005, https://www.epi.org/publication/webfeatures _snapshots_20050831/. Defining "hard living" in strictly economic terms is conceptually valuable, with important consequences for understanding the working class as a whole. But this does not mean that living cannot be hard within settled-living families, especially for children of alcoholics or parents with other toxic maladies. Thomas Gorman, for example, recounts in *Growing up Working Class: Hidden Injuries and the Development of Angry White Men and Women* (Cham, Switzerland: Palgrave Macmillan, 2017), that what by economic standards was a settled-living family was made hard by his father's chronic alcoholism and the uncertainty and insecurity that introduces into a child's world.

30. Michael Zweig, *The Working Class Majority: America's Best Kept Secret*, 2nd ed. (Ithaca, NY: Cornell University Press, 2012), 90.

31. Herbert Gans, *The Urban Villagers: Group and Class in the Life of Italian-Americans* (New York: Free Press, 1962), 28–32. For a more recent application of Gans's categories, see Sherry Ortner, "Reading America: Preliminary Notes on Class and Culture," in *Anthropology and Social Theory: Culture, Power, and the Acting Subject*, 19–41 (Durham, NC: Duke University Press, 2006).

32. See Betsy Leondar-Wright, *Class Matters: Cross-Class Alliance Building for Middle-Class Activists* (Gabriola Island, Canada: New Society Publishers, 2005). In the chapter titled "Are There Class Cultures?," Leondar-Wright develops the notion that working-class and middle-class cultures share a pragmatic realism that can often be limiting, while both low-income and owning classes, in different ways, are more likely to dream big, often too big to be useful in achieving better conditions.

33. For a comprehensive history from Manchester, England, in the nineteenth century to Foxconn in China in the twenty-first century, see Freeman, *Behemoth*. For a centuries-long history of the struggles of one working-class family in the south of England, see Alison Light, *Common People: The History of an English Family* (London: Fig Tree Penguin Books, 2014). For a three-generation portrait of an immigrant steel-working family in Chicago from the late nineteenth century until after the mills were gone, see Christine Walley, *Exit Zero: Family and Class in Postindustrial Chicago* (Chicago: University of Chicago Press, 2013).

34. Gorman, *Growing Up Working Class*, 63–68.

35. The concept of a "culture of poverty" was initially articulated by Oscar Lewis, *Five Families: Mexican Culture in the Culture of Poverty* (n.p.: Basic Books, 1959), and then picked up by Michael Harrington, *The Other America: Poverty in the United States* (New York: Scribner, 1962). Thus, though used by political conservatives to preach boot-strap government policies of inaction, the concept comes out of the US progressive tradition up to today and has often been extended to cover the entirety of "the working class." Recent examples include Robert Putnam, *Our Kids: The American Dream in Crisis* (New York: Simon & Schuster, 2015); Richard Reeves, *Dream Hoarders: How the American Upper Middle Class Is Leaving Everyone Else in the Dust, Why That Is a Problem, and What to Do about It* (Washington, DC: Brookings Institution Press, 2017). For a probing critical history of more recent usage of the concept, see Jessi Streib, "The Unbalanced Theoretical Toolkit:

Problems and Partial Solutions to Studying Culture and Reproduction but Not Culture and Mobility," *American Journal of Cultural Sociology* 5, nos. 1–2 (March 2017): 127–53.

36. See, for example, Charles Murray, *Coming Apart: The State of White America, 1960–2010* (New York: Crown Forum, 2012).

37. Sarah Smarsh, *Heartland: A Memoir of Working Hard and Being Broke in the Richest Country on Earth* (New York: Scribner, 2018); J. D. Vance, *Hillbilly Elegy: A Memoir of a Family and Culture in Crisis* (New York: HarperCollins, 2016).

38. For an insightful survey of the literature of deindustrialized places, see Sherry Lee Linkon, *The Half-Life of Deindustrialization: Working-Class Writing about Economic Restructuring* (Ann Arbor: University of Michigan Press, 2018). For a useful survey of people in declining small-town and rural areas, see Robert Wuthnow, *The Left Behind: Decline and Rage in Rural America* (Princeton, NJ: Princeton University Press, 2018).

39. Allison J. Pugh, *The Tumbleweed Society: Working and Caring in an Age of Insecurity* (Oxford: Oxford University Press, 2015), 100 and 16.

40. Though focused only on officially poor women, not on a broader working class, Kathryn Edin and Maria Kefalas, *Promises I Can Keep: Why Poor Women Put Motherhood before Marriage,*2nd ed. (Berkeley: University of California Press, 2011), documents these women's positive attitudes toward living free of male dependency (chap. 4) and how centrally important caring for their children has been to their lives (chap. 6).

41. Kim Parker and Renee Stepler, "As U.S. Marriage Rate Hovers at 50%, Education Gap in Marital Status Widens," Pew Research Center, September 14, 2017, https://www.pewresearch.org/fact-tank/2017/09/14/as-u-s-marriage-rate-hovers-at-50-education-gap-in-marital-status-widens/; Pugh, *The Tumbleweed Society*, 16.

42. "The Majority of Children Live with Two Parents, Census Bureau Reports," US Census Bureau, November 17, 2016, https://www.census.gov/newsroom/press-releases/2016/cb16-192.html.

43. See Robert Putnam, *Our Kids: The American Dream in Crisis* (New York: Simon & Schuster, 2015).

44. Anne Case and Angus Deaton, "Rising Morbidity and Mortality in Midlife among White Non-Hispanic Americans in the 21st Century," *Proceedings of the National Academy of Sciences* 112, no. 49 (December 8, 2015): 15078–83. Though focused only on the white part of the working class in their initial study, in their subsequent book Case and Deaton point out that black mortality rates are still nearly 50 percent higher than that of whites even after forty years of steeper declines in death rates. What's more, black death rates have more recently started to increase instead of decline. Anne Case and Angus Deaton and, *Deaths of Despair and the Future of Capitalism* (Princeton, NJ: Princeton University Press, 2020), 64.

45. Case and Deaton (*Deaths of Despair*, 123) make it even clearer that the tripling of deaths of despair reflects a much larger "disintegration of working-class lives" as a whole, not simply middle-aged white men.

46. Julia Belluz, "Nobel Winner Angus Deaton Talks about the Surprising Study on White Mortality He Just Co-authored," Vox, November 7, 2015, https://www.vox.com/2015/11/7/9684928/angus-deaton-white-mortality. A *Washington Post* investigation of 2014 data found that though the "white working class are more likely to use opioids" than the white middle class, the percentage of reported drug users among working-class whites was only 2.2 percent. Max Ehrenfreund and Jeff Guo, "If You've Ever Described People as 'White Working Class,' Read This," *Washington Post*, November 23, 2016, https://www.washingtonpost.com/news/wonk/wp/2016/11/22/who-exactly-is-the-white-working-class-and-what-do-they-believe-good-questions/.

47. See Tamara Draut, *Sleeping Giant: How the New Working Class Will Transform America* (New York: Doubleday, 2016); Steven Greenhouse, *Beaten Down, Worked Up: The Past, Present, and Future of American Labor* (New York: Knopf, 2019), part 4; An-

nelise Orleck, *"We Are All Fast-Food Workers Now": The Global Uprising against Poverty Wages* (Boston: Beacon, 2018).

48. Marianne Cooper, *Cut Adrift: Families in Insecure Times* (Berkeley: University of California Press, 2014), 88.

49. Thomas F. X. Noble, *The Foundations of Western Civilization* (Chantilly, VA: Teaching Company, 2002), 85.

50. Mindah-Lee Kumar, "Mindfulness: Finding Joy in the Present Moment," The Enthusiastic Buddhist, August 15, 2013, https://www.enthusiasticbuddhist.com/mindfulness -finding-joy-in-the-present-moment/.

51. See Tim Lott, "Zen Buddhism Teaches Us of the Importance of Living in the Present," *The Guardian*, September 21, 2012, https://www.theguardian.com/commentisfree /belief/2012/sep/21/zen-buddhism-lessons.

52. Sarah Blackwell, *At the Existentialist Café: Freedom, Being, and Apricot Cocktails* (New York: Other Press, 2016), 20.

53. Even Seymour Martin Lipset recognizes this possibility in a footnote: "It may be argued, though I personally doubt it, that this capacity to establish personal relationships, to live in the present, may be more 'healthy' (in a strictly medical, mental-health sense) than a middle-class concern with status distinctions, one's own personal impact on one's life situation, and a preoccupation with the uncertain future." Lipset, *Political Man*, 110.

54. William Deresiewicz, *Excellent Sheep: The Miseducation of the American Elite & The Way to a Meaningful Life* (New York: Free Press, 2014), 24–25.

55. Quoted from *Gravity's Rainbow* in Edward Mendelson, "In the Depths of the Digital Age," *The New York Review of Books*, June 23, 2016.

56. Cf. Betsy Leondar-Wright, *Missing Class: Strengthening Social Movement Groups by Seeing Class Cultures* (Ithaca: Cornell University Press, 2014). Though Leondar-Wright never uses the word "headstrong," it is one of the themes of her study of how various traditions, including class cultures but also class trajectories, race/ethnicities, and movement traditions, affect how activists understand and frame issues in different ways— issues from whether to serve food or talk at meetings to whether to use direct action or formal petition. To be more effective, Leondar-Wright demonstrates, requires everybody to be open to other ways of seeing and doing—not to abandon your own way, but simply to allow that others' ways may be legitimate and insightful too, which is what I mean by "less headstrong."

57. Nancy MacLean wrote about this effort in "Bringing the Organizing Tradition Home: Campus-Labor-Community Partnerships for Regional Power," in *Labor Rising: The Past and Future of Working People in America*, edited by Daniel Katz & Richard Greenwald (New York: The New Press, 2012).

9. WORKING-CLASS REALISM

1. Jennifer Artis's conception is similar to what British researchers saw as the "concept of 'enough'" among working-class parents and their daughters, an aspiration to simply have "enough materially and emotionally." Valerie Walkerdine, Helen Lucey, and June Melody, *Growing Up Girl: Psychosocial Explorations of Gender and Class* (New York: New York University Press, 2001), 47.

2. John Lennon, "Working Class Hero," *John Lennon/Plastic Ono Band* (1970).

3. See Didier Eribon, *Returning to Reims*, trans. Michael Lucey (South Pasadena, CA: Semiotext(e), 2013); Edouard Louis, *The End of Eddy*, trans. Michael Lucey (New York: Farrar, Straus and Giroux, 2014).

4. John Bodnar, "Immigration and Modernization: The Case of Slavic Peasants in Industrial America," in *American Working Class Culture*, ed. Milton Cantor (Westport, CT: Greenwood, 1979), 334–38.

5. John Bodnar, "Immigration, Kinship, and the Rise of Working-Class Realism in Industrial America," *Journal of Social History* 14, no. 1 (Autumn 1980): 56.

6. John Bodnar, *Workers' World: Kinship, Community, and Protest in an Industrial Society, 1900–1940* (Baltimore: John Hopkins University Press, 1982).

7. Nicole Stephens, Jessica Cameron, and Sarah Townsend, "Lower Social Class Does Not (Always) Mean Greater Interdependence: Women in Poverty Have Fewer Social Resources Than Working-Class Women," *Journal of Cross-Cultural Psychology* 45, no. 7 (May 2014): 1061–73.

8. The exclusive focus on marriage rates, single parents, and absent fathers in Andrew Cherlin, *Labor's Love Lost: The Rise and Fall of the Working-Class Family* (New York: Russell Sage Foundation, 2014), and Charles Murray, *Coming Apart: The State of White America, 1960–2010* (New York: Crown Forum, 2012), cannot capture what is going on in working-class extended families, where so much anecdotal information (including in memoirs mentioned throughout my notes as well as in my own observation and experience) recounts children being raised for a time by aunts and grandmothers and grandfathers—not to mention Elizabeth Warren's famous Aunt Bee who moved in with her to help Warren mother her children when she first taught law school. See Elizabeth Warren, *A Fighting Chance* (New York: Metropolitan Books, 2014), 20–23. The strength of the working-class family, traditionally and still now, is in its extension, and a middle-class focus exclusively on nuclear families systematically ignores this.

9. Annette Lareau, *Unequal Childhoods: Class, Race, and Family Life*, 2nd ed. (Berkeley: University of California Press, 2011). See also Michael Ignatieff's early twenty-first-century investigations around the world as evidence of the connections between peasant culture and working-class realism in *Ordinary Virtues: Moral Order in a Divided World* (Cambridge, MA: Harvard University Press, 2017).

10. Alison Light, *Common People: The History of an English Family* (London: Fig Tree Penguin Books, 2014), 67.

11. Diane Ravitch, *The Death and Life of the Great American School System: How Testing and Choice Are Undermining Education* (New York: Perseus Books, 2010).

12. Raj Chetty, Nathaniel Hendren, Patrick Kline, Emmanuel Saez, and Nicholas Turner, "Is the United States Still a Land of Opportunity? Recent Trends in Intergenerational Mobility," *American Economic Review* 104, no. 5 (2014): 141–47.

13. Chetty et al., "Is the United States Still a Land of Opportunity?"

14. Chetty et al., "Is the United States Still a Land of Opportunity?"

15. "America's Elite: An Hereditary Meritocracy," *The Economist*, January 22, 2015.

16. Raj Chetty, David Grusky, Maximilian Hell, Nathaniel Hendren, Robert Manduca, and Jimmy Narang, "The Fading American Dream: Trends in Absolute Income Mobility since 1940," *Science* 356, no. 6336 (2017): 398–406.

17. For example, Emmanuel Saez, "Income and Wealth Inequality: Evidence and Policy Implications," *Contemporary Economic Policy*, January 35, no. 1 (2017): 7–25. For a more thoroughly prescriptive analysis, see Emmanuel Saez and Gabriel Zucman, *The Triumph of Injustice: How the Rich Dodge Taxes and How to Make Them Pay* (New York: Norton, 2019).

18. Chetty et al., "Is the United States Still a Land of Opportunity?"

19. See Daniel Markovits, *The Meritocracy Trap: How America's Foundational Myth Feeds Inequality, Dismantles the Middle Class, and Devours the Elite* (New York: Penguin, 2019).

20. See Jack Metzgar, *Striking Steel: Solidarity Remembered* (Philadelphia: Temple University Press, 2000), chap. 1.

21. Observing many different campaigns through the 1980s in a variety of industries, I found that most antishutdown campaigns *did* result in substantially better treatment in the closing, both by the companies and by local governments. In the long run that didn't

matter much, but it usually made the transition to joblessness less stark and ruinous in the short term. And fighting back almost always seemed to have some positive psychological benefits.

22. See Staughton Lynd, *The Fight Against Shutdowns: Youngstown's Steel Mill Closings* (San Pedro: Singlejack Books, 1982); Dan Swinney and Jack Metzgar, "Expanding the Fight against Shutdowns," in *The Imperiled Economy: Through the Safety Net*, 153–60 (New York: Union of Radical Political Economics, 1988).

23. See Daniel Nelson, *Shifting Fortunes: The Rise and Decline of American Labor from the 1820s to the Present* (Chicago: Ivan R. Dee, 1997); Steve Babson, *The Unfinished Struggle: Turning Points in American Labor, 1877–Present* (Lanham, MD: Rowman & Littlefield, 1999); Dan Clawson, *The Next Upsurge: Labor and the New Social Movements* (Ithaca, NY: Cornell University Press, 2003).

24. A telling example of this cross-class fertilization is that in the 1940s when only one of ten adults "had been to college" (not necessarily graduating), one of three CIO organizers and one of four AFL organizers had been. See Martin Trow, *Twentieth-Century Higher Education: From Elite to Mass to Universal* (Baltimore: John Hopkins University Press, 2010), 234. On the other hand, key CIO strategists such as Bob Travis "never made it past the eighth grade." Toni Gilpin, *The Long Deep Grudge: A Story of Big Capital, Radical Labor, and Class War in the American Heartland* (Chicago: Haymarket Books, 2020), 90.

25. Franklin Folsom, *Impatient Armies of the Poor: The Story of Collective Action of the Unemployed, 1808–1942* (Niwot: University Press of Colorado, 1991), chaps. 18–36.

26. Alexis de Tocqueville, *The Ancien Regime and the French Revolution*, trans. and ed. Gerald Bevan (London: Penguin Books, 2008, first published in 1856), 174–175. For a full discussion of the evidence from the twentieth century that supports Tocqueville's view, see chapter 1 in this volume.

27. The best comprehensive account of this period is still Irving Bernstein, *Turbulent Years: A History of the American Worker, 1933–1941* (Boston: Houghton Mifflin, 1969), esp. chaps. 10–12 for the relative speed of the upsurge when it came.

28. For the period of upsurge in the civil rights movement, see the first seven episodes of the PBS documentary series *Eyes on the Prize* (1987 and 1990), and the first two volumes of Taylor Branch's trilogy *Parting the Waters: America in the King Years, 1954–63* (New York: Simon & Schuster, 1988), and *Pillar of Fire: America in the King Years, 1964–65* (New York: Simon & Schuster, 1998). As importantly, for the later period when the movement was consolidating its gains, see Nancy MacLean, *Freedom Is Not Enough: The Opening of the American Workplace* (Cambridge, MA: Harvard University Press, 2006).

EPILOGUE

1. Benjamin M. Friedman, *The Moral Consequences of Economic Growth* (New York: Vintage Books 2005), 4.

2. See Barbara Jensen, *Reading Classes: On Culture and Classism in America* (Ithaca, NY: Cornell University Press, 2012), esp. chaps. 4 and 5; Annette Lareau, *Unequal Childhoods: Class, Race, and Family Life*, 2nd ed. (Berkeley: University of California Press, 2011), esp. chaps. 10 and 11.

3. See Emmanuel Saez and Gabriel Zucman, *The Triumph of Injustice: How the Rich Dodge Taxes and How to Make Them Pay* (New York: Norton, 2019). Thomas Piketty, *Capital and Ideology*, trans. Arthur Goldhammer (Cambridge, MA: Harvard University Press, 2020), brilliantly surveys the politics of what he calls "inequality regimes" around the world and makes a strong case for the necessity today of transnational political economic approaches. In the United States the politics may actually be simpler than that, because we lack so many elements of what is a standard social wage in Europe and elsewhere. Plus, as Piketty documents, in the United States as "the most inegalitarian country

in the developed world after 1980," our top income and wealth groups are accumulating such magnificent sums that taking even a small percentage of their money in fairer taxes could produce huge amounts of government revenue for redistribution (522).

4. Alison Light, *Common People: The History of an English Family* (London: Fig Tree Penguin Books, 2014), 189.

Index

"accomplishment of natural growth," 91–94
action-seeking. *See* "working class culture."
AFL-CIO, 184
African-American freedom struggle, 136
Allegretto, Sylvia, 219n29
Amazon warehouses, 142
American Psychiatric Association, 36
American Revolution, 39
Arnold, Andrew, 159
Artis, Jennifer, 172–75
Attfield, Sarah, 204n8
"authenticity dramas," 47–48

Bakewell, Sarah, 47, 202n13
Balay, Anne, 156–57
Baldwin, James, 47
Bardacke, Frank, 140
Barrett, James, 120–21
Beard, Mary, 196n8, 211n16
Beats, the, 169
being vs. doing, 103–10
belonging vs. becoming, 77–78, 103t, 110–16
Berry, Chuck, 47
Bethlehem Steel, 23, 140
Bettie, Julie, 85, 193n9, 195n19, 208n21
binaries, uses of, 126–27
Bledstein, Burton, 201n6
Bluestone, Barry, 199n26
Bodnar, John, 175
Bohm, Svetlana, 196n4
Bosnia, 122
Boucher, Jean, 127
Bourdieu, Pierre, 19, 130, 210n34
Brexit, 123
Bright, Geoff, 22
Brinkman, Svend, 115
Buddhism, 169–170
Burawoy, Michael, 142, 215n17
Bureau of Labor Statistics, 11
Burgess, Anthony, 172–73
Bush, George W., 178
"busting balls," 129–30

Calarco, Jessica, 107,137–38, 195n19, 215n7
Camus, Albert, 47, 49

career culture vs. job culture, 86
careers vs. callings, 83
careers vs. jobs, 84–88, 102–03
Case, Anne, 145, 166, 216n30, 220n44
ceding control to gain control, 106–07
Cherlin, Andrew, 107, 160, 222n8
Chetty, Raj, 179–80
Chicago, 15–16, 21, 117, 121, 141, 171, 173, 182
civil rights movement, 28, 34, 136–37
class cultures, 50, 80, 103t, 189
    Anywheres and Somewheres, 124
    becoming vs. belonging, 77–78, 110–16
    being vs. doing, 103–10
    careers vs. jobs, 83–88
    cosmopolitan vs. parochial, 121–26
    and delaying gratification, 150–55
    differences in, 103t
    future-oriented vs. present-oriented, 168–70
    independence vs. interdependence, 112–14
    individualism vs. solidarity, 113–14
    mono-class vs. class hybrids, 127
    and race, 12, 194–95n19
    status vs. anti-status, 116–20, 141–47
class crossovers, 63, 78–79, 88–96, 102, 117, 130
class culture clash, 79, 96, 128, 189
class culture sharing, 71, 98–99, 189
    during Glorious Thirty, 62–63
class identity vs. class position, 89–90
class sensibilities, 96
class straddlers, 88–96
class struggle, 74
class vernacular, American, 13
code-switching, 63, 78
collective action, 147
    golden age of, 34, 41
    and women, 167–68
"concerted cultivation," 91—94
Congress of Industrial Organizations (CIO), 37, 185
Cooper, Marianne, 116, 168–69, 212n33
consumer debt, 31
consumerism, 53–54
consumer sovereignty, 64
Cowie, Jefferson, 67, 70
Cronkite, Walter, 49

culture, definition of, 8–10, 100–03
cultural capital, 24, 53, 90, 111, 113
cultural repertoires, 94–95
cultural rules, 100–02
"culture of poverty," 187–88, 219n35
Currid-Halkett, Elizabeth, 216n26

Daniels, Jim, 98
Davis, Miles, 47
"deaths of despair," 145, 166–67
Deaton, Angus, 145, 166–67, 216n30, 220n44
Debs, Eugene, 65
Delgado, Laura, 116
deficit culture, definition of, 79
democratic socialism, 64
Democrats, 52
delayed gratification, 150–55
DeMott, Benjamin, 81, 207n10
Deresiewicz, William, 169–70
discretionary income, 19, 29, 64, 67, 146–48
    difference from disposable income, 31–32
    and freedom, 68
discretionary time and money, 51
disposable income
    difference from discretionary income, 31–32
dominated culture, definition of, 79
Dostoyevsky, Fyodor, 47
Double V campaign, 37
downward mobility, involuntary and voluntary, 96
doxa, 210n34
Draut, Tamara, 200n47
Duckworth, Angela, 157
Dylan, Bob, 49

economic growth, US history of, 28–29
Economic Policy Institute, 30, 161, 219n28
Edin, Kathryn, 160, 220n40
Eisenhower, Dwight, 25, 70, 151
Engels, Friedrich, 53
English Revolution, 39
Epicurean, 169–70
Eribon, Didier, 209n31

Faderman, Lillian, 199n27
Fair Labor Standards Act (FLSA), 32
family economic self-sufficiency, 161
family income, US history of, 30
Father Knows Best, 49
fear of falling, 180–81
feeling rules, 96, 100–01
Fischer, Claude, 81–82, 208n15
Fourastié, Jean, 27, 30

Franklin, Benjamin, 5, 13, 43, 71
Freedom Summer, 136
Freeman, Joshua, 71, 156, 206n12, 219n33
free time for what you will, 19, 29, 67, 87, 94, 146–47
free wage labor, 10, 28, 42, 48, 49, 51, 54, 63–64, 72—75, 88, 156, 171, 180
French Revolution, 5, 35, 39
Friedan, Betty, 49
Friedman, Benjamin, 39, 67, 188
Fukushima, 158

Galbraith, John Kenneth, 46, 49, 201n4
Gans, Herbert, 58, 162, 203n6
Garagiola, Joe, 177
gay liberation movement, 34
General Social Survey, 13
Ginsberg, Alan, 47
Glorious Thirty, definition of, 27–28
Glosser Brothers Department Store, 17
golden-age thinking, 24–26
Goodhart, David, 124, 213n52
Gordon, Robert, 33, 198n11
Gorman, Thomas, 214n3, 219n29
Great Depression, 32, 110, 184
Great Recession, 38
Greene, David, 89
Guendelsberger, Emily, 142

Habits of the Heart, 9, 77, 80–83, 97
Hacker, Jacob, 25, 31
Haidt, Jonathan, 121
Hanley, Lynsey, 113
Hamper, Ben, 140, 142
hard-living. See "working class."
hardship thresholds, 161
Harrison, Bennett, 199n26
Heartland, 165
Hegel, Georg, 6
Hillbilly Elegy, 165
Hoggart, Richard, 53
Horace, 169
Howell, Joseph, 218n26
Huntington, Samuel, 39, 200n45
Hyman, Louis, 31

Idle, Eric, 126
Ignatieff, Michael, 122, 158, 213n46
imposter syndrome, 78
Isbell, Jason, 50

Jacobins, 5
Jencks, Christopher, 204n14

Jensen, Barbara, 77–78, 80, 102, 110, 114–15, 126, 146, 170, 193n9, 211n15
Johnstown, PA, 2, 15, 17, 23, 66, 133
Judt, Tony, 25, 71

Kefalas, Maria, 220n40
Kelley, Robin D.G., 214n3
Kennedy, John F., 25
Kennedy, Randall, 37–38
Khurana, Rakesh, 202n7, 208n15
Kimbley, George, 136
Kiner, Ralph, 177
King, Colby, 194n17
King, Martin Luther Jr., 34
Krugman, Paul, 25
Ku Klux Klan, 36
Kuttner, Robert, 25–26
Kynaston, David, 52

labor market rules, 138
labor movement, 36
Labor Research Review, 16
"lads," 7–8, 108, 193n9
Lamont, Michele, 144, 152, 194n19, 204n13, 208n21
Lareau, Annette, 99, 176, 195n19
    and "accomplishment of natural growth," 91–94
    and "concerted cultivation," 91–94
Lennon, John, 174
Leondar-Wright, Betsy, 95–96, 210n35, 219n32, 221n56
Levin, Yuval, 195n1
Levinson, Marc, 67, 205n1
Levy, Frank, 29
liberatory movements
    African-American freedom struggle, 34–39, 136
    civil rights movement, 28, 34, 36–38, 43, 136–37
    gay liberation, 34
    labor movement, 36
    relation to economic prosperity, 39–40
    women's liberation, 34
life expectancy, 33
life as highway or river, 154–55
lifestyle, 9
Light, Alison, 105, 120, 178, 189, 219n33
Lind, Michael, 203n17
Linkon, Sherry, 210n35
Lipset, Seymour Martin, 150–52, 160, 217n1, 221n53
living-wage levels, 161

living-wage movement, 25–26
"long revolution," 5
Lubrano, Alfred, 88–89
Luce, Henry, 71

MacLean, Nancy, 200n47, 221n57
MacLeod, Jay, 111, 208n19
Mailer, Norman, 47, 49
management as a profession, 46
managerial capitalism, 46, 202n7
managerial workers, 11, 45t
managerial and professional workers, 29, 44–46, 45t
Markovits, Daniel, 195n25
Marmot, Michael, 142–46, 216nn22
Marx, Karl, 10, 53, 73–75, 147
McIvor, Arthur, 59, 158
mediocrity, 3–8, 13, 28, 43, 71–72, 177–78
Metzgar, Judd, 92–94
Metzgar, Judith, 17–18, 66, 168–69
Mexican Revolution, 39
Meyer, Stephen, 54
middle-class imperialism, 81, 119
Midwest Center for Labor Research, 16, 182
Mikula, Albert, 21–23
Mischel, Walter, 152–53
Moore, Amzie, 136–37

National Election Survey, 13–14
National Industrial Recovery Act, 186
National Labor Relations Act, 186
Needleman, Ruth, 136
New York University, 61
Nietzsche, Friedrich, 40, 169–70
No Child Left Behind, 62
Northwestern University, 15, 17, 172
nostalgia, 22–25, 33–34, 64, 66–67
    and golden-age thinking, 24–26
    restorative, 70

Oak Park, IL, 15
Obama, Barack, 178
Offer, Avner, 49, 203n16
Ohio University, 17
O'Nan, Stewart, 194n15
ordinary virtues, 122–23
Osterman, Paul, 97–98

Patterson, James, 28, 36, 199n29
Payne, Charles, 136
Pearce, Diana, 218n28
Pearlstein, Steven, 26
Perkins, Frances, 186

Persky, Joe, 21–22
Petigny, Alan, 202n13
Pickett, Kate, 119, 142–45
Piercy, Marge, 193n9
Pierson, Paul, 25, 31
Piff, Paul, 109, 209n23
Piketty, Thomas, 5, 25, 69, 206n11, 223n3
Pipes, Richard, 122
Pittsburgh Pirates, 177
Playboy, 49
Pizzigati, Sam, 25, 69, 71
"preexisting relationships," 115
professional middle class
    business and communications/education
        wings, 46–50, 126
    business wing, 46, 48, 53–54,
    careers vs. callings, 83
    communications/education wing, 47–49,
        53–54, 72, 80–81
    definition of, 10–14, 42–44, 73–76
    elite and standard-issue parts, 126
    rise of, 44–46
    standard-issue part, 6, 15, 20, 22, 80, 98, 130,
        188
    working-class perception of, 86
professional middle-class culture, 4, 103
    aspiration, 19
    becoming, 17, 110–16
    doing as achievement or accomplishment,
        45, 103–10
    doing and becoming, 45, 102–03
    as dominant mainstream culture, 81–83
    meritocratic, 42
    narrowing of, 19, 22, 51, 87
    proactive, 93, 105, 109, 171, 185
    and social evaluative threat, 116–20
    and status, 116–20
    strategies of influence, 107, 137–38
    vs. working-class culture, 103t
    unintended homogeneity, 4, 125
poverty, US history of, 29–30
power, formal and informal, 135, 139–42
productivity growth, 56, 69
    sharing of, 68–70
professional workers, 11, 44–45
Progressive Era, 25
progressive taxes, 68–70
proletarian wager, 95
Protestant Reformation, 39
Pugh, Allison, 165
Putnam, Robert, 114–16
Pynchon, Thomas, 170

Ramapo College, 89
Reagan Revolution, 6, 44
real hourly compensation, 68
real wages, US history of, 29
Reeves, Richard, 214n7
Reich, Robert, 25
residual culture, 80, 161, 207n6
retirement as new stage of life, 33
Riesman, David, 204n14
"ritual mockery," 129–30
Roosevelt, Franklin, 184
Roosevelt University, 15–17, 172
routine-seeking. *See* "working-class
    culture."
Royko, Mike, 121
Rubin, Lillian Breslow, 203n6, 218n26
Russian Revolution, 39
Russians, 122

Saez, Emmanuel, 206n11
Sartre, Jean-Paul, 47
Second New Deal, 5
Second Reconstruction, 37–38
settled-living. *See* "working-class."
Shennum, Jill, 140, 142,
Silva, Jennifer, 158, 208n15
Smarsh, Sarah, 112
social capital, 24, 87, 90, 111, 113
    bonding vs. bridging, 114
social classes, 73–76
    definition of, 10–14
social democracy, 25, 31, 71
social evaluative threat, 116–20, 189. *See*
    "status, and anxiety."
"soldiering, industrial," 139–42
Soria, Krista, 108
Sousa, Xavier de, 115
Starr, Paul, 202n6
status, 6, 116–20, 141–47
    and anxiety, 143–45, 189
Stearns, Peter, 81
steel strike, 1959, 150–51
Steelworkers Organizing Committee (SWOC),
    136
Stephens, Nicole, 112–14
Stonewall Riots, 34
Strangleman, Tim, 98, 130, 196n2
Streib, Jessi, 96, 100–01, 153, 160
strikes, labor, 35, 181, 184–86
survivor guilt, 6, 78
Swan, William, 105
Swift, Adam, 201n49

t-Hartley Act of 1947, 36
aking it, 148–49, 151, 153–59, 173–74
  aguantar in Spanish, 158–159
  as delayed gratification, 157–58
  difference in hard-living and settled-living, 164–65
  difference in men and women, 165–68
  ganbaru in Japanese, 158
taxes, progressive, 70
Taylor, Frederick Winslow, 139
Theriault, Reg, 140
Tocqueville, Alexis de, 5, 9, 35–37, 47, 184
Tolstoy, Leo, 47
Torlina, Jeff, 120
Townsend, Sarah, 112–14
Trump, Donald, 123

Unequal Childhoods, 91–94
United Parcel Service (UPS), 85, 142
United Steelworkers (USWA), 21, 136, 150
upward mobility
  difference between absolute and relative, 40–41, 44, 178–181
U.S. Steel, 23

Vance, J. D., 112

Wagner, Robert F., 186
Walkerdine, Valerie, 221n2
Wallace, Henry, 71
Walley, Christine, 219n33
Warren, Tracey, 98
Weil, David, 26
White Citizens Councils, 36
Whyte, William Foote, 110
Williams, Joan C., 83
Williams, Raymond, 5, 9, 161, 207n6, 209n31
Willis, Paul, 7, 85, 108, 148
Wilkinson, Richard, 119, 142–45
Wilson, August, 57
women's liberation movement, 28, 34
World War II, 32–33, 36
Woodard, Colin, 82
working class
  craftsmen and laborers, 54–55
  definition of, 10–14, 73–76
  hard-living, 10–11, 17, 90, 176
  hard-living and settled-living, 5, 90, 118, 126, 158, 218n26

  definition of, 161–62
  relation to action-seeking and routine-seeking, 163
  respectable and rough, 54–55
  settled-living, 5, 58–59, 63, 90, 92, 173, 179, 186
  increase of, 54–58
working-class culture, 4
  action-seeking, 58
  action-seeking and routine-seeking, 55
    definition of, 162–63
    relation to hard-living and settled-living, 163
  anti-status, 46, 116–20, 142–47
  aspiration, 3, 172–74, 176–78
  authenticity, 3, 8, 101, 109, 208n21, 210n35
  being, 103–10
  being and belonging, 102–03
  belonging, 110–16
  breadwinner/homemaker ideology, lack of, 57–58
  ceding control to gain control, 122, 133–34
  and character, 104–09, 138
  and collective action, 114, 147, 167–68, 181–85
  college option in, 59–62
  deference, uses of, 135—39
  as deficit, 79
  as dominated, 79
  and integrity, 8, 85–86, 95, 101, 108–09, 138, 208n21
  maladapted, 162
  middle-class seeking, 162
  present-oriented, 168–70
  reactive, 80, 105, 154–55
  realism, 3–4
  respectability, 54–57
  as residual, 80, 161
  routine-seeking, 19, 55, 58, 162–63
  and solidarity, 114
  strategies of deference, 107–08, 138–39
  toughness, 105, 165. *See* "taking it."
  unavoidable diversity, 125–26
  values, 6–7
working-class studies, 19

Zucman, Gabriel, 206n11
Zweig, Michael, 10, 161